# The Other Half of
# Macroeconomics and the Fate
# of Globalization

# The Other Half of Macroeconomics and the Fate of Globalization

### RICHARD C. KOO

# WILEY

This edition first published 2018
© 2018 John Wiley & Sons, Ltd

*Registered office*
John Wiley & Sons Ltd, The Atrium, Southern Gate, Chichester, West Sussex, PO19 8SQ, United Kingdom

For details of our global editorial offices, for customer services and for information about how to apply for permission to reuse the copyright material in this book please see our website at www.wiley.com.

Wiley publishes in a variety of print and electronic formats and by print-on-demand. Some material included with standard print versions of this book may not be included in e-books or in print-on-demand. If this book refers to media such as a CD or DVD that is not included in the version you purchased, you may download this material at http://booksupport.wiley.com. For more information about Wiley products, visit www.wiley.com.

Designations used by companies to distinguish their products are often claimed as trademarks. All brand names and product names used in this book are trade names, service marks, trademarks or registered trademarks of their respective owners. The publisher is not associated with any product or vendor mentioned in this book.

Limit of Liability/Disclaimer of Warranty: While the publisher and author have used their best efforts in preparing this book, they make no representations or warranties with respect to the accuracy or completeness of the contents of this book and specifically disclaim any implied warranties of merchantability or fitness for a particular purpose. It is sold on the understanding that the publisher is not engaged in rendering professional services and neither the publisher nor the author shall be liable for damages arising herefrom. If professional advice or other expert assistance is required, the services of a competent professional should be sought.

*Library of Congress Cataloging-in-Publication Data is Available:*

ISBN 978-1-119-48215-4 (paperback) ISBN 978-1-119-48216-1 (ePub)
ISBN 978-1-119-48213-0 (ePDF) ISBN 978-1-119-48212-3 (Obook)

Cover Design: Wiley
Cover Image: © anigoweb/Shutterstock

Set in 10/12pt Garamond by SPi Global, Chennai, India

Printed in United States of America.

V305735_080519

*"To my dearest wife, Chyen-Mei"*

# Contents

# Contents

# Preface

The advanced countries today face a highly unusual economic environment in which zero or negative interest rates and astronomical amounts of monetary easing have failed to produce vibrant economies or the targeted level of inflation. Simply trying to understand what zero or negative interest rates *mean* in a capitalist system sets the head spinning. One wonders how Karl Marx or Thomas Piketty would explain negative interest rates.

It was twenty years ago that the author came up with the concept of balance sheet recessions in Japan to explain why post-bubble economies suffer years of stagnation and why conventional monetary remedies are largely ineffective in such recessions. The key point of departure for this concept was the realization that the private sector is not always maximizing profits, as assumed in textbook economics, but will actually chose to minimize debt when faced with daunting balance sheet challenges. Once this fundamental assumption of traditional macroeconomics is overturned and the possibility of debt minimization is acknowledged, everything that was built on the original assumption—including many standard policy recommendations—must also be reconsidered.

It recently occurred to the author that the same insight can be used to explain periods of long-term economic stagnation throughout history because there is another reason for the private sector to be minimizing debt—or simply refraining from borrowing—in spite of very low interest rates. The reason is that businesses cannot find investment opportunities attractive enough to justify borrowing and investing. After all, there is nothing in business or economics that guarantees such opportunities will always be available. When businesses cannot find investments, they tend to minimize debt (except when tax considerations argue against it) because the firm's probability of long-term survival increases significantly if it carries no debt.

This shortage of investment opportunities, in turn, has two possible causes. The first is a lack of technological innovation or scientific breakthroughs, which makes it difficult to find viable investment projects. This probably explains the economic stagnation observed for centuries prior to the Industrial Revolution in the 1760s. Some also attribute the recent slowdown in advanced economies to an absence of innovative, must-have, "blockbuster" products.

The second cause is higher returns on capital overseas, which forces businesses to invest abroad instead of at home. For companies in the advanced countries, the rise of Japan in the 1960s and of emerging economies in the 1990s has changed the geographic focus of their investments. Businesses continue to invest in order to satisfy shareholder expectations for ever-higher returns on capital, but the bulk of their investments, especially in the job-creating manufacturing sector, are no longer taking place in their home countries. This probably explains the economic stagnation and slow productivity growth observed in advanced countries during the last two to three decades.

The bursting of debt-financed bubbles in Japan in 1990 and in the West in 2008 caused even more borrowers to disappear as these economies fell into balance sheet recessions. Advanced countries today are therefore suffering from two ailments, both of which discourage businesses from borrowing and investing at home.

The economics profession, however, failed to consider the macro-economic implications of private-sector balance sheet problems until very recently. It never envisioned a world where businesses no longer invest domestically because the return on capital is higher abroad.

Even though all of the developed countries suffer from both of these issues, economists continue to recommend policies such as monetary easing and balanced budgets based on the assumption that the private sector is maximizing profits. But for that to be the case, the private sector must have a clean balance sheet and plenty of viable domestic investment opportunities. Neither assumption holds today.

The fact that most advanced countries are going through the same stagnation problems at the same time while emerging economies continue to attract capital from around the world also suggests that the effectiveness of monetary and fiscal policy changes as an economy undergoes different stages of development. This means those policies that were effective just a few decades ago many not be effective or appropriate today.

Because promised economic recoveries took far longer than expected or, for many, did not materialize at all, the public is losing confidence in the competence of established political parties and is starting to vote for outsiders and extremists, a dangerous sign in any society. Although a much-improved social safety net means that today's democracies are more resilient to recessions than those in the 1930s, democracy cannot survive if center-left and center-right leaders continue to pursue fundamentally flawed economic policies while people at the bottom suffer.

Once the root cause of stagnation and the failure of conventional economic policies is understood, the remedies turn out to be remarkably straightforward. To get there, however, we must discard conventional notions about monetary and fiscal policy that were developed at a time when the developed economies were not facing balance sheet problems or challenges from emerging markets.

The problem is that the discipline of macroeconomics was founded in the postwar years, when private-sector balance sheets were in pristine shape and new products ranging from television sets to washing machines were being brought to market one after another. That led economists to believe that the only *modus operandi* for the private sector was profit maximization. Convincing these believers that the private sector might sometimes behave differently has proven to be a challenging task because profit maximization is the pattern the discipline is identified with.

But rediscovering this "other half" of macroeconomics should not be too difficult inasmuch as the discipline's origins lie in Keynes' concept of aggregate demand, which was developed during the Great Depression, at a time when the private sector was aggressively minimizing debt.

The author first used the phrase "the other half of macroeconomics" to describe a world in which the private sector is minimizing debt in his 2008 book, *The Holy Grail of Macroeconomics*, which introduced the concept of yin and yang business cycles. The term has been chosen for the title of this book because its relevance goes far beyond post-bubble balance sheet issues.

Physics and chemistry evolved over the centuries as new phenomena that defied existing theories were discovered. In many of these cases, it was eventually realized that what people thought they knew was not wrong but was in fact a subset of a bigger truth. Similarly, the economics taught in schools is not wrong, but it applies only to situations where the private sector has a clean balance sheet and enjoys an abundance of attractive investment opportunities. When these conditions are not met, we have to look at the other half of macroeconomics, which is not based on those two assumptions.

This book started life as Part II of a joint book project with my brother John Koo, a well-known dermatologist, who came up with some fascinating insights on where civilization might be headed by applying scientific methods to analyze the evolution of religion and morality. Unfortunately, speaking engagements related to newly developed drugs for psoriasis have prevented him from completing his section of the book. But because the original target audience for this book was the non-specialist public, the author has tried to use as few specialized economic terms as possible so that those with minimal training in economics will still be able to follow the arguments. Besides, it is the author's belief that any economic phenomenon or theory must be explainable in plain language because its actors are all ordinary human beings going about their daily lives.

The author has also tried not to repeat the arguments put forth in his previous three books (eight in Japanese), but some of the fundamental

concepts of balance sheet recessions are repeated in Chapter 2 for readers
who are also encountering this concept for the first time. The challenges
facing the Eurozone are also revisited in Chapter 7 because the fundamental
defect in the system remains unaddressed, even though some European
countries are doing better than before.

   The times have changed, and everyone, economists included, must
open their minds and broaden their vision to understand what is happening. There are also right ways and wrong ways to respond to that change.
It is the author's hope that this book will help explain why policies that
worked so well in the past no longer work today, and why nostalgia for the
"good old days" is no solution for the future. Once the key drivers of change
are identified and understood, individuals and policymakers alike should be
able to respond correctly to today's new environment without wasting time
on remedies that are no longer relevant.

# About the Author

**Richard C. Koo** is the Chief Economist of Nomura Research Institute, with responsibilities to provide independent economic and market analysis to Nomura Securities, the leading securities house in Japan, and its clients. Before joining Nomura in 1984, Mr. Koo, a US citizen, was an economist with the Federal Reserve Bank of New York (1981–84). Prior to that, he was a Doctoral Fellow of the Board of Governors of the Federal Reserve System (1979–81). In addition to conducting financial market research, he has also advised several Japanese prime ministers on how best to deal with Japan's economic and banking problems. In addition to being one of the first non-Japanese to participate in the making of Japan's five-year economic plan, he was also the only non-Japanese member of the Defense Strategy Study Conference of the Japan Ministry of Defense for 1999–2011. Currently he is serving as a Senior Advisor to Center for Strategic and International Studies (Washington D.C.). He is also an Advisory Board Member of Institute for New Economic Thinking (N.Y.C.) and a frequent contribution to *The International Economy Magazine*, Washington, D.C.

Author of many books on Japanese economy, his *The Holy Grail of Macroeconomics—Lessons from Japan's Great Recession* (John Wiley & Sons, 2008) has been translated into and sold in six different languages. Mr. Koo holds BAs in Political Science and Economics from the University of California at Berkeley (1976) and an MA in Economics from the Johns Hopkins University (1979). From 1998 to 2010, he was a visiting professor at Waseda University in Tokyo. In financial circles, Mr. Koo was ranked first among over 100 economists covering Japan in the Nikkei Financial Ranking for 1995, 1996, and 1997, and by the *Institutional Investor* magazine for 1998. He was also ranked 1st by Nikkei Newsletter on Bond and Money for 1998, 1999, and 2000. He was awarded the Abramson Award by the National Association for Business Economics (Washington, D.C.) for the year 2001. Mr. Koo, a native of Kobe, Japan, is married with two children.

# CHAPTER 1

# Introduction to the Other Half of Macroeconomics

The discipline of macroeconomics, which was founded in the late 1940s and was based on the assumption that the private sector always seeks to maximize profits, considered in its short history only one of the two phases an actual economy experiences. The largely overlooked other phase, in which the private sector may instead seek to minimize debt, can help explain why economies undergo extended periods of stagnation and why the much-touted policies of quantitative easing and zero or even negative interest rates have failed to produce the expected results. With sluggish economic and wage growth becoming a pressing issue in many developed countries, it is time for economists to leave their comfort zones and honestly confront the other half of macroeconomics.

The failure of the vast majority of economists in government, academia, and the private sector to predict either the post-2008 Great Recession or the degree of its severity has raised serious credibility issues for the profession. The widely varying opinions of these "experts" on how this recession should be addressed, together with the repeated failures of central banks and other policymakers to meet inflation or growth targets in spite of truly astronomical levels of monetary accommodation, have left the public rightfully suspicious of the establishment and its economists.

This book seeks to elucidate what was missing in economics all along and what changes are needed to make the profession relevant to the economic challenges of today. Once the other half of macroeconomics is understood both as a post-bubble phenomenon and as a phase of post-industrial economies, it should be possible for policymakers to devise appropriate measures to overcome the difficulties faced by advanced countries today, including stagnation and deflation.

Human progress is said to have started when civilizations sprang up in China, Egypt, and Mesopotamia over 5,000 years ago. The Renaissance,

1

which began in Europe in the 13th century, accelerated the search for both a better understanding of the physical world and better forms of government. But for centuries that progress benefited only the fortunate few who had enough to eat and the leisure to ponder worldly affairs. Life for the masses was little better in the 18th century than it was in the 13th century when the Renaissance began. Thomas Piketty noted in his book *Capital in the 21st Century* that economic growth was basically at a standstill during this period, averaging only 0.1 percent per year[1].

Today, on the other hand, economic growth is largely taken for granted, and most economists only talk about "getting back to trend" without asking how the trend was established in the first place. To understand how we got from centuries of economic stagnation to where we are today, with economic growth taken for granted, we need to review certain basic facts about the economy and how it operates.

## Basic Macroeconomics: One Person's Expenditure Is Another Person's Income

One person's expenditure is another person's income. It is this unalterable linkage between the expenditures and incomes of millions of thinking and reacting households and businesses that makes the study of the economy both an interesting and a unique undertaking. It is interesting because the interaction between thinking and reacting households and businesses creates a situation where one plus one does not necessarily equal two. For example, if A decides to buy less from B in order to set aside more savings for an uncertain future, B will have less income to buy things from A. That will lower A's income, which in turn will reduce the amount A can save.

This interaction between expenditure and income also means that, at the national level, if one group is saving money, another group must be doing the opposite—"dis-saving"—to keep the economy running. In most cases, this dis-saving takes the form of borrowing by businesses that seek to expand their operations. If everyone is saving and no one is dis-saving on borrowing, all of those savings will leak out of the economy's income stream, resulting in less income for all.

For example, if a person with an income of $1,000 decides to spend $900 and save $100, the $900 that is spent becomes someone else's income and continues circulating in the economy. The $100 that is saved is typically deposited with a financial institution such as a bank, which then lends it

---

[1] Piketty, Thomas (2014) *Capital in the Twenty-First Century*, Cambridge, MA: Harvard University Press.

to someone else who can make use of it. When that person borrows and spends the $100, total expenditures in the economy amount to $900 plus $100, which is equal to the original income of $1,000, and the economy moves forward.

In a normal economy, this function of matching savers and borrowers is performed by the financial sector, with interest rates moving higher or lower depending on whether there are too many or too few borrowers. If there are too many, interest rates will rise and some will drop out. If there are too few, interest rates will fall and prompt potential borrowers who stayed on the sidelines to step forward.

The government also has two types of policy, known as monetary and fiscal policy, that it can use to help stabilize the economy by matching private-sector savings and borrowings. The more frequently used is monetary policy, which involves raising or lowering interest rates to assist the matching process. Since an excess of borrowers is usually associated with a strong economy, a higher policy rate might be appropriate to prevent overheating and inflation. Similarly, a shortage of borrowers is usually associated with a weak economy, in which case a lower policy rate might be needed to avert a recession or deflation.

With fiscal policy, the government itself borrows and spends money on such projects as highways, airports, and other social infrastructure. While monetary policy decisions can be made very quickly by the central bank governor and his or her associates, fiscal policy tends to be very cumbersome in a peacetime democracy because elected representatives must come to an agreement on how much to borrow and where to spend the money. Because of the political nature of these decisions and the time it takes to implement them, most recent economic fluctuations were dealt with by central banks using monetary policy.

## Two Reasons for Disappearance of Borrowers

Now that we have covered the basics, consider an economy in which everyone wants to save but no one wants to borrow, even at near-zero interest rates. There are at least two sets of circumstances where such a situation might arise.

The first is one in which private-sector businesses cannot find investment opportunities that will pay for themselves. The private sector will only borrow money if it believes it can pay back the debt with interest. And there is no guarantee that such opportunities will always be available. Indeed, the emergence of such opportunities depends very much on scientific discoveries and technological innovations, both of which are highly irregular and difficult to predict.

In open economies, businesses may also find that overseas investment opportunities are more attractive than those available at home. If
the return on capital is higher in emerging markets, for example, pressure from shareholders will force businesses to invest more abroad while
reducing borrowings and investments at home. In modern globalized
economies, this pressure from shareholders to invest where the return on
capital is highest may play a greater role than any technological breakthroughs, or lack thereof, in the decision as to whether to borrow and
invest at home.

In the second set of circumstances, private-sector borrowers have sustained huge losses and are forced to rebuild savings or pay down debt to
restore their financial health. Such a situation may arise following the collapse of a nationwide asset price bubble in which a substantial part of the
private sector participated with borrowed money. The collapse of the bubble leaves borrowers with huge liabilities but no assets to show for the debt.
Facing a huge debt overhang, these borrowers have no choice but to pay
down debt or increase savings in order to restore their balance sheets,
regardless of the level of interest rates.

Even when the economy is doing well, there will always be businesses that experience financial difficulties or go bankrupt because of poor
business decisions. But the number of such businesses explodes after a
nationwide asset bubble bursts.

For businesses, negative equity or insolvency implies the potential loss
of access to all forms of financing, including trade credit. In the worst case,
all transactions must be settled in cash, since no supplier or creditor wants
to extend credit to an entity that may seek bankruptcy protection at any
time. Many banks and other depository institutions are also prohibited by
government regulations from extending or rolling over loans to insolvent
borrowers in order to safeguard depositors' money. For households, negative equity means savings they thought they had for retirement or a rainy
day are no longer there. Both businesses and households will respond to
these life-threatening conditions by focusing on restoring their financial
health—*regardless of the level of interest rates*—until their survival is no
longer at stake.

What happens when borrowers disappear for either or both of the
above reasons? If there are no borrowers for the $100 in savings in the above
example, even at zero interest rates, total expenditures in the economy will
drop to $900, while the saved $100 remains unborrowed in financial institutions or under mattresses. The economy has effectively shrunk by 10 percent, from $1,000 to $900. That $900 now becomes someone else's income.
If that person decides to save 10 percent and there are still no borrowers,
only $810 will be spent, causing the economy to contract to $810. This cycle

will repeat, and the economy will shrink to $730, if borrowers remain on the sidelines. This process of contraction is called a "deflationary spiral."

The $100 that remains in the financial sector could still be invested in various asset classes. It could even create mini-bubbles in certain asset classes from time to time. But without borrowers in the real economy, it will never be able to leave the financial sector and support transactions that add to GDP (changes in ownership of assets do not add to GDP).

The deflationary process described above does not continue forever, since the savings-driven leakages from the income stream end once people become too poor to save. For example, if a person cannot save any money on an income of $500, the entire $500 will naturally be spent. If the person who receives that $500 as income is in the same situation, she will also spend the entire amount. The result is that the economy finally stabilizes at $500, in what we typically call a depression.

## Paradox of Thrift as Fallacy-of-Composition Problem

Keynes had a name for this state of affairs, in which everyone wants to save but is unable to do so because no one is borrowing. He called it the paradox of thrift. It is a paradox because if everyone tries to save, the net result is that no one can save.

The phenomenon of right behavior at the individual level leading to a bad result collectively is known as the "fallacy of composition." An example would be a farmer who strives to increase his income by planting more crops. If all farmers do the same, and their combined efforts result in a bumper crop, crop prices will fall, and the farmers will end up with far less income than they originally expected.

The paradox of thrift is one such fallacy-of-composition problem, but macroeconomics is full of such examples. Indeed, the *real* reason to study macroeconomics as opposed to microeconomics or business administration is to be able to identify (counter-intuitive) fallacy-of-composition problems such as paradox of thrift so as to avoid their pitfalls.

Put differently, if one plus one is always equal to two, one only needs to add up the actions of individual households and businesses to obtain an aggregate result. But when interactions and feedback among the various actors cause fallacy-of-composition problems, one plus one does not always equal two, and that is where the discipline of macroeconomics (as opposed to the simple aggregation of microeconomic results) has a role to play. In that sense, macroeconomics can be considered a "science of interaction," whereas microeconomics takes the outside world as a given.

Indeed, before Keynes came up with the concept of aggregate demand, most people thought that one plus one always equaled two, and there was no macroeconomics. These fallacy-of-composition problems become particularly acute when the economy is in what might be called "the other half of macroeconomics," i.e., when borrowers disappear because of balance sheet problems or a lack of domestic investment opportunities.

## Disappearance of Borrowers Finally Recognized After 2008

Until 2008, the economics profession considered a contractionary equilibrium (the $500 economy) brought about by a lack of borrowers to be an exceptionally rare occurrence—the only recent example was the Great Depression, which was triggered by the stock market crash in October 1929 and during which the U.S. lost 46 percent of nominal GNP. Although Japan fell into a similar predicament when its asset price bubble burst in 1990, its lessons were almost completely ignored by the economics profession until the Lehman shock of 2008[2].

Economists failed to consider the case of insufficient borrowers because when macroeconomics was emerging as a separate academic discipline in the 1940s there were plentiful investment opportunities for businesses in the West: new "must-have" household appliances ranging from washing machines to television sets were being invented one after another. With businesses trying to start or expand production of all these new products, there were plenty of borrowers in the private sector, and interest rates were quite high.

With borrowers never in short supply, economists' emphasis was very much on the availability of savings and the correct use of monetary policy to ensure that businesses obtained the funds they needed at interest rates low enough to enable them to continue investing. Economists also disparaged fiscal policy—i.e., government borrowing and spending—when inflation became a problem in the 1970s because they were worried the public sector would squander the precious savings of the private sector on inefficient pork-barrel projects.

During this period economists also assumed the financial sector would ensure that all saved funds were automatically borrowed and spent, with interest rates moving higher when there were too many borrowers relative to savers and lower when there were too few. It is because of this assumed

---

[2] One exception was the National Association of Business Economists in Washington, D.C., which awarded its Abramson Award to a paper by the author titled "The Japanese Economy in Balance Sheet Recession," published in its journal *Business Economics* in April 2001.

automaticity that most macroeconomic theories and models developed prior to 2008 contained no financial sector.

However, the advent of major recessions in 1990 in Japan and in 2008 in the West demonstrated that private-sector borrowers can disappear altogether—even at a time of zero or negative interest rates—when they face daunting financial problems after the collapse of a debt-financed bubble. In both post-1990 Japan and the post-2008 Western economies, borrowers vanished due to a similar sequence of events.

It all starts with people leveraging up in an asset price bubble in the hope of getting rich quickly. For example, if the value of a house bought entirely with cash rises from $1 million to $1.2 million in a year, the buyer enjoys a 20 percent return. But if the same person buys the house with a 10 percent down payment and borrows the rest, she will have increased an initial investment of $100,000 in down payment to $300,000, for a return of 200 percent. If the interest rate on the $900,000 is 5 percent, she will have made $200,000 less the interest cost of $45,000, or $155,000, representing an annual return of 155 percent. The prospect of easily doubling or tripling one's money leads many to leverage up during bubbles by borrowing and investing more.

When the bubble bursts and asset prices collapse, however, these people are left with huge debts and no assets to show for them. In the above example, if the value of the house falls by 30 percent to $700,000 but the buyer is still carrying a mortgage worth $900,000, the owner will be $200,000 underwater. If she has little in the way of other assets, she will be effectively bankrupt. People whose balance sheets are underwater have no choice but to pay down debt or rebuild savings to restore their financial health.

With their financial survival at stake, they are in no position to borrow even if interest rates are brought down to zero. There will not be many willing lenders, either, especially when the lenders themselves have balance sheet problems, which are frequently the case after the bursting of a bubble. That means these households and businesses shift their priorities from profit maximization to *debt minimization* once they face the solvency constraint. Since asset bubbles can collapse abruptly, the private sector's shift to debt minimization can also happen quite suddenly.

## No Name for Recession Driven by Private-Sector Debt Minimization

Although it may come as a shock to non-economist readers, the economics profession did not envision a recession driven by private-sector debt minimization until quite recently. In other words, the $1,000–$900–$810–$730 deflationary process fueled by the balance sheet concerns of over-leveraged borrowers was never discussed. Economists simply ignored the whole issue of financial health or the need to restore it when building their macroeconomic theories and models because they assumed the private sector would always try to maximize profits.

But two conditions must be satisfied for the private sector to maximize profits: it must have a clean balance sheet, and there must be attractive investment opportunities. By taking it as given that the private sector is always maximizing profits, economists assumed, mostly unconsciously, that both of these two conditions are always satisfied. And that was in fact the case for many decades—until asset bubbles burst in Japan in 1990 and in the Western economies in 2008. When that happened, millions of private-sector balance sheets were impaired, resulting not only in the disappearance of borrowers, but also in many borrowers starting to pay down debt in spite of record low interest rates.

Flow-of-funds data for the advanced economies indeed show a massive shift in the private sector's behavior before and after 2008 (Figure 1.1). Flow-of-funds data indicate whether a particular sector of an economy is

FIGURE 1.1  Private-sector[1] Savings Behavior Changed Dramatically After 2008

Average Annual Private Sector Financial Surplus (+) or Deficit (−)

|  | 5 years to Q3 2008 | from Q4 2008 to present[4] | latest 4 quarters (% of GDP) |  | 5 years to Q3 2008 | from Q4 2008 to present[4] | latest 4 quarters (% of GDP) |
|---|---|---|---|---|---|---|---|
| UK | 1.63 | 3.38 | −2.97 | Germany | 8.46[3] | 7.04 | 12.13 |
| U.S. | 0.48 | 5.21 | 4.12 | France | 2.54 | 2.36 | −0.07 |
| Canada | −0.02 | −1.21[5] | −1.77 | Italy | 1.48 | 2.75 | 6.19 |
| Japan | 7.68[2] | 8.57 | 6.24 | Spain | −8.02 | 7.15 | 6.40 |
| Korea | −1.89 | 4.04 | 4.58 | Greece | −1.53 | 2.64 | 0.64 |
| Australia | −7.77 | 0.09 | 0.39 | Ireland | −5.41 | 7.28 | 0.40 |
| Eurozone | 1.65 | 5.01 | 4.62 | Portugal | −3.97 | 4.42 | 3.61 |

Notes: *Based on these countries' flow-of-funds and national accounts data. 1. Private sector = household + corporate + financial sectors. 2. In balance sheet recession since 1990. 3. In balance sheet recession since 2000. 4. Until Q1 2017. Only for France, Greece, and Ireland, Q4 2016. 5. Except Canada.

Source: Nomura Research Institute

a net supplier or borrower of funds by looking at changes in its financial assets and financial liabilities.

If the sector's financial assets increased more than its financial liabilities, it is considered to be in financial surplus—in other words, it is a net saver, or a net supplier of funds to the economy. If the sector's financial assets increased less than its financial liabilities, it is considered to be in financial deficit, which means it is a net borrower of funds. It should be noted that the concept of financial surplus in the flow-of-funds data is not the same as the frequently used "savings rate" because the latter is adjusted for depreciation and other factors that affect net additions to the saver's wealth.

Flow-of-funds data typically divide the economy into five sectors: household, non-financial corporate, financial, government, and the rest of the world. The data are compiled in such a way that these five sectors always add up to zero. The data therefore show who saved and who borrowed within the economy.

In the U.S., however, the five sectors do not sum to zero. This is because the compiler of these data, the Federal Reserve, believes that it is better to share with the public the raw data it collected rather than go through the additional iteration of adjustments and estimations needed to ensure that the numbers add up to zero.

These data, like many macroeconomic statistics, are frequently revised as more complete information becomes available. And as noted in the author's previous work[3], these revisions can be quite large. Anyone who uses these data must therefore view each statistic with a certain amount of latitude given the possibility of subsequent revisions. The numbers used in this book reflect what was available on the internet on August 2nd, 2017. In this book, the term "private sector" is used to mean the sum of the household, non-financial corporate, and financial sectors.

According to these data, which are shown in Figure 1.1, the entire U.S. private sector has been saving an average of 5.21 percent of GDP since the third quarter of 2008, when interest rates fell almost to zero in the wake of Lehman Brothers' collapse. The corresponding figures are 7.15 percent for Spain's private sector, 7.28 percent for Ireland's, and 4.42 percent for Portugal's. In Japan, where the bubble burst in 1990 and interest rates have been essentially zero or negative since 1997, the private sector was saving an average of 7.68 percent of GDP even *before* Lehman's failure and 8.57 percent of GDP in the eight years afterwards. In Germany, where the dotcom bubble in the Neuer Markt, the local equivalent of Nasdaq, burst

---

[3] For example, see Koo, Richard (2015) *The Escape from Balance Sheet Recession and the QE Trap*, Singapore: John Wiley & Sons, Chapter 3.

in 2000, the private sector was saving a full 8.46 percent of GDP *before* the Lehman bankruptcy and 7.04 percent thereafter.

These are very disturbing numbers because businesses and households should be massive *borrowers* at today's ultra-low interest rates. Instead, they have been saving huge amounts in an attempt to rebuild their damaged balance sheets. In effect, the private sectors in all the advanced countries except Canada are operating outside the realm of textbook economics.

The abrupt shift from the pre-Lehman to the post-Lehman world, shown in the third column of Figure 1.1, was nothing short of spectacular. In both Spain and Ireland, for example, the shift in private-sector behavior from borrowing to saving amounted to well over 10 percent of GDP. And that is comparing the five-year average before Lehman and the eight-year average after Lehman.

The shift in private-sector behavior immediately before and after the Lehman failure was even bigger, reaching well over 20 percent of GDP in many countries. Such a huge and abrupt shift from net borrowing to net saving will throw any economy into a recession. And households and businesses will not start borrowing again until they feel comfortable with their financial health. These disturbing numbers will be revisited throughout this book.

Yet economists continue to assume (often implicitly) that borrowers are plentiful because their models and theories all assume that the private sector is maximizing profits. Their forecasts for growth and inflation, which are based on those models and theories, have consistently and repeatedly missed the mark since 2008 because the assumption of a profit-maximizing private sector is no longer valid in the post-bubble world. Moreover, because the assumption of a profit-maximizing private sector is so fundamental to their models and theories, most economists failed to suspect that their models have foundered because this basic assumption about private-sector behavior is no longer valid.

Mikhail Gorbachev famously said, "You cannot solve the problem until you call it by its right name." When the economic crisis hit in 2008, the economics profession had not only neglected to consider the possibility of a recession caused by a debt-minimizing private sector, but it did not even have a name for the phenomenon. Indeed, the author had to coin the term *balance sheet recession* in the late 1990s to describe this economic disease in a Japanese context[4]. This term finally entered the lexicon of economics in

---

[4] The author acknowledges the inspiration given to him by Mr. Edward Frydl, his former boss at the Federal Reserve Bank of New York, who used the term "balance sheet-driven recession" when we were discussing the U.S. economy of the early 1990s.

the West with the 2008 collapse of Lehman Brothers and the global financial crisis that followed.

Economists' inability to consider the possibility that borrowers might stop borrowing or actually start paying down debt has already resulted in some very bad outcomes, including the Great Depression in the U.S. and the rise of the National Socialists in Germany in the 1930s. European policymakers' continued failure to understand balance sheet recessions has enabled the emergence of similar far-right political groups in the Eurozone since 2008. These economic and political issues are addressed in Chapter 7.

## Paradox of Thrift Was Norm Before Industrial Revolution

For thousands of years before the Industrial Revolution in the 1760s, however, economic stagnation due to a lack of borrowers was much closer to the norm. As shown in Figure 1.2, economic growth had been negligible for centuries before 1760. Even then, there were probably millions who tried

FIGURE 1.2 Economic Growth Became the Norm Only After the Industrial Revolution

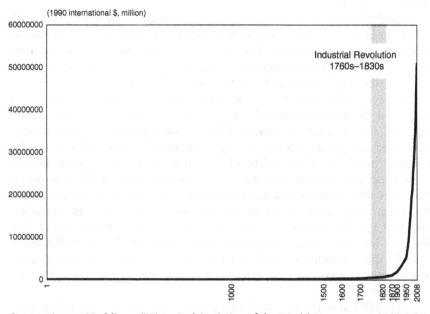

*Source:* Angus Maddison, "Historical Statistics of the World Economy: 1-2008 AD", www.ggdc.net/maddison/Historical_Statistics/Verticel-file_02-2010.xls

to save—after all, human beings have always worried about an uncertain future. Preparing for old age and the proverbial rainy day is an ingrained aspect of human nature. But if it is only human to save, the centuries-long economic stagnation prior to the Industrial Revolution must have been due to a lack of borrowers.

The private sector must have a clean balance sheet and promising investment opportunities to borrow. After all, businesses will not borrow unless they feel sure the debt can be paid back with interest. But before the Industrial Revolution, which was essentially a technological revolution, there was little or no technological innovation, and therefore few investments capable of paying for themselves.

Businesses also tend to minimize debt when they see no investment opportunities because the probability of bankruptcy can be reduced drastically by eliminating debt. Japanese firms dating back several centuries, many of which can be found in and around Kyoto and Nagoya, typically do not borrow money for this reason. And if they do, they pay it back at the earliest opportunity to minimize the risk of bankruptcy. It is therefore appropriate for businesses to minimize debt until investment opportunities present themselves, with the possible exception of tax considerations. Given the dearth of investment opportunities prior to the Industrial Revolution, it is not hard to understand why there were so few willing borrowers.

Amid this absence of investment opportunities in the pre-1760 world, efforts to save only caused the economy to shrink. The result was a permanent paradox of thrift in which people tried to save but their very actions and intentions kept the national economy in a depressed state. This state of affairs lasted for centuries in both the East and the West.

Powerful rulers sometimes borrowed funds saved by the private sector and used them to build social infrastructure or monuments. The vicious cycle of the paradox of thrift was then suspended as the government borrowed the private sector's savings (the initial savings of $100 in the example above) and injected them back into the income stream, fueling rapid economic growth. But unless the project paid for itself—and politicians are seldom good at selecting investments that pay for themselves—the government, facing a mounting debt load, would at some point get cold feet and discontinue its investment. The broader economy would then fall back into the stagnation that characterizes the paradox of thrift. Consequently, these regimes were often outlived by the monuments they created. The challenging task of selecting viable public works projects is revisited in Chapter 4.

Countries also tried to achieve economic growth by expanding their territories, i.e., by acquiring more land, which was the key factor of production in pre-industrial agricultural societies. Indeed, for centuries until

1945, people believed that territorial expansion was essential for economic growth (the significance of this date is explained in Chapter 3). This territorial drive for prosperity was the economic rationale for colonialism and imperialism. But both were basically a zero-sum proposition for the global economy and also resulted in countless wars and deaths.

Ironically, the wars and resulting destruction produced investment opportunities in the form of postwar reconstruction activity. And wars were frequent occurrences in those days. But without a continuous flow of innovation, investment opportunities soon exhausted themselves and economic growth petered out.

## Four Possible States of Borrowers and Lenders

The discussion above suggests that an economy is always in one of four possible states depending on the presence or absence of lenders (savers) and borrowers (investors). They are as follows: (1) both lenders and borrowers are present in sufficient numbers, (2) there are borrowers but not enough lenders even at high interest rates, (3) there are lenders but not enough borrowers even at low interest rates, and (4) both lenders and borrowers are absent. These four states are illustrated in Figure 1.3.

Of the four, only Cases 1 and 2 are discussed in traditional economics, which implicitly assumes there are always enough borrowers as long as real interest rates are low enough. Or, more precisely, economists who argue that lower real interest rates are needed to stimulate the economy are assuming that the economy is in Case 1 or Case 2. Of the two, only Case 1 requires a minimum of policy intervention—such as slight adjustments to interest rates—to match savers and borrowers and keep the economy going. Case 1, therefore, is associated with ordinary interest rates and can be considered the ideal textbook case.

The causes of Case 2 (insufficient lenders) can be traced to both macro and financial factors. The most common macro factor is when the central bank tightens monetary policy to rein in inflation. The tighter credit conditions that result certainly leave lenders less willing to lend. Once inflation is under control, however, the central bank typically eases monetary policy, and the economy returns to Case 1.

A country may also be too poor or underdeveloped to save. If the paradox of thrift leaves a country too poor to save, the situation would be classified as Case 3 or 4 because it is actually attributable to a lack of borrowers.

Financial factors weighing on lenders may also push the economy into Case 2. One such factor is an excess of non-performing loans (NPLs) in the banking system, which depresses banks' capital ratios and prevents

FIGURE 1.3 Borrowers and Lenders—Four Possible States

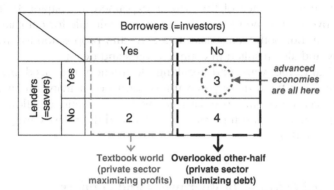

1. Lenders and borrowers are present in sufficient numbers (textbook world) ⇒ **Ordinary interest rates.**
2. Borrowers are present but not lenders due to the latter's bad loan problems (financial crisis, credit crunch) ⇒ **Loan rates much higher than policy rate.**
3. Lenders are present but no borrowers, due to the latter's balance sheet problems and/or lack of investment opportunities (balance sheet recession, "secular" stagnation) ⇒ **Ultra-low interest rates.**
4. Borrowers and lenders both absent due to balance sheet problems for the former and bad loan problems for the latter (aftermath of a bubble burst) ⇒ **Ultra-low interest rates, but only for highly rated borrowers**

them from lending. This is what is typically called a "credit crunch." Over-regulation of financial institutions by the authorities can also lead to a credit crunch. When many banks encounter NPL problems at the same time, mutual distrust may lead not only to a credit crunch but also to a dysfunctional interbank market, a state of affairs typically referred to as a "financial crisis."

When lenders have NPL problems, the central bank's policy rate could diverge significantly from actual lending rates set by the banks, and only those willing to pay the high actual rates will be able to borrow. Monetary authorities may also allow such "fat spreads" deliberately in certain circumstances to strengthen banks' balance sheets.

Cultural norms discouraging savings, as well as income (and productivity) levels that are simply too low to allow people to save, are developmental phenomena typically found in pre-industrialized societies. An underdeveloped financial system, due in some cases to religious considerations, may also constrain lending. These developmental issues can take many years to address.

However, non-developmental causes of a shortage of lenders all have well-known remedies in the literature. For example, the government can inject capital into the banks to restore their ability to lend, or it can relax regulations preventing financial institutions from serving as financial intermediaries.

In the case of a dysfunctional interbank market, the central bank can act as lender of last resort to ensure the clearing system continues to operate. It can also relax monetary policy. The conventional emphasis on monetary policy and concerns over the crowding-out effect of fiscal policy are justified in Cases 1 and 2, where there are borrowers but (for a variety of reasons in Case 2) not enough lenders. Lender-side problems such as credit crunches and financial crises are discussed in more detail in Chapter 8.

The problem comes with Cases 3 and 4, where the bottleneck is a shortage of *borrowers*. This is the *other half of macroeconomics* that has been overlooked by traditional economists.

As noted above, there are two main reasons why private-sector borrowers might disappear. The first is that they cannot find attractive investment opportunities at home, and the second is that their financial health has deteriorated to the point where they cannot borrow until they repair their balance sheets. Examples of the first case would include the world that existed prior to the Industrial Revolution or a country where the return on capital was much higher abroad than at home, while examples of the second case can be observed following the collapse of debt-financed asset bubbles.

Most advanced countries today suffer from both of these factors, which have served to reduce the number of borrowers. Because balance sheet problems are more urgent in the sense that they can depress the economy very quickly, they are discussed first, in Chapter 2, although the main thrust of this book involves the second case and is explored in Chapters 3, 4, and 5. Those already familiar with the concept of balance sheet recessions and who aware of where the major countries stand on this issue may wish to proceed directly to Chapter 3.

# Balance Sheet Problems Create Shortage of Borrowers

As noted in Chapter 1, there are two main reasons why an economy can end up in the "other half" of macroeconomics with no private-sector borrowers. The first is that borrowers cannot find attractive investment opportunities at home, and the second is that their financial health has deteriorated to the point where they are unable to borrow until they repair their balance sheets.

Today all advanced countries confront both factors, which have reduced the number of borrowers. Because balance sheet issues have become so acute since the housing bubble collapsed in 2008 and are more urgent in the sense that they can quickly destroy an economy, they will be discussed first. Readers who are already familiar with the concept of balance sheet recessions and the progress that major economies have made in addressing this ailment may wish to skip this section and move on to the next chapter.

Borrowers who have absented themselves because of underwater balance sheets will not return until their negative equity problems are resolved. Depending on the size of the bubble, this can take many years even under the best of circumstances. For example, if the borrower in Chapter 1 who was $200,000 underwater has an after-tax income of $150,000 and a savings rate of 20 percent, she is saving $30,000 per year. If she is able to earmark two-thirds of that amount to address the debt overhang issue, it will still take her ten years to repair her balance sheet.

With so many people trying to repair their balance sheets at the same time, however, the economy will be in constant danger of entering the $1000-$900-$810-$730 deflationary scenario described in Chapter 1. If a recession reduces the income of the person in the example above, she will have even less money to pay down debt and will therefore require more time to repair her balance sheet. And if house prices fall further, it will take her even longer to restore her financial health. Both factors—reduced income and falling house prices—can easily double the time needed for balance sheet repairs.

## Japan in Balance Sheet Recession

Japan was the first advanced country to experience a private-sector shift to debt minimization for balance sheet reasons since the Great Depression. After the bubble burst in 1990, nationwide commercial real estate prices fell 87 percent to levels last seen in 1973 (Figure 2.1), devastating the balance sheets of businesses and financial institutions across the country. Figure 2.2 shows the funds procured by Japanese non-financial businesses from both the banking system and the capital markets. From 1985 to 1990, when the Japanese bubble was rapidly expanding, these businesses were leveraging up by borrowing massive amounts to invest in a wide variety of assets. The Bank of Japan (BOJ), realizing that the bubble was on and the economy was overheating, steadily raised short-term interest rates in an attempt to contain the bubble.

Demand for funds shrank rapidly when the bubble finally burst in 1990. Noting that the economy was also slowing sharply, the BOJ took interest rates down from 8 percent at the height of the bubble to almost zero by 1995. But demand for funds not only failed to recover but actually turned

FIGURE 2.1 Japan's GDP Grew Despite Major Loss of Wealth and Private-Sector Deleveraging

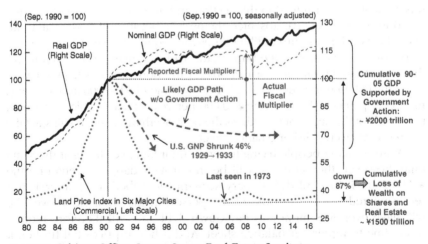

*Sources:* Cabinet Office, Japan; Japan Real Estate Institute

FIGURE 2.2 Japan's Corporate Deleveraging with Zero Interest Rates Lasted for Over 10 Years, Until 2005

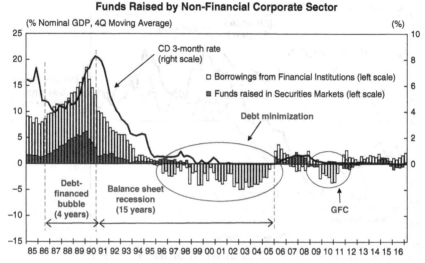

**Funds Raised by Non-Financial Corporate Sector**

Sources: Bank of Japan; Cabinet Office, Japan

negative that year. Negative demand for funds means that Japan's entire corporate sector was paying down debt at a time of zero interest rates, a world that no economics department in university or business school had ever envisioned. The borrowers not only stopped borrowing but began moving in the opposite direction by paying down debt and continued doing so for a full ten years, until around 2005.

Figure 2.3 provides a more general view of the Japanese economy during this period, based on flow-of-funds data. Flow-of-funds data, which divide the economy into five sectors—household, non-financial corporate, financial, government, and the rest of the world—indicate whether a given sector is a net supplier or net borrower of funds. Sectors above the horizontal line at zero are net suppliers (financial surplus = savers) of funds, while those below the line are net borrowers (financial deficit = investors). The data are compiled in such a way that the five sectors sum to zero and show which sectors saved money and which sectors borrowed money in each year.

To simplify presentation, the original five sectors are reduced to four in this book by combining non-financial and financial companies into a single "corporate sector." All national flow-of-funds data in this book (the figures with four lines) are presented as four-quarter moving averages to smooth out seasonal fluctuations, a fairly common practice when using flow-of-funds data.

FIGURE 2.3 Japan's Challenge: Persuade Traumatized Businesses to Borrow Again

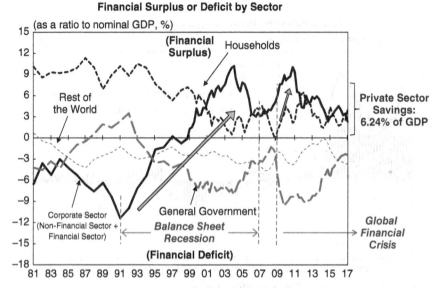

**Financial Surplus or Deficit by Sector**

*Notes:* All entries are four-quarter moving averages. For the latest figures, four-quarter averages ending in 2017 Q1 are used.

*Sources:* Bank of Japan, *Flow of Funds Accounts*, and Government of Japan, Cabinet Office, *National Accounts*

It should also be noted that shifts within financial assets or liabilities are netted out in flow-of-funds data. For example, businesses issuing debt to buy back shares will have zero net impact on the flow-of-funds data because both debt and equity represent financial liabilities. This means that corporate leverage may still be growing even if there is no change in corporate sector financial deficit if the companies are engaged in share buybacks using borrowed funds.

Figure 2.3 shows that Japan's post-bubble economy was indeed driven by massive corporate deleveraging (the large arrow). While in a textbook economy the household sector saves and the corporate sector borrows, both sectors became net savers in post-1999 Japan, with the corporate sector becoming the largest saver in the country from 2002 onward in spite of zero interest rates. The deflationary impact of businesses' swing from borrowing to saving was over 20 percent of GDP (from a financial deficit of 11.4 percent of GDP in 1991 to a financial surplus of 10.2 percent of GDP in 2004.) This massive corporate shift from profit maximization to debt minimization is the cause of the prolonged economic stagnation that continues to this day in Japan. Fully 27 years after the bubble burst, Japan's private sector is still saving over 6 percent of GDP at a time of negative interest rates.

## The West in Balance Sheet Recession

Western economies also experienced huge housing bubbles (Figure 2.4). When those bubbles collapsed on both sides of the Atlantic in 2008, the balance sheets of millions of households and many financial institutions were devastated. The resulting loss of wealth reached well into the tens of trillions of dollars, while the liabilities incurred during the bubble remained on the books at their original values.

As Figure 1.1 shows, the private sectors in virtually all major advanced nations have been increasing savings or paying down debt since 2008 in spite of record low interest rates. According to the latest data, the U.S. private sector saved 4.1 percent of GDP at near-zero interest rates in the four quarters through Q1 2017 (Figure 2.5). The corresponding figure for Spain was 6.4 percent (Figure 2.6). Although the Irish data are affected by that nation's volatile financial sector, Ireland's non-financial private sector is saving 2.43 percent of GDP (Figure 2.7) at a time of zero or negative interest

FIGURE 2.4 The West (Excluding Germany) Also Saw Collapse of Housing Bubbles

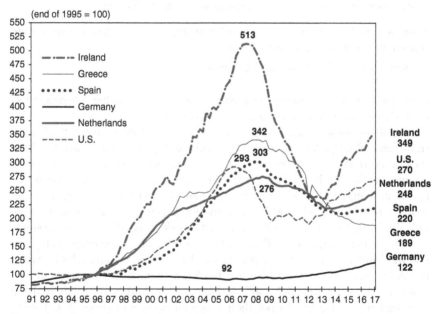

*Notes:* 1. Ireland's figures before 2005 are existing house prices only. 2. Greece's figures are flats' prices in Athens and Thessaloniki.

*Sources:* Nomura Research Institute, calculated from Bank for International Settlements and S&P Dow Jones data

FIGURE 2.5 U.S. Private Sector Has Been Saving 5.21 Percent of GDP Since 2008 in Spite of Zero Interest Rates

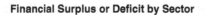

**Financial Surplus or Deficit by Sector**

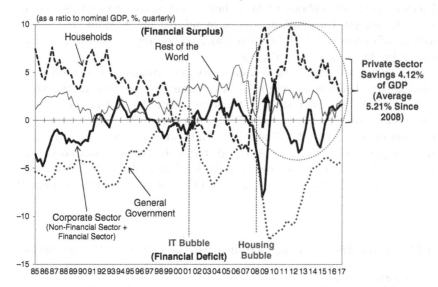

*Notes:* All entries are four-quarter moving averages. For the latest figures, four-quarter averages ending in 2017 Q1 are used.

*Sources:* FRB, U.S. Department of Commerce

rates. Indeed, the Eurozone's overall private sector is saving 4.6 percent of GDP (Figure 2.8) in spite of negative interest rates.

In all of these countries, not only the household sector but also the non-financial corporate sector is increasing savings or paying down debt at these record low interest rates. Such corporate sector behavior runs totally counter to the textbook insistence that profit-maximizing firms should be taking advantage of record low interest rates by borrowing more. In other words, the developed world is experiencing private-sector behavior that falls totally outside the conventional framework of neoclassical economics.

The private sectors in all of these countries are increasing savings or paying down debt because their balance sheets were damaged badly when the debt-financed asset bubbles burst. With a huge debt overhang and no assets to show for that debt, affected businesses and households realized they had no choice but to put their financial houses in order. A failure to do so would mean a loss of access to credit if not to society altogether. As such, they will be increasing savings or paying down debt until they safely emerge from negative equity. This also means they will be forced to change their focus from maximizing profit to minimizing debt.

FIGURE 2.6 Spanish Households Increased Borrowings After Dotcom Bubble, But Are Now Deleveraging

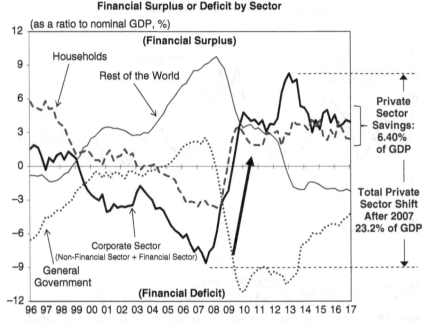

**Financial Surplus or Deficit by Sector**

*Notes:* All entries are four-quarter moving averages. For the latest figures, four-quarter averages ending in 2017 Q1 are used.

*Sources:* Banco de España and National Statistics Institute, Spain

The shift here has been nothing short of spectacular. The U.S. private sector went from saving a net 1.3 percent of GDP in Q4 2008 to saving a net 7.6 percent of GDP in Q1 2010 in spite of the lowest interest rates in U.S. history. The U.S. economy not only suffered an exodus of borrowers but also lost private-sector demand equal to 6.3 percent of GDP in just five quarters, plunging the economy into a serious recession. The UK lost private-sector demand equal to 8.2 percent of GDP from Q3 2006 to Q3 2010. Spain lost 19.4 percent of GDP from the shift in private-sector behavior between Q3 2007 and Q1 2010, also at a time of record low interest rates. These private sectors' scramble to repair damaged balance sheets tipped the global economy into the Great Recession.

In other words, the problems began with the private sector, not the government. The government sectors in all of these countries are simply responding to the recession caused by the collapse of private-sector demand, which in turn was triggered by the sudden swing to debt minimization.

FIGURE 2.7  Irish Households Increased Borrowings After Dotcom Bubble, But Are Now Deleveraging

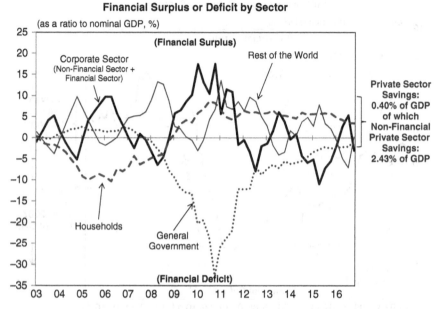

**Financial Surplus or Deficit by Sector**

*Notes:* All entries are four-quarter moving averages. For the latest figures, four-quarter averages ending in 2016 Q4 are used.

*Sources:* Central Bank of Ireland and Central Statistics Office, Ireland

# The First Casualty of Borrowers' Disappearance: Monetary Policy

When borrowers disappear and the economy is in Case 3 or 4, there is very little that monetary policy, economists' preferred policy tool, can do to support the real economy. For monetary policy to help stimulate GDP, there has to be someone willing to borrow money from financial institutions and spend or invest it in the *real* economy.

Figures 2.9 to 2.11 show that the close relationship observed prior to 2008 between central-bank-supplied liquidity, known as the monetary base, and growth in money supply and private-sector credit broke down completely after the bubbles burst and the private sector began minimizing debt. Here, money supply refers to the sum of all bank accounts plus bills and coins circulating in the economy, and credit means the amount of money lent to the private sector by financial institutions.

These figures make it clear that the monetary base, money supply, and credit supplied to the private sector were closely correlated prior to 2008, just as economics teaches. In this textbook world, a 10 percent increase in

FIGURE 2.8 Eurozone's Flow of Funds

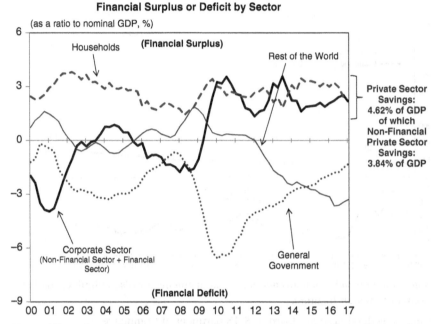

**Financial Surplus or Deficit by Sector**

(as a ratio to nominal GDP, %)

*Notes:* All entries are four-quarter moving averages. For the latest figures, four-quarter averages ending in 2017 Q1 are used.

*Sources:* ECB and Eurostat

central bank liquidity would increase both the money supply and credit by 10 percent. This means there were enough borrowers in the private sector to borrow all the funds supplied by the central bank, and economies were in Case 1 of Figure 1.3.

But after the bubble burst, which forced the private sector to minimize debt in order to repair its balance sheet, no amount of central bank accommodation was able to increase private-sector borrowings. The U.S. Federal Reserve, for example, expanded the monetary base by 349 percent after Lehman Brothers went under. But the money supply grew by only 76 percent and credit by only 27 percent. A 27 percent increase in private-sector credit over a period of nearly nine years represents an average annual increase of only 2.75 percent, which is next to nothing.

A central bank can always add liquidity to the banking system by purchasing assets from financial institutions. But for that liquidity to enter the real economy, banks must lend out those funds: they cannot give them away because the funds are ultimately owned by depositors. A 27 percent increase in lending since 2008 means new money entering the real economy from the financial sector has grown by only 27 percent. In other words,

FIGURE 2.9 Drastic Liquidity Injections Resulted in Minimal Increases in Money Supply and Credit (I)—U.S.

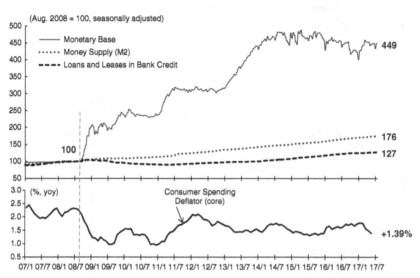

*Note:* Commercial bank loans and leases, adjustments for discontinuities made by Nomura Research Institute.

*Sources:* Federal Reserve Board; U.S. Department of Commerce

most of the liquidity supplied by the central bank (the 349 percent) remains stuck in the financial sector due to a lack of borrowers. Similar de-couplings have been observed in all post-bubble economies, including the Eurozone (Figure 2.10) and the UK (Figure 2.11).

This explains why inflation and growth rates in the advanced economies have all failed to respond to zero interest rates and astronomical injections of central bank liquidity since 2008. The lack of borrowers has meant that the actual money circulating in the economy has increased only modestly. Some economists argue that inflation is always and everywhere a monetary phenomenon, and that a central bank in charge of monetary policy can therefore create inflation at will. If that were the case, the 349 percent growth in the monetary base should have led to similar increases in the money supply and credit, driving a corresponding surge in inflation. But nothing of the sort happened after 2008.

# Great Depression as Balance Sheet Recession

Not surprisingly, the same decoupling of monetary aggregates was observed in the U.S. after the Great Crash of 1929, which led to the Great Depression,

FIGURE 2.10 Drastic Liquidity Injections Resulted in Minimal Increases in Money Supply and Credit (II)—Eurozone

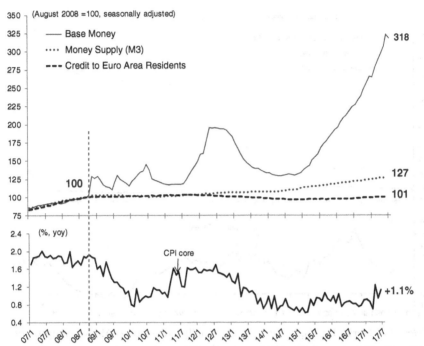

*Note:* Base money's figures are seasonally adjusted by Nomura Research Institute.

*Sources:* European Central Bank; Eurostat

and in Japan after its bubble burst in 1990. Figure 2.12 illustrates the monetary base, the money supply, and credit supplied to the private sector before and after the October 1929 stock market crash. It shows that the three were moving in tandem until the crash, just as textbooks teach, but then decoupled in exactly the same way as they did in the post-2008 economies. Thus the line for the loans to the private sector is at the bottom of the figure, which fell as much as 54.7 percent from its 1929 peak as the U.S. private sector sought to pay down debt in order to repair its battered balance sheet. The line for the money supply is just above the line for the loans and the line for the monetary base is at the top of the graph.

The money supply contracted as much as 33 percent during this period because people withdrew money from their bank accounts to pay down debt. A 54.7 percent decline in lending means there was a corresponding withdrawal of money from bank deposits to pay down debt. Since the money supply consists mainly of bank deposits, a large net withdrawal of bank deposits to pay down debt led to a contraction of the money supply.

FIGURE 2.11 Drastic Liquidity Injections Resulted in Minimal Increases in Money Supply and Credit (III): UK

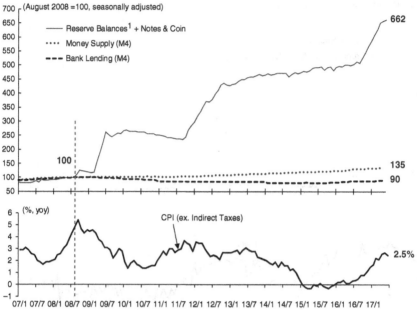

*Notes:* 1. Reserve balances data are seasonally adjusted. 2. Money supply and bank lending data exclude intermediate financial institutions.

*Sources:* Bank of England; Office for National Statistics, UK

Milton Friedman and other believers in monetary policy argued that the Fed did not quickly expand the monetary base in the 1930s (unlike its post-Lehman behavior), and that this lack of early action contributed to the severity of the subsequent depression in the 1930s. Since monetary base is largely bank reserves, a close look at the reserve data shown at the bottom of Figure 2.12, indicates that American banks were *paying back* borrowed reserves to the Fed in huge amounts immediately after the stock market crash. Between June 1929 and March 1930, bank borrowings from the Fed fell 95 percent, plunging from $801 million to just $43 million (circled area in bottom graph). This was most likely in response to the post-crash collapse in loan demand, which left banks with no reason to hold borrowed reserves. With lenders so eager to return their reserves to the Fed, there was no reason for the Fed to supply *more* reserves to the banks.

Monetary policy believers also argued that the post-1933 U.S. recovery was made possible not by President Roosevelt's New Deal policies but rather by the Fed's monetary easing. They pointed out that while the

FIGURE 2.12  Same Decoupling of Monetary Aggregate Observed in 1930s

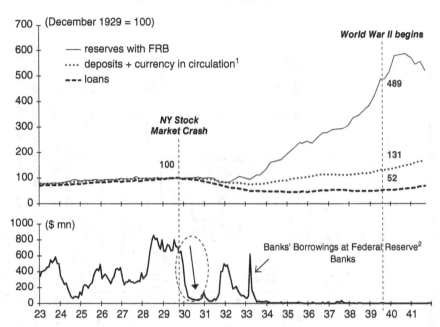

*Notes:* 1. Deposits = demand deposits adjusted + other time deposits. 2. Only this data series is based on member banks in 101 leading cities. All other data series are for all member banks.

*Sources:* Nomura Research Institute, based on data from Board of Governors of the Federal Reserve System (1976) *Banking and Monetary Statistics 1914–1941*, pp. 72–75, 138–163, 409–413

deficit-to-GDP ratio did not grow substantially after 1933, the money supply did. However, as noted by the author in his 2008 book *The Holy Grail of Macroeconomics*, the money supply is a liability of the banking system and can only grow if the asset side of the banking system also increases. A look at the asset side of U.S. banks' post-1933 balance sheets (Figure 2.13) clearly indicates that only lending to the government expanded during this period. And that was a direct result of President Roosevelt's New Deal policies.

The U.S. money supply grew after 1933 because the government presented itself as borrower of last resort. With the government now willing to borrow the unborrowed $100 in the earlier example, the economy was finally able to emerge from the $1,000–$900–$810 deflationary spiral.

Lending to the private sector actually continued to shrink until 1936 (Figure 2.12). The gap between money supply growth and private-sector credit growth was due to government borrowing. The correct interpretation

FIGURE 2.13 Reflationists Overlooked Fact that Government's New Deal Borrowings Enabled Post-1933 Growth in U.S. Money Supply

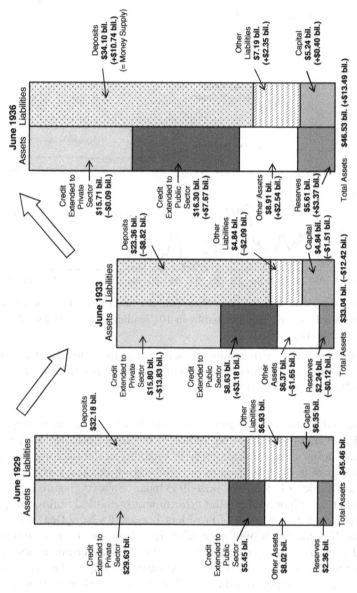

*Source:* Koo, Richard (2008) *The Holy Grail of Macroeconomics: Lessons from Japan's Great Recession,* Singapore: John Wiley & Sons, p. 112; based on data from The Board of Governors of the Federal Reserve System (1978) *Banking and Monetary Statistics 1914–1941,* pp. 72–78

FIGURE 2.14 Drastic Liquidity Injections Resulted in Minimal Increases in Money Supply and Credit (IV): Japan

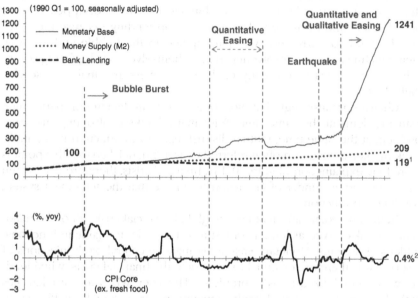

Notes: 1. Figures for bank lending are seasonally adjusted by Nomura Research Institute. 2. Excluding the impact of consumption tax.

Source: Bank of Japan

of the post-1933 U.S. recovery, therefore, is that New Deal-driven government borrowing and spending boosted *both* GDP and the money supply.

The same decoupling of monetary aggregates was also observed in Japan after its bubble burst in 1990, as shown in Figure 2.14. Here, too, the Bank of Japan's massive injections of reserves to the banking system, especially after 2013, failed to increase lending to the private sector or boost inflation (shown at the bottom of Figure 2.14). Instead, it was government borrowing that kept the Japanese money supply from contracting after 1990 when private-sector borrowing was rapidly shrinking.

The decoupling of monetary aggregates following a bubble's collapse suggests that monetary policy loses its effectiveness when the private sector is minimizing debt, i.e., when the economy is in Case 3 or 4 in Figure 1.2. Central banks have continued to miss their inflation targets since 2008 because their private sectors are all minimizing debt. And they are doing so because their balance sheets are impaired. The fact that a number of central bank governors continue to insist that further monetary easing will enable them to meet their inflation targets suggests they still do not understand why their models and forecasts have failed.

## Lender of Last Resort Needed in Case 4

It should be noted that in the immediate aftermath of a bubble collapse, the economy is usually in Case 4, characterized by a disappearance of both lenders and borrowers. The lenders stop lending because they provided money to borrowers who participated in the bubble and are now facing technical or real insolvency. Banks themselves may be facing severe solvency problems when many of their borrowers are unable to service their debts.

Chances are also high that most or all banks are facing non-performing loan problems at the same time. With many banks confronting the same problem at the same time, mutual distrust leads to dysfunction in the inter-bank market, a condition often referred to as a "financial crisis" (this point is more fully explained in Chapter 8). In a financial crisis, therefore, the central bank must act as lender of last resort to ensure that the settlement system continues to function.

In the immediate aftermath of the global financial crisis, all of the major central banks served as lenders of last resort in order to maintain functional settlement systems. Monetary easing via massive central bank injections of reserves was therefore essential to overcome the financial crisis, when lenders were immobilized by NPL problems. However, when the problem lies with the borrowers, central bank monetary policy is largely ineffective in stimulating the economy, as described above.

## Government Must Act as Borrower of Last Resort in Cases 3 and 4

Once the bubble bursts and households and businesses are left facing debt overhangs, no amount of monetary easing by the central bank will persuade them to resume borrowing until their balance sheets are fully repaired. Some are badly traumatized by the years of painful deleveraging experience and may never borrow again—even after they restore their balance sheets. Indeed, most of the Americans who lived through the Great Depression never borrowed again because of this kind of trauma. The economy then falls into the $1000-$900-$810-$730 deflationary spiral described above because an absence of borrowers prevents saved and deleveraged funds from re-entering the economy's income stream.

When private-sector borrowers disappear and monetary policy stops working, the correct way to prevent a deflationary spiral is for the government to borrow and spend the excess savings of the private sector ($100 in the example above). In other words, the government should mobilize fiscal policy and serve as *borrower of last resort* when the economy is in Case 3 or 4.

If the government borrows and spends the $100 left unborrowed by the private sector, total expenditures will amount to $900 plus $100, or $1,000, and the economy will move on. This way, the private sector will have the income it needs to pay down debt or rebuild savings. The government's borrowing will also keep the money supply from shrinking because it allows the deleveraged funds to re-enter the economy via government borrowing and spending. This policy should be continued until the private sector is ready to borrow again.

Any premature fiscal consolidation when the economy is in Case 3 or 4 risks restarting the deflationary spiral. Such risks actually materialized in Japan in 1997 (discussed later with Figure 2.19) and in the Eurozone in 2010 (discussed in Chapter 7).

## Self-Corrective Mechanism of Economies in Balance Sheet Recessions

The bond market will encourage the government to act as borrower of last resort during this type of recession by pushing government bond yields down to an exceptionally low level. This happens because in a balance sheet recession (1) the government is the only remaining borrower and (2) the financial sector will be flooded with funds from private-sector deleveraging, newly generated household savings, and central bank monetary easing.

Fund managers at life insurers and pension funds who must earn an investment return but are not allowed to take on excessive foreign exchange risk or principal risk (i.e., they cannot invest all their money in stocks or foreign assets) have little choice but to buy government bonds during this type of recessions. This is because the government is the only borrower issuing debt denominated in the domestic currency. Their rush into government debt pushes yields to exceptionally low levels and encourages the government to act as borrower of last resort in what may be called the *self-corrective mechanism* of economies in balance sheet recessions (and in the other half of macroeconomics in general).

This mechanism is self-corrective in two senses. First, when the private sector is generating excess savings in spite of zero or negative interest rates, the funds required to finance fiscal stimulus to stabilize the economy are already sitting in financial institutions as unborrowed funds. Since those funds will necessarily flow into bonds issued by the last borrower standing— the government—there is no need for the central bank or any other entity to worry about financing government deficits. In other words, financing government deficit should never be a problem in balance sheet recessions. (Unfortunately this does not always hold true in the Eurozone, where nineteen government bond markets use the same currency. A solution to this Eurozone-specific problem is discussed in Chapter 7.)

Second, it is self-corrective in the sense that the bond market will encourage the government to borrow by sending bond rates down to unusually low levels. These ultra-low yields are a message to the government that, if there is any social infrastructure needed for the future, now is the time to build it because the cost of financing will never be lower. If the government heeds the bond market's message and serves as borrower of last resort, not only will the economy and money supply be supported, but the burden on future taxpayers will also be minimized because of the lower cost of financing necessary infrastructure investment.

Exceptionally low government bond yields were first observed in post-1990 Japan even as the country's budget deficit and public debt skyrocketed. By 2009, Japan's public debt had surpassed 200 percent of GDP but its 10-year bond yield had fallen to 1.34 percent. Just before the Bank of Japan unveiled the policy of quantitative and qualitative easing (QQE) in 2013, the 10-year yield slipped to 0.735 percent, even though the country's public debt had risen to 240 percent of GDP.

The same drastic fall in bond yields has also been observed in Western economies since 2008. With the bond market making it possible for governments to borrow at exceptionally low rates, the real challenge for the latter is to ensure that (1) all saved funds are borrowed and spent, and (2) this policy is maintained until the financial health of the private sector is restored.

In November 2008, just two months after Lehman Brothers went under, the G20 countries agreed at an emergency meeting in Washington to implement fiscal stimulus. That decision kept the world economy from falling into a deflationary spiral. But in 2010, the fiscal orthodoxy of those who did not understand balance sheet recessions reasserted itself at the Toronto G20 meeting, where members agreed to cut deficits in half even though private-sector balance sheets were nowhere near a healthy state. The result was a sudden loss of forward momentum for the global economy that prolonged the recession unnecessarily in many parts of the world. After 2010, those countries that understood the danger of balance sheet recessions did well, while those that did not fell by the wayside.

## Four Central Banks' Track Records

In addition to the post-November 2008 fiscal stimulus, the U.S., the UK, Japan, and Europe also implemented their own massive monetary easing measures, known as quantitative easing (QE), as shown by the movement of monetary bases in Figures 2.9 to 2.11. But the understanding of how these policies work appears to differ greatly from country to country, leading to very different outcomes. There has also been some debate in Europe as to why the U.S. economy is doing better than the rest[1].

When most people hear the term quantitative easing, they think of Professor Milton Friedman's famous statement that inflation is "everywhere and always a monetary phenomenon," the implication being that the central bank—which is responsible for monetary policy—should be able to control the inflation rate.

According to this view, inflation can always be created if the central bank runs the printing presses and prints enough money. Professor Paul Krugman emphasized this point repeatedly in a two-hour debate with the author that was published in the November 1999 issue of *Bungei Shunju*, a leading monthly magazine in Japan[2]. The heads of central banks in post-2008 Japan, the UK, and Europe also declared that QE would increase lending and the money supply, thereby making it possible to reach their inflation targets.

In the UK, Paul Fisher, an official at the Bank of England when quantitative easing was launched in March 6, 2009, stated explicitly that the policy was intended to produce an economic recovery by increasing bank lending and expanding the money supply[3]. Bank of Japan Governor Haruhiko Kuroda declared on April 12, 2013 in his first speech as governor that QE would boost lending and allow the Bank to reach its 2 percent inflation target in two years[4]. Deputy Governor Kikuo Iwata was so confident in his belief that inflation is a monetary phenomenon[5] that he declared he would resign if the Bank were unable to achieve its inflation target within two years. Similarly, ECB President Mario Draghi, who unveiled a quantitative easing policy for the Eurozone on January 22, 2015, argued that this policy would "support money supply and credit growth, and thereby contribute to a return of inflation rates toward 2%."[6]

---

[1] Greenwood, John (2016) "Successful central banks focus on greater purchasing," *Financial Times*, May 31, 2016. https://next.ft.com/content/f7a98fb2-241f-11e6-9d4d-c11776a5124d.

[2] Koo, Richard & Krugman, Paul (1999) Gekitotsu Taidan: Nihon Keizai Endaka wa Akuka ("Big Debate on Japan's Economy: Is Strong Yen a Bad Thing?"), *Bungeishunju*, November 1999, edited by Yasuhara Ishizawa, pp. 130–143.

[3] Oakley, David (2009) "A bold bid to revive lending," *Financial Times*, March 7, 2009. https://next.ft.com/content/9b3fd930-0a90-11de-95ed-0000779fd2ac.

[4] Kuroda, Haruhiko (2013) "Quantitative and Qualitative Monetary Easing," speech at a meeting held by Yomiuri International Economic Society in Tokyo, April 12, 2013. www.boj.or.jp/en/announcements/press/koen_2013/ko130412a.htm/.

[5] Iwata, Kikuo, (2001), *Defure no Keizaigaku* ("The Economics of Deflation"), Tokyo: Toyo Keizai.

[6] Draghi, Mario, (2015), "Introductory statement to the press conference (with Q&A)," ECB's press conference in Frankfurt am Main, January 22, 2015. www.ecb.europa.eu/press/pressconf/2015/html/is150122.en.html.

## QE Did Not Boost Money Supply in Japan, UK, or Europe

All of these countries, however, have been in severe balance sheet recessions since their asset bubbles burst in 2008 (1990 in the case of Japan). Their private sectors have been collectively undergoing massive deleveraging—i.e., they have been running a large financial surplus—in spite of zero or negative interest rates. And they have been deleveraging because the collapse of debt-financed bubbles left them with a huge debt overhang.

Even though a central bank can always inject as much liquidity into the banking sector as it wants via QE, banks must lend that money for it to enter the real economy: they cannot give it away because it belongs to depositors. But if the private sector as a group is deleveraging, an absence of borrowers will prevent that liquidity from entering the real economy. The liquidity remains trapped within the financial system, leaving the central bank with no way to expand the money supply in the real economy[7].

More specifically, the money supply consists mostly of bank deposits, which are a liability of the banking system. But for the banking system's liabilities to grow, its assets must also increase—i.e., banks must lend more, as mentioned earlier. And if the private sector is not borrowing, the banks cannot increase lending. Consequently, as indicated in Figures 2.9 to 2.11, growth in both the money supply and bank lending in all of these countries has been modest at best.

In the UK, which Paul Fisher boldly declared would not repeat Japan's mistakes, the BOE increased the monetary base by 562 percent. But lending remains nearly 10 percent *below* pre-Lehman levels, and the nation's economy continues to seesaw between periods of no inflation and periods of outright deflation (Figure 2.9), much like Japan. The UK inflation rate did

---

[7] Technically, a central bank can increase the money supply by buying financial assets directly from non-bank private entities. However, such actions will only increase the savings component of the money supply since the non-bank entity that sold the assets to the central bank was presumably holding those assets as a form of savings. Changing the form of that savings from, say, government bonds to bank deposits is unlikely to prompt that entity to increase consumption. Accordingly, even if the money supply increases due to such purchases by the central bank, that growth will not add to GDP or lift inflationary pressures. In contrast, if the central bank buys cars and cameras from the non-bank private sector, such purchases will increase the transaction component of the money supply and thereby boost GDP. But the public purchase of goods and services is usually considered to lie within the realm of fiscal policy.

pick up after the Brexit vote, but that was due largely to the sharp fall in the value of the pound following the vote. In the Eurozone, where Draghi expanded the monetary base by 122 percent after introducing QE in 2015, bank lending has grown only 3 percent, and the inflation rate has remained around zero (Figure 2.10).

In Japan, Kuroda has expanded the monetary base by 227 percent since introducing QE in 2013, but bank lending has increased by just 14 percent. That 14 percent growth represents zero acceleration from the era of his predecessor, Masaaki Shirakawa. This can be seen in Figure 2.15 as a continuous straight line for both credit and the money supply before and after the change in governorship. Zero acceleration means the massive expansion of the monetary base under Kuroda has had no impact on the real economy, and the inflation rate remains at around zero.

This should help to demonstrate that the argument that "inflation is everywhere and always a monetary phenomenon" may be valid when there

FIGURE 2.15 No Acceleration of Private-Sector Credit or Money Supply Growth After BOJ's QQE

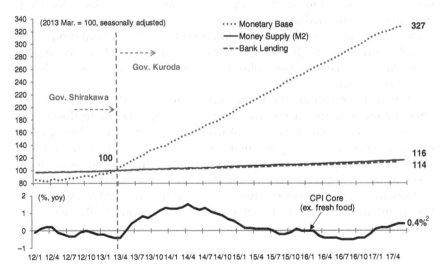

*Notes:* 1. Figures for bank lending are seasonally adjusted by Nomura Research Institute. 2. Excluding the impact of consumption tax.

*Sources:* Bank of Japan; Ministry of Internal Affairs and Communications

is strong private-sector demand for funds (Cases 1 and 2), but is basically irrelevant when the private sector refuses to borrow despite zero or even negative interest rates (Cases 3 and 4). While it can be argued that realized inflation is everywhere and always a monetary phenomenon, it makes no sense to say that the central bank can always create inflation by expanding the money supply.

## Fed Officials Did Not Claim They Would Raise Inflation by Expanding Money Supply

Fed officials such as former Chairman Ben Bernanke and current Chair Janet Yellen, on the other hand, said something very different when they introduced QE. While they, too, were among the pioneers of quantitative easing, they have never—to the author's knowledge, at least—claimed they would increase inflation by expanding the money supply. On the contrary, Bernanke made the opposite point in an article in the November 4, 2010 *Washington Post*[8] titled "What the Fed did and why: supporting the recovery and sustaining price stability." The article sought to explain QE2, which was intended to stimulate the economy, as opposed to QE1, which was originally implemented as a "lender of last resort" injection of reserves in response to the financial crisis that followed the Lehman bankruptcy. The liquidity provided by QE1, however, was deliberately left in the market even after the financial crisis subsided in the hope that it would help the economy recover.

Unlike his counterparts at the other three central banks, Bernanke does not mention increasing the money supply even once in this article. Instead, he says "Our earlier use of this policy approach had little effect on the amount of currency in circulation or on other broad measures of the money supply, such as bank deposits. Nor did it result in higher inflation." In effect, he is saying that all of the liquidity supplied under QE1 had *not* increased the money supply and that that is why QE2 would *not* lead to inflation. And, in fact, neither QE2 nor subsequent QE3 generated inflation.

---

[8]Bernanke, Ben S. (2010) "What The Fed Did and Why: Supporting the Recovery and Sustaining Price Stability," *Washington Post*, November 10, 2010. www.washingtonpost.com/wp-dyn/content/article/2010/11/03/AR2010110307372.html.

## Bernanke Rescued U.S. Economy with Policy That Ran Contrary to His Teacher's Views

Bernanke understood that the U.S. was in a balance sheet recession. The flow-of-funds data published by the Fed when QE2 was introduced showed the U.S. private sector was saving close to 8 percent of GDP in spite of zero interest rates. That U.S. businesses and households were saving so much meant that the money multiplier[9] for the private sector was negative at the margins. In other words, the U.S. money supply would have shrunk if no other borrower had emerged to take up the slack.

The U.S. money supply actually contracted 33 percent between 1929 and 1933 in the wake of the New York stock market crash (Figure 2.12) as the private sector collectively paid down debt and no one else was borrowing. Under such circumstances, the only way to prevent a contraction in GDP and the money supply is for the government to borrow and spend.

Bernanke and Yellen both understood this, and they used the expression "fiscal cliff" to warn Congress about the danger posed by fiscal consolidation, which the Republicans and many orthodox economists supported. The extent of Bernanke's concerns about fiscal consolidation can be gleaned from a press conference on April 25, 2012, when he was asked what the Fed would do if Congress pushed the U.S. economy off the fiscal cliff. He responded, "There is . . . absolutely no chance that the Federal Reserve could or would have any ability whatsoever to offset that effect on the economy."[10] Bernanke clearly understood that the Fed's monetary policy not only cannot offset the negative impact of fiscal consolidation, but would also lose its effectiveness if the government refused to act as borrower of last resort.

Even though the U.S. came frighteningly close to falling off the fiscal cliff on a number of occasions, including government shutdowns, sequesters, and debt-ceiling debates, it ultimately managed to avoid that outcome thanks to the efforts of officials at the Fed and the Obama administration. And that is why the U.S. economy is doing so much better than Europe, where virtually every country did fall off the fiscal cliff.

Bernanke had previously stated that he was a direct disciple of Milton Friedman, who was stridently opposed to fiscal stimulus. In the

---

[9] This concept is described in more detail in Chapter 8.

[10] Board of Governors of the Federal Reserve System (2012) "Transcript of Chairman Bernanke's Press Conference," Washington D.C., April 25, 2012. www.federalreserve .gov/mediacenter/files/FOMCpresconf20120425.pdf.

end, however, he saved the U.S. economy from its single worst postwar economic crisis by supporting a policy that ran contrary to the views of his teacher. In short, he understood that an economy in a balance sheet recession is doomed unless the government acts as borrower of last resort and that the impact of quantitative easing is limited to the portfolio rebalancing effect[11], which is far from sufficient to offset the headwinds from fiscal austerity. He understood that when the private sector is not borrowing money, the effectiveness of monetary policy is dependent on the last borrower standing, i.e., the government. The U.S. economy is doing better precisely because Bernanke and Yellen prevented the government from abdicating its responsibility to serve as borrower of last resort.

Even though the U.S. came close to falling off the fiscal cliff on several occasions, it is doing better now because, after eight years of fiscal support, private-sector balance sheets are growing healthier, and some households are actually starting to borrow again.

This can be seen from Figure 2.16, which shows U.S. household sector financial assets and liabilities separately. In this chart, a white bar above zero means the household sector is increasing its financial assets, i.e., increasing its savings. A white bar below zero means the household sector is reducing its financial assets, i.e., withdrawing its savings. Similarly, a shaded bar below zero means the sector is increasing its financial liabilities, i.e., increasing its borrowings. A shaded bar above zero means the sector is reducing its financial liabilities, i.e., paying down debt. The net number is shown by the broken line.

Traditional textbooks on economics say the household sector should save and the corporate sector should borrow. But during the bubble the U.S. household sector was a huge net borrower, as shown in Figure 2.16. Once the bubble burst, household sector not only became a huge net saver, but also stopped borrowing altogether for about four years. Now some U.S. households have resumed borrowing (circled areas in Figure 2.16). Even though the amounts are small compared to the pre-bubble era and the sector as a whole continues to run a substantial financial surplus, at least some have started borrowing again. This represents major progress compared to the situation in Europe, where there is still very little recovery in borrowings[12].

---

[11] This effect refers to the support the economy gets from higher asset prices brought about by central bank purchases of assets via quantitative easing.
[12] This point is discussed in more detail in Chapter 7.

FIGURE 2.16 Some U.S. Households Are Starting to Borrow

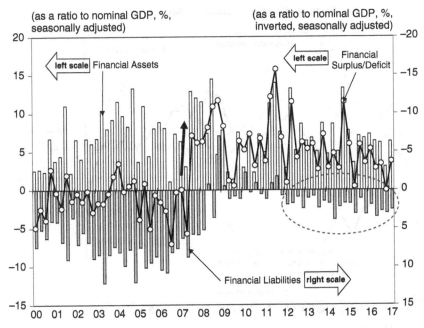

*Notes:* Latest figures are for 2017 Q1.

*Sources:* Nomura Research Institute, based on flow-of-funds data from FRB and U.S. Department of Commerce

## Other Central Banks Supported Austerity

The warnings about the fiscal cliff set the Fed apart from its counterparts in Japan, the UK, and Europe. In the UK, then-BOE Governor Mervyn King publicly supported David Cameron's rather draconian austerity measures, arguing that his bank's QE policy would provide necessary support for the British economy. At the time, the UK private sector was saving a full 9 percent of GDP (Figure 2.17) when interest rates were at their lowest levels in 300 years. That judgment led to the disastrous performance of the UK economy during the first two years of the Cameron administration and prompted George Osborne, Cameron's Chancellor of the Exchequer, to ask a Canadian to head the BOE.

BOJ Governor Haruhiko Kuroda also argued strongly in favor of hiking the consumption tax rate, believing a Japanese economy supported by

FIGURE 2.17  UK's Private Savings Shot Up After 2008 But Came Down Recently

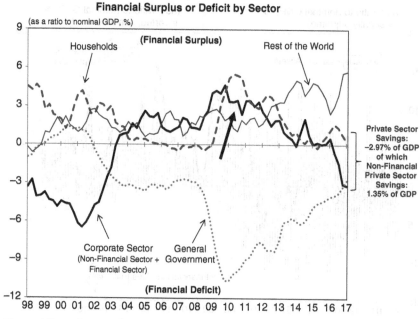

**Financial Surplus or Deficit by Sector**

*Notes:* All entries are four-quarter moving averages. For the latest figures, four-quarter averages ending in 2017 Q1 are used.

*Source:* Office for National Statistics, UK

his quantitative easing regime would be strong enough to withstand the shock of fiscal consolidation. This was in spite of the fact that the Japanese private sector was saving 6.2 percent of GDP at a time of zero interest rates (Figure 2.3). The tax hike, which was carried out in April 2014, threw the Japanese economy back into recession, and global enthusiasm for Abenomics evaporated completely thereafter.

ECB President Mario Draghi has admonished member governments to meet the austerity target imposed by the Stability and Growth Pact at every press conference, even though his own inflation forecasts have been revised downwards almost every time they are updated. He seems to be completely oblivious to the danger posed by fiscal austerity when the Eurozone private sector has been saving an average of 5 percent of GDP since 2008 despite zero or even negative interest rates (Figure 2.8).

These consistent failures suggest that these central bankers do not (or did not in the case of Mervyn King) possess an accurate model of their economies. Not only did they not realize the extent to which the private sector was saving (or minimizing debt), but they also pushed their governments to abdicate their role as borrower of last resort. The U.S. is doing better than the rest not because it had a better version of QE, but because it is the only country with a central bank that openly opposed fiscal austerity.

## People in Real Economy Fully Aware That QE Is Meaningless

How do people outside the rarefied world of central banking view quantitative easing? Households and businesses in the real economies of Japan, the U.S., the UK, and Europe are either in the process of repairing their balance sheets or are still suffering from the after-effect of debt trauma. Consequently, quantitative easing has not prompted any change in their behavior. If it had, they would have resumed borrowing, producing a measurable pick-up in both bank lending and money supply growth.

In other words, households and businesses facing balance sheet problems remain unimpressed by the argument made by Friedman, Krugman, and the three central bankers named above—namely, that there are always willing borrowers as long as real interest rates are low enough. They know that such arguments do not apply to them or to anyone else facing similar balance sheet problems. And that group of people tends to represent a large portion of society after a nationwide asset bubble bursts.

## Market Participants Still Acting Based on Illusion That Inflation Is Monetary Phenomenon

Participants in the foreign exchange and equity markets, however, hold a very different view. Indeed, the majority of them continue to act based on the assumption that the global economy remains in the textbook world, i.e., Cases 1 and 2. Evidence of this is offered by the fact that every time a central bank announces another round of QE, they sell that country's currency while buying its equities. They do so on the assumption that the money supply in QE countries will grow far faster than those in non-QE countries, and the currency of a country with a rapidly expanding money supply should fall against that of a country where the money supply is not growing so quickly.

When the U.S. and UK implemented QE policies after the GFC, for example, the dollar fell 30 percent against the Japanese yen and the pound plunged 40 percent, both to historical lows (Figure 2.18, left graph). These moves were based on the assumption that money supply growth in the U.S. and UK would massively outpace that in Japan, and that the vastly increased supply of dollars and pounds should weaken their exchange rates versus the yen.

**FIGURE 2.18** Foreign Exchange Market Participants Still Believe in Textbook World

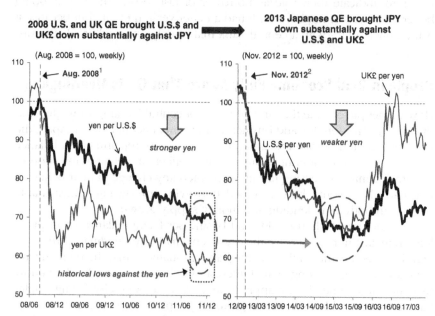

*Notes:* 1. One month before the Lehman Shock. 2. One month before the start of Abenomics.

*Source:* Nomura Research Institute, based on the data from Nikkei

When Japan implemented its own version of QE four years later, the yen dropped 35 percent against the dollar and the pound (Figure 2.18, right graph), also on the assumption that money supply growth would diverge significantly as a result of QE. The euro fell sharply on the same logic when Draghi announced the ECB was prepared to introduce QE.

In reality, however, credit and money supply growth did not accelerate meaningfully in any of these nations under QE. Although interest rate differentials did widen somewhat, they were nowhere near large enough to justify 30 to 40 percent movements in exchange rates.

It is because so many people in the foreign exchange and stock markets act based on mistaken textbook views that equity prices and exchange rates move so dramatically each time another round of QE is announced. Their movements, in turn, affect the behavior of households and businesses in these countries and enable QE proponents to claim their policy actually worked.

Bernanke reportedly said that quantitative easing does not work in theory, but it does work in practice. He was probably referring to the behavior of market participants who continue to hold a Friedman-like textbook view of the world.

It is worth asking just how long this disconnect between the real economy and the beliefs of market participants can continue. If the expected money supply growth and inflation never materialize, the market participants who have been acting based on the assumption that they would will eventually be forced to change course. And that could mean a nasty surprise for countries that have benefited from QE.

## Fiscal Policy's Track Record

If the track record of monetary policy in balance sheet recessions is clear, so is that of fiscal policy. As noted above, the first country to experience a balance sheet recession after the Great Depression was post-1990 Japan. The Japanese bubble was absolutely massive. At the peak, it was said that the gardens of the Imperial Palace in central Tokyo (with a circumference of about 5 kilometers) were worth as much as the entire state of California. When the bubble burst, commercial real estate prices fell 87 percent nationwide, touching levels last seen in 1973. And since real estate was always used as collateral for borrowing money in Japan, the collapse of land prices devastated private-sector balance sheets, and the economy started to implode.

The Liberal Democratic Party (LDP) government was quick to administer fiscal stimulus to stop the implosion. But this was not because they understood the horrors and mechanics of balance sheet recessions, but rather because they thought government spending would "prime the pump" and get the economy moving again.

The economy responded positively each time fiscal stimulus was implemented, but lost momentum each time the stimulus was removed. The expected pump priming never materialized because, after an 87 percent decline in real estate values, the private sector was far from regaining financial health, and businesses and households were using every yen that could be spared to pay down debt.

The orthodox fiscal hawks who dominated the press and academia also tried to stop fiscal stimulus at every step of the way, arguing that large deficits would soon lead to skyrocketing interest rates and a fiscal crisis. These hawks forced politicians to cut stimulus as soon as the economy showed signs of life, prompting another downturn. The resulting on-again, off-again fiscal stimulus did not imbue the public with confidence in the government's handling of the economy. Fortunately, the LDP had enough pork-barrel politicians to keep a minimum level of stimulus needed in place, and as a result Japanese GDP never once fell below its bubble peak (Figure 2.1). Nor did the Japanese unemployment rate ever exceed 5.5 percent.

That was a fantastic achievement in view of the fact that the Japanese private sector was saving an average of 8 percent of GDP from 1995 to 2005, and the Japanese lost three times as much wealth (as a share of GDP) as Americans did during the Great Depression, when nominal GNP fell 46 percent as a result of the $1000-$900-$810-$730 deflationary process.

But in 1997, seven years into the recession, the IMF and OECD—who understood nothing about balance sheet recessions—started pressuring Japan to cut its fiscal deficit because the population was aging and all those well-publicized roads and bridges "to nowhere" were leading the economy to nowhere. These institutions completely failed to understand that without fiscal stimulus the Japanese economy would have collapsed long ago.

Unfortunately, the Hashimoto Administration listened to them and embarked on a fiscal austerity program amounting to 3 percent of GDP, or 15 trillion yen, in April 1997. The resultant tax hikes and spending cuts, however, were an utter disaster for both the economy and the banking system. Japan's GDP contracted for five consecutive quarters and the deficit, instead of shrinking by 15 trillion yen, actually *increased* by 16 trillion yen, or 72 percent. It took the country 10 years to bring the deficit back to where it had been in 1996, and during that time the public debt increased by nearly 100 trillion yen (Figure 2.19). Japanese banks, which successfully endured the first seven years of the recession, finally threw in the towel in late 1997, and a full-blown banking crisis ensued.

Hashimoto realized his mistake by December of that year and started to reverse the direction of fiscal policy while injecting capital into the banking system to arrest the nationwide credit crunch. Subsequent Obuchi and Mori administrations also implemented sufficient fiscal stimulus to keep the economy going, but fiscal orthodoxy made a comeback with the Koizumi and the first Abe administrations, and the economy stagnated again. Prime Minister Taro Aso, who understood well the importance of deficit spending during a balance sheet recession, administered fiscal stimulus, but had the misfortune to be in power when the Lehman crisis erupted, and the LDP was voted out of office in 2009. The Democratic Party of Japan (DPJ) administrations that followed had learned nothing from the 1997 disaster, and the economy languished again under fiscal orthodoxy.

When the LDP returned to power in 2012, Taro Aso, now finance minister, included fiscal stimulus as the second arrow of Abenomics to get the economy moving again. However, even this effort was torpedoed by the return of fiscal orthodoxy as many pushed for a consumption tax hike in 2014, and the economy lost its forward momentum once again.

In the U.S., Larry Summers, the Obama administration's first NEC chairman, initially thought a large jolt of fiscal stimulus would be enough to prime the economy's pump, just like the Japanese had 18 years earlier. Thus, he talked about the "three Ts" of fiscal stimulus, declaring that it

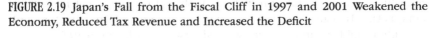

FIGURE 2.19 Japan's Fall from the Fiscal Cliff in 1997 and 2001 Weakened the Economy, Reduced Tax Revenue and Increased the Deficit

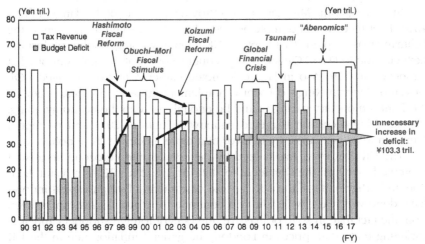

*Notes:* Latest figures (*) are estimated by MOF. From FY2011, figures include reconstruction taxes and bonds for rebuilding after tsunami.

*Source:* Ministry of Finance, Japan

should be timely, targeted, and temporary. But he soon had a change of heart and began pushing for the "three Ss," saying fiscal stimulus really needed to be speedy, sustained, and substantial[13]. He also recognized that the problem faced by the U.S. was the same problem Japan had confronted 18 years earlier.

At the Fed, Chairman Bernanke also realized within the first two years of the Lehman crisis that the economy was suffering from a balance sheet recession and that fiscal stimulus was absolutely essential. He then went on to warn Congress about the dangers of the fiscal cliff, as noted earlier.

Although the Fed and the Obama administration had to fight fiscal orthodoxy in the Congress through government shutdowns, debt-ceiling debates, and the sequester, they managed to keep the U.S. economy away from the fiscal cliff, which is why it is doing so much better than the rest. In fact, the U.S. is the only advanced country that managed to avoid falling off the fiscal cliff by actually utilizing the lessons from Japan's disaster with

---

[13] Summers, Lawrence, H. (2009) "Rescuing and Rebuilding the U.S. Economy: A Progress Report," remarks at the Peterson Institute for International Economics, July 17, 2009. https://piie.com/commentary/speeches-papers/rescuing-and-rebuilding-us-economy-progress-report?ResearchID=1264.

premature fiscal consolidation in 1997. It should be noted that Larry Summers, as U.S. Treasury Secretary, was one of the very few who, together with the author, publicly argued against fiscal austerity in Japan in 1997.

In the UK, Prime Minister Gordon Brown was aware of the danger of balance sheet recession and implemented a large fiscal stimulus as soon as the Lehman crisis erupted. That kept the UK economy going, but he still lost the next election to David Cameron in a sequence of events reminiscent of what happened to Taro Aso in Japan. As noted earlier, Cameron received BOE Governor Mervyn King's consent to implement austerity policies, believing the Bank's monetary easing would be enough to keep the economy going. The resulting recession triggered nationwide riots in 2011 and prompted Cameron to jettison austerity in favor of a more moderate fiscal policy.

The UK, however, was helped by the crisis in the Eurozone because it prompted many on the Continent to shift funds to the UK. As a result, London and other parts of the UK capable of attracting foreign capital inflows have done very well, while the rest continue to struggle. This can be seen from the fact that, in spite of massive numbers of foreign shoppers and skyrocketing real estate prices in London, the general inflation rate in the UK fell to almost zero (Figure 2.11, bottom graph)—much like Japan—until the Brexit vote sent the pound sharply lower.

Chapter 7 is devoted entirely to the Eurozone economies' continuing problems, but for now, suffice it to say that the Maastricht Treaty, which created the euro, prohibited member governments from running fiscal deficits in excess of 3 percent of GDP *regardless* of the level of savings generated in the private sector. That constraint prevented the region from properly addressing balance sheet recessions, in which private sectors can save well over 5 percent of GDP, as noted in Figures 1.1 and 2.8. The long stagnation experienced by Eurozone economies is testimony to that fact.

Experience shows that when private-sector borrowers disappear, fiscal stimulus is absolutely essential in keeping the economy going. Every time fiscal stimulus was implemented, the economy improved, and every time it was removed, the economy collapsed. The above experience also underlines the difficulty of maintaining fiscal stimulus in a democracy during peacetime, a topic discussed further in Chapter 10.

## Difficulty of Measuring Fiscal Multiplier in Balance Sheet Recessions

The above experience also indicates that, unlike in Cases 1 and 2, where fiscal stimulus can crowd out private-sector investments and end up having a low multiplier effect, the fiscal multiplier in Cases 3 and 4 tends to be very large. However, there are two difficulties in accurately measuring the multiplier. First the measurement must start from where the economy would have been in the absence of fiscal stimulus. But it is difficult to establish such a counter-factual case because there are no statistical examples of past balance sheet recessions to establish the counter-factual path of GDP.

The second difficulty is that the measurement must start the moment the private sector shifts its focus from profit maximization to debt minimization. Any measurement that includes data from before that shift, when the economy was still in Case 1 or 2, should not be used because it will underestimate the actual size of the fiscal multiplier in Cases 3 and 4.

These two statistical limitations make quantifying the size of the fiscal multiplier almost impossible at the beginning of a balance sheet recession, when fiscal stimulus is most urgently needed. However, even in a rather optimistic counter-factual scenario for Japan in Figure 2.1 where the GDP returns to pre-bubble levels (i.e., to the level of 1985) without fiscal stimulus, the fiscal multiplier turns out to be very large.

In this example, the cumulative difference between actual GDP and the counter-factual GDP from 1990 to 2005 (i.e., before the GFC) is over 2,000 trillion yen, whereas the cumulative increase in public debt during the same period was 460 trillion yen. In other words, the Japanese government spent 460 trillion yen to buy the GDP equivalent of 2,000 trillion yen, which suggests the fiscal multiplier was actually in the range of 4 to 5 instead of the figure of around 1 suggested by orthodox fiscal hawks. The bottom line is that, even though it is difficult to quantify the actual size of the fiscal multiplier at the beginning of a balance sheet recession, government must act as borrower of last resort when the private sector is not borrowing or, even worse, is minimizing debt.

## Tax Cuts or Government Spending?

It has been argued that fiscal stimulus is essential when the economy is in Case 3 or 4. But there are two kinds of fiscal stimulus: government spending and tax cuts. If the economy is in a balance sheet recession, the correct form of fiscal stimulus is government spending. If the economy is suffering from a lack of domestic investment opportunities, the proper response would be a combination of tax cuts and deregulation to encourage innovation and risk taking (this point is discussed in more detail in Chapter 4) augmented by government spending.

Government spending is essential during a balance sheet recession because when the private sector is minimizing debt for balance sheet reasons, any tax cut will be used to pay down debt. Although that will help the private sector regain its financial health sooner than it would have otherwise, it will not help eliminate the economy's deflationary gap. And if the economy is allowed to fall into a deflationary spiral, both incomes and asset prices will decline further, making the task of repairing private-sector balance sheets that much more difficult. The government's highest priority should therefore be to stop the deflationary spiral. If it succeeds in keeping GDP from contracting, the private sector will have the income it needs to pay down debt and eventually repair its balance sheet.

It should be noted that if the debt overhang at borrowers is small enough for the rest of society to absorb, tools such as debt forgiveness, debt-for-equity swaps, and straightforward liquidations can be used to address the problem. But if a large portion of society is facing such an overhang at the same time—which is usually the case when a nationwide asset bubble bursts—such measures merely transfer the problem from one part of society to another without solving it. When the problems are broad-based, therefore, measures to help all borrowers rebuild their balance sheets are needed, and this process necessarily takes time.

## Oil Price Declines in Balance Sheet Recession

The importance of not using tax cuts during balance sheet recessions was demonstrated recently in the most unexpected quarters. When oil prices started falling in late 2014, most economists predicted it would lift economic growth in developed countries reliant on imported oil. They argued that a fall in the price of oil is equivalent to a tax cut for importing nations, which should increase disposable income and therefore consumption.

In spite of such expectations, these economies remained weak despite a fall in oil prices that was nothing short of spectacular. This was because they were all in balance sheet recessions, and their private sectors were busy minimizing debt. The fact that they were deleveraging at a time of zero or negative interest rates shows how urgently people feel the need to repair their balance sheets. For many it was indeed a matter of life or death.

When the "tax cut" presented itself in the form of lower oil prices, most people used the extra cash to repair or strengthen their balance sheets. In other words, most of the bounty from lower oil prices was used for stock adjustments—repairing balance sheets—leaving very little for flow items such as increasing consumption. This example demonstrates that tax cuts are not particularly useful in supporting the economy during balance sheet recessions.

Borrowers may also remain traumatized by the long and painful experience of deleveraging even after they have repaired their balance sheets. Under such conditions, which were observed in the U.S. for decades after the Great Depression and in Japan more recently, the authorities may need to provide accelerated depreciation allowances or other incentives to borrow and invest. Such tax breaks, however, are useful only after balance sheets have been fully repaired and only the psychological issue of debt trauma remains. Any tax cuts implemented before balance sheets have been nursed back to health will only be used to speed up the repair process.

Since the political capital needed for deficit spending in a democracy during peacetime is limited, the government should direct all its energy toward infrastructure spending instead of tax cuts to ensure that it gets the maximum boost to GDP from each dollar of deficit spending.

## Fiscal Stimulus Must Be Maintained Despite Large Public Debt

In contrast to lender-side problems, there are no quick fixes for borrower-side problems, whether they are due to balance sheet difficulties or to a lack of domestic investment opportunities. An economy in Case 3 can therefore remain there for years, if not decades, until the private sector regains both its financial health and the self-confidence needed to borrow and invest again[14].

The fact that recovery takes time means that fiscal support may have to be administered for years. With the level of public debt already so high in so many countries, the prospect of the government running large deficits for a prolonged period would almost certainly elicit strong opposition not just from the fiscal hawks but also from the general public, who would argue that the country cannot continue spending money it does not have. Even those who agree that government should act as borrower of last resort during a balance sheet recession might worry that it would take on too much debt. Since the issue of debt sustainability is even more acute when the absence of borrowers is due to a lack of investment opportunities—the problem that plagued the human race for *centuries* before the Industrial Revolution—this challenge is discussed in conjunction with the issue of domestic investment opportunities in Chapter 4.

---

[14] This phase of the economy corresponds to what the author called the Yin-phase of Yin-Yang economic cycles mentioned in his *Holy Grail of Macroeconomics: Lessons from Japan's Great Recession*, Singapore: John Wiley & Sons, 2008, pp. 160.

# CHAPTER 3

# Dearth of Investment Opportunities Can Deter Borrowers

If there are no borrowers because businesses cannot find attractive investment opportunities, which was why the world experienced centuries of economic stagnation before the Industrial Revolution, a very different mindset is needed to address the problem. To begin with, there can be various reasons for this problem in the various stages of economic development, and each requires a different policy response.

Today's developed economies all started out as agrarian societies, and the centuries-long paradox of thrift only ended with the arrival of the Industrial Revolution. The invention of new products and the machines needed to make them produced a huge number of investment opportunities for the first time in history. Private-sector businesses that would not borrow money unless they were certain that they could pay it back found numerous promising projects and started borrowing. The financial sector also developed to meet the newfound demand for funds. This process continued as long as there were debt-financed projects sound enough to pay for themselves.

Thus began a virtuous cycle in which investment created more jobs and income, which in turn created more savings to finance more investment. Unlike the government investments in earlier centuries that eventually ran into financing difficulties, private-sector-led investments could sustain themselves as long as attractive new products were continuously brought to market. With new household appliances, cars, airplanes, and a host of other goods invented and developed in rapid succession, a lack of investment opportunities was seldom a constraint to growth. The end result was the rapid economic growth observed since the Industrial Revolution.

At the beginning of the Industrial Revolution, constraints to growth included insufficient social infrastructure (e.g., transportation networks), inadequate savings to fund investments, an illiterate work force, and the slow pace of technological innovation. But some of these constraints were soon transformed into investment opportunities in the form of railways and other utilities. The urbanization of the population alone created massive investment opportunities as rural workers needed accommodation when they migrated to the cities to work in factories.

Household savings also became a virtue instead of a vice from a macroeconomic perspective, and economies where people felt responsible for their own future and saved more tended to grow more rapidly than those where people saved less.

## Borrower Availability and the Three Stages of Economic Development

The availability of investment opportunities, however, is never guaranteed. It depends on myriad factors, including the pace of technological innovation and scientific breakthroughs, the ability of businesspeople to identify such opportunities and their willingness to borrow, the cost of labor and other inputs, the availability of reasonably priced financing, the protection of intellectual property rights, the stage of economic development as well as the state of the economy and world trade.

The importance of each factor also depends on a nation's stage of economic development. The pace of innovation and breakthroughs is probably more important for countries already at the forefront of technology, while in emerging economies the availability of financing and the protection of intellectual property rights might be equally important.

When Germany was emerging as an industrial power, for instance, the UK accused it of copying its products and demanded the use of "Made in Germany" labels to distinguish its products from the British originals. Japan faced similar accusations from Western countries, as did China from both the West and Japan. Today, many Chinese businesses are demanding that the Beijing government implement stronger intellectual property rules because they worry that any product they develop will be quickly copied by domestic competitors, rendering their research and development efforts worthless. In this way, the ability to copy goes from being a huge positive at one stage of economic development to a major negative later on.

In terms of the availability of investment opportunities, it may be useful to divide the industrialization process into three stages: urbanizing economies, which have yet to reach the Lewis Turning Point (LTP), maturing economies, which have already passed the LTP, and pursued economies, where the return on capital is higher abroad than at home. The LTP refers to the point at which urban factories have finally absorbed all the surplus rural labor. (In this book, the term "LTP" is used only because it is a well-known expression for a specific point in a nation's economic development; the use of this term does not refer to the model of economic growth proposed by Sir Arthur Lewis.)

At the advent of industrialization, most people are living in rural areas. Only the educated elite, who are very few in number, have the technical knowledge needed to produce and market goods. Families whose ancestors have lived on depressed farms for centuries have no such knowledge. Most of the gains during the initial stage of industrialization therefore go to the educated few, while the rest of the population simply provides labor for the industrialists. And with so many surplus workers in the countryside, worker wages remain depressed for decades until the LTP is reached.

Figure 3.1 illustrates this from the perspective of labor supply and demand. The labor supply curve is almost horizontal (DHK) until the Lewis Turning Point (K) is reached because there is an essentially unlimited supply of rural laborers seeking to work in the cities. A business owner can attract any number of such laborers simply by paying the going wage (DE).

In this graph, capital's share is represented by the area of the triangle formed by the vertical axis on the left, the labor demand curve, and

**FIGURE 3.1** Three Phases of Industrialization/Globalization

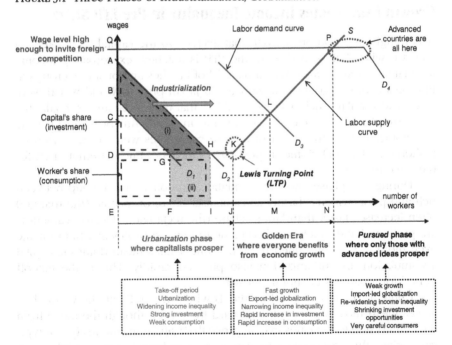

*Source:* Nomura Research Institute

the labor supply curve, while labor's share is represented by the rectangle below the labor supply curve. At labor demand curve $D_1$, capital's share is the triangle BDG and labor's share is the rectangle DEFG. During this phase of industrialization, the capital share BDG may be shared by only a few persons or families, whereas the labor share DEFG may be shared by millions of workers. With depressed wages leaving workers unable to save much, most investment has to be self-financed by the capitalist class, i.e., the amount capitalists save is the amount they can invest.

Successful businesses continue investing in an attempt to make even more money. That raises the demand for labor, causing the labor demand curve to shift steadily to the right (from $D_1$ to $D_2$) even as the labor supply curve remains flat. As the labor demand curve shifts to the right, total wages received by labor increase from the area of the rectangle DEFG at time $D_1$ to the area of the rectangle DEIH at time $D_2$ as the length of the rectangle below the labor supply curve grows. However, the growth is linear. The share of capital, meanwhile, is likely to increase at more than a linear rate as the labor demand curve shifts to the right, expanding from the area of the triangle BDG at $D_1$ to the area of the triangle ADH at $D_2$.

## Growth Exacerbates Income Inequality in Pre-LTP Stage

Accordingly, the portion of GDP that accrues to the capitalists is likely to increase with GDP growth until the LTP is reached, exacerbating income inequalities. A key reason why a handful of families and business groups in Europe a century ago and the zaibatsu in Japan prior to World War II were able to accumulate such massive wealth is that they faced an essentially flat labor supply curve (wealth accumulation in North America and Oceania was not quite as extreme because these economies were characterized by a shortage of labor). Some in post-1978 China became extremely rich for the same reason.

During this phase, income inequality, symbolized by the gap between rich and poor, widens sharply as capitalists' share of income (the triangle) often increases faster than labor's share (the rectangle). Because capitalists are profiting handsomely, they continue to reinvest profits in a bid to make even more money. Sustained high investment rates mean domestic capital accumulation and urbanization also proceed rapidly. This is the takeoff period for a nation's economic growth.

Until the economy reaches the Lewis Turning Point, however, low wages mean most people still lead hard lives, even though the move from the countryside to the cities may improve their situations modestly. For typical workers this was no easy transition, with 14-hour factory workdays not at all uncommon until the end of the 19th century. According to the OECD, the annual working time in Western countries averaged around 2,950 hours in 1870, or double the current level of 1,450 hours[1]. Business owners, however, were able to accumulate tremendous wealth during this period.

## Stage II of Industrialization: The Post-LTP Maturing Economy

As business owners continue to generate profits and expand investment, the economy eventually reaches the LTP. Once that happens, urbanization is largely finished and the total wages of labor—which had grown only linearly until then—start to increase much faster because any additional demand for labor pushes wages higher. In other words, the post-LTP labor supply curve takes on a significant positive slope.

Even if labor demand increases only modestly in Figure 3.1, from J to M, total wages accruing to labor will rise dramatically, from the area of rectangle DEJK to the area of rectangle CEML. This means labor's share of output is likely to be expanding relative to capital's share. It is at this point that the income inequality problem begins to correct itself.

Once the LTP is reached, labor also gains the bargaining power to demand higher wages for the first time in history, which reduces the share of output accruing to business owners. But businesses will continue to invest as long as they are achieving good returns, leading to further tightness in the labor market.

A significant portion of the U.S. and European populations still lived in rural areas until World War I, as shown in Figure 3.2. Even in the U.S., where—unlike in Europe—workers were always in short supply, nearly half the population was living on farms as late as the 1930s. Continued industrialization as well as the mobilizations for two world wars then pushed these economies beyond the LTP, and the standard of living for the average worker began to improve dramatically.

As labor's share increases, consumption's share of GDP will increase at the expense of investment. At the same time, the explosive increase in the purchasing power of ordinary citizens means that most businesses are able to increase profits simply by expanding existing productive capacity. Consequently, both consumption and investment will increase rapidly.

From that point onward the economy begins to "normalize" in the sense in which the term is used today. Inequality also diminishes as workers' share

---

[1] Maddison, Angus (2006) *The World Economy: A Millennial Perspective (Vol. 1), Historical Statistics (Vol. 2)*. Paris: OECD, p. 347.

FIGURE 3.2  Western Urbanization* Continued Until 1960s

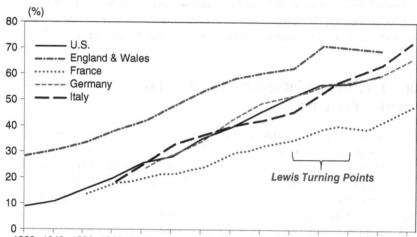

*Note:* *Percentage of population living in urban areas with 20,000 people or more in England & Wales, 10,000 or more in Italy and France, 5,000 or more in Germany and 2,500 or more in the U.S.

*Sources:* U.S. Census Bureau (2012) *2010 Census*; Flora, P., Kraus F. and Pfenning W. (eds) (1987) *State, Economy and Society in Western Europe 1815–1975*, Frankfurt am Main: Campus Verlag

of output increases relative to that of capital. In the U.S., that led to the so-called "Golden Sixties" where everyone benefited from economic growth. With incomes rising and inequality falling, this post-LTP maturing phase may be called the *golden era* of economic growth.

Once the economy reaches the LTP and wages start growing rapidly, workers begin to utilize their newfound bargaining power. The numerous strikes experienced by many Western countries from the 1950s to the 1970s reflect this development.

Capitalists initially respond to labor movements with union busters and strike busters. But as workers grow increasingly scarce and expensive, the capitalists must back down and begin accepting some of labor's demands if they want to keep their factories running. After 20 years or so of such struggles, a new political order is established as both employers and employees begin to understand what can be reasonably expected from the other side. The current political order in the West and Japan, which is dominated by center-left and center-right political parties, reflects this learning process.

Higher wages force businesses to look harder for profitable investment opportunities. On the other hand, the explosive increase in the purchasing

FIGURE 3.3  Western Urbanization Slowed in 1970s

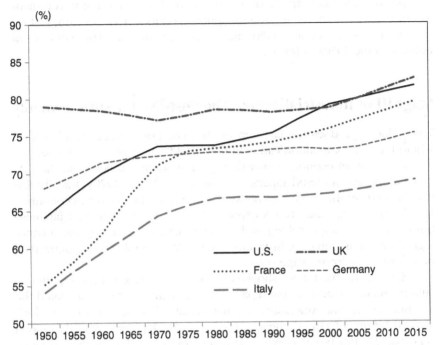

*Sources:* United Nations, Department of Economic and Social Affairs, Population Division (2014). *World Urbanization Projects: The 2014 Revision,* custom data acquired via website

power of ordinary workers who are paid ever-higher wages creates major investment opportunities. This prompts businesses to invest for two reasons. First, they seek to increase worker productivity so that they can pay ever-higher wages. Second, they want to expand capacity to address workers' increasing purchasing power. Both productivity- and capacity-enhancing investments increase demand for labor and capital that add to economic growth. In this phase, business investment increases workers' productivity even if their skill level remains unchanged.

When the West was at the forefront of technology, it was also in an export-led globalization phase as it exported consumer and capital goods to the rest of the world. American cars and German cameras were the global standard to which other countries aspired to.

With rapid improvements in the living standards of most workers, the post-LTP maturing phase is characterized by broadly distributed benefits from economic growth. Even those with limited skills are able to make a good living, especially if they belong to a strong union. Government tax receipts also increase rapidly during this period, allowing the government to offer an ever-expanding range of public services. That, in turn, further reduces the sense of inequality among the population. This golden era lasted into the 1970s in the West.

## Stage III of Industrialization: The Post-LTP Pursued Economy

This golden age does not last forever. At some point, wages reach a level where foreign competition can gain a foothold. The first signs of a serious threat to Western economic growth appeared when businesses in the U.S. and Europe encountered Japanese competition in the 1970s. Initially this was blamed on the wage gap between Japan and the Western economies. But the wage gap had always existed. The real reason was that Japanese businesses were approaching and, in some cases, surpassing the technological and marketing sophistication of the West while at the same time benefiting from lower wage costs.

Many in the West were shocked to find that Japanese cars required so little maintenance and so few repairs. The Germans may have invented the automobile, and the Americans may have established the process by which it could be manufactured cheaply, but it was the Japanese who developed cars that did not break down. The arrival of Nikon F camera also came as a huge shock to the German camera industry in the 1960s because it was so much more rugged, adaptable, easy to use and serviceable than German Leicas and Exaktas, and professional photographers around the world quickly switched to the Japanese brand. For the first time since the Industrial Revolution, the West found itself being pursued by a formidable competitor from the East.

Once a country is being chased by a technologically savvy competitor, often with a younger and less expensive labor force, it has entered the third or "pursued" stage of economic development. In this phase, it becomes far more challenging for businesses to find attractive investment opportunities at home because it often makes more sense for them to buy directly from the "chaser" or to invest in that country themselves. In other words, the return on capital is higher abroad than at home.

Many U.S. and European companies happily added Japanese products to their product lines or sold them through their dealerships starting in the 1970s. These products carried proud American or European brand names but were actually made in Japan. For example, General Motors was buying cars from Toyota, Ford from Mazda, and Chrysler from Mitsubishi. Ford acquired a large ownership stake in Mazda, and Chrysler did the same with Mitsubishi. In the "German" camera industry, Leicas were increasingly made with Minolta components—if not produced entirely by the Japanese company—and cameras with such venerable names such as Exakta and Contax were made entirely in Japan.

Businesses in the pursued country no longer have the same incentive to invest in productivity- or capacity-enhancing equipment at home because there is now a viable alternative—investing in or buying directly from lower-cost production facilities abroad. In this phase, capital invested abroad, especially in manufacturing, earns a higher return than capital invested at home. With constant pressure from shareholders to improve the return on capital, firms are forced to shift investments to locations with a higher return on capital.

Once this stage is reached, productivity gains at home from investment in productivity-enhancing equipment slow significantly. According to U.S. Bureau of Labor Statistics data compiled by Stanley Fischer at the Fed[2], productivity growth in the non-farm business sector averaged 3.0 percent from 1952 to 1973, before falling to 2.1 percent for the 1974 to 2007 period and 1.2 percent for 2008–2015. These numbers not only confirm the trend mentioned above, but also suggest that worker productivity in the future will depend increasingly on the efforts of individual workers to improve their skills instead of on corporate investment in productivity-enhancing equipment.

In a post-LTP pursued economy, labor demand curve ($D_4$ in Figure 3.1) becomes largely horizontal at wage level EQ, where outsourcing to foreign production sites becomes a viable alternative. This means real wage growth will be minimal from this point onward, except for those workers with abilities that are not easily replicated abroad. It should be noted that the level of EQ depends not just on domestic wage inflation, but also on foreign productivity gains. For example, if the Japanese products in the 1970s were not so competitive, EQ for the West would have been much higher.

With domestic investment opportunities shrinking, economic growth also slows in the pursued countries. The country is now in an import-led globalization phase as capital seeks higher returns abroad and imports flood the domestic market. This is very much the reality facing most advanced countries today, while a steadily increasing number of emerging countries are joining the rank of chasers.

---

[2] Fischer, Stanley (2016) "Reflections on Macroeconomics Then and Now," remarks at "Policy Challenges in an Interconnected World" 32nd Annual National Association for Business Economics Economic Policy Conference, Washington D.C., March 7, 2016. www.federalreserve.gov/newsevents/speech/fischer20160307a.htm.

## Japan's Ascent Forced Changes in the West

Japan's emergence in the 1970s shook the U.S. and European industrial establishments. As manufacturing workers lost their jobs, ugly trade frictions ensued between Japan and the West. This marked the first time that Western countries that had already passed their LTPs had been chased by a country with much lower wages.

Zenith, Magnavox, and many other well-known U.S. companies folded under the onslaught of Japanese competition, and household names such as GE and RCA stopped producing household products. The West German camera industry, the world's undisputed leader until around 1965, had all but disappeared by 1975. While Western companies at the forefront of technology continued to do well, the disappearance of many well-paying manufacturing jobs led to worsening income inequality in these countries.

Initially there was tremendous confusion in the West over what to do about the Japanese threat. As the Japanese took over one industry after another, industry and labor leaders sought protection via higher tariffs and non-tariff barriers. France, for example, ruled that all Japanese video recorders must clear customs in the remote countryside village of Poitiers, which not surprisingly had few customs officers, to discourage their entry into the country. This was done even though there were no French manufacturers of video recorders. Others argued for exchange rate realignments that were realized in the Plaza Accord of 1985, which halved the dollar's value against the yen.

Still others said the West should study Japan's success and learn from it, resulting in a Western infatuation with so-called "Japanese management." Many well-known business schools in the U.S. actively recruited Japanese students so they could discuss Japanese management practices in the classroom. Some even argued that eating fish—and sushi in particular—would make them as smart as the Japanese. All in all, Western nations' confidence that they were the world's most technically advanced economies was shattered.

Some of the pain Western workers felt was naturally offset by the fact that, as consumers, they benefited from cheaper imports from Asia, which is one characteristic of import-led globalization. Businesses with advanced technology continued to do well, but it was no longer the case that everyone in society was benefiting from economic growth. Those whose jobs could be transferred to lower-cost locations abroad saw their living standards stagnate or even fall.

## Inequality Worsens in Post-LTP Pursued Stage

Figure 3.4 shows the real income of the lowest quintile of U.S. families from 1947 to 2015. Even in this group, incomes grew rapidly in the post-LTP golden era that lasted until around 1970. But income growth subsequently stagnated as the country entered the post-LTP pursued phase. Figure 3.5, which illustrates the income growth of other quintiles relative to the lowest 20 percent, demonstrates that the ratios remain remarkably stable until 1970 but diverge thereafter.

Figure 3.6 shows annualized income growth by income quintile in the post-LTP golden era from 1947 to 1970 and the post-LTP pursued phase from 1970 to 2015. It shows that the lowest 60 percent actually enjoyed slightly faster income growth than those at the top before 1970, indicating a reduction in income inequality. This was indeed a golden era for the U.S. economy in which everyone was becoming richer and enjoying the fruits of economic growth.

FIGURE 3.4  Incomes of Lowest 20 Percent of U.S. Families Shot Up Until 1970 But Stagnated Thereafter

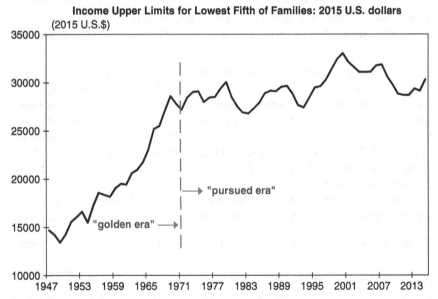

*Source:* U.S. Census Bureau, *Current Population Survey; 2016 Annual Social and Economic (ASEC) Supplement*

FIGURE 3.5  U.S. Income Inequality Began to Worsen After 1970

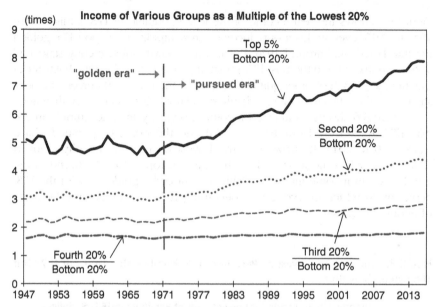

*Source:* Nomura Research Institute, based on data from the U.S. Census Bureau's *Current Population Survey, 2016 Annual Social and Economic (ASEC) Supplement*

The situation changed drastically, however, once Japan started chasing the U.S. Figure 3.4 shows that income growth for the lowest quintile has been stagnant ever since. Figures 3.5 and 3.6 show that income growth for other groups was only slightly better—except for the top 5 percent, which continued to experience significant income gains even after 1970. This group probably includes those who were at the forefront of innovation along with those who were able to take advantage of Japan's emergence.

Figure 3.7 demonstrates that income growth for different income quintiles was quite similar during the golden era but began to diverge significantly

FIGURE 3.6  Annualized Growth Rates of U.S. Family Income by Income Quintile

|  |  |  |  |  | (annualized, %) |
|---|---|---|---|---|---|
|  | lowest 20% | second 20% | third 20% | fourth 20% | top 5% |
| Post-LTP maturing phase 1947–1970 | 2.805 | 2.854 | 2.861 | 2.719 | 2.496 |
| Post-LTP pursued phase 1970–2015 | 0.189 | 0.436 | 0.737 | 0.996 | 1.298 |

*Source:* Nomura Research Institute, based on data from the U.S. Census Bureau's *Current Population Survey, 2016 Annual Social and Economic (ASEC) Supplement*

FIGURE 3.7  Real Wages in Six European Countries After WWII

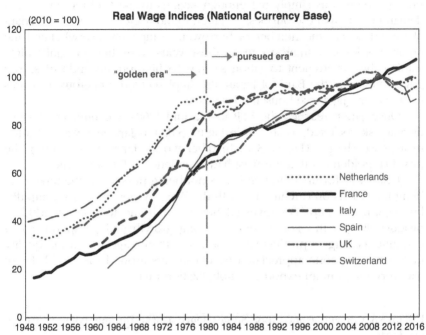

*Sources:* Nomura Research Institute, based on data from the IMF, *International Financial Statistics*, Office for National Statistics, UK, *Analysis of Real Earnings*, and Swiss Federal Statistics Office, *Swiss Wage Index*

once the U.S. became a pursued economy. Income growth for the top five percent dropped from 2.50 percent per year during the golden age to just 1.30 percent during the pursued phase, but that is still seven times the rate for the lowest 20 percent.

Similar developments were observed in Europe. Figure 3.7 shows real wages in six European countries. All of these countries experienced rapid wage growth until the 1970s followed by significantly slower growth thereafter.

## The Three Stages of Japanese Industrialization

Japan reached the LTP in the mid-1960s, when the mass migration of rural graduates to urban factories and offices, known in Japanese as *shudan shushoku*, finally came to an end. Investment opportunities in Japan were plentiful during this period because the hard work needed to develop new products and processes had already been done in the West. All Japan had to do was make those products better and less expensive, a task the Japanese system was well suited for. Rapid urbanization and the need to rebuild cities devastated by U.S. bombing during the war also offered plenty of low-hanging fruit in terms of investment opportunities.

Indeed, the main constraint on Japanese growth at the time was savings—there was simply not enough savings to meet all the investment demand from Japanese businesses. Japan found itself in an extreme variant of Case 1 where the number of borrowers completely overwhelmed the number of lenders. Interest rates in those years were therefore quite high, leading the government to ration savings to high-priority industries. The government and the Bank of Japan also implemented numerous measures to encourage Japanese households to save.

Once Japan reached the LTP in the mid-1960s, the number of labor disputes skyrocketed, as shown in Figure 3.8, and Japanese wages started to increase sharply (Figure 3.9). In other words, Japan was entering the post-LTP golden era that the West had experienced 40 years earlier.

Japan was fortunate in that it was not being pursued at the time, enabling it to focus on catching up with the West. Wages were rising rapidly, but Japanese companies invested heavily at home to boost workforce productivity. Japan's golden era of strong growth and prosperity could continue as long as productivity rose faster than wages. With the quality of Japanese exports appreciated by consumers around the world, Japan was very much in an export-led globalization phase.

FIGURE 3.8 Demand from Labor Surges Once Lewis Turning Point Is Passed (1): Japan

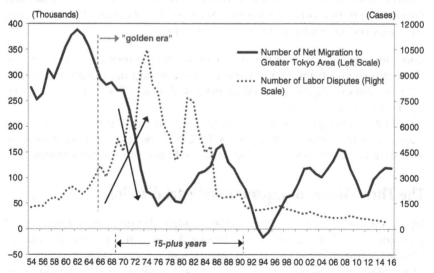

*Note:* Greater Tokyo Area consists of Tokyo Metropolis, Kanagawa Prefecture, Saitama Prefecture, and Chiba Prefecture.

*Sources:* Ministry of Internal Affairs and Communications, *Report on Internal Migration in Japan,* and Ministry of Health, Labour and Welfare, *Survey on Labour Disputes*

FIGURE 3.9 Japanese Wages Peaked in 1997 When Country Entered Post-LTP Pursued Stage

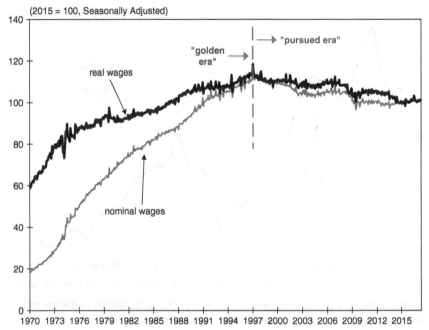

*Source:* Ministry of Health, Labour and Welfare, Japan, *Monthly Labour Survey*

Labor's share of profits rose along with wages, and Japan came to be known as the country of the middle class, with more than 90 percent of the population identifying itself as such. The Japanese were proud of the fact that their country had virtually no inequality. Some even quipped in those days that Japan was how Communism was supposed to work.

The happy days for Japan lasted until the mid-1990s, when Taiwan, South Korea, and China emerged as serious competitors. By then, Japanese wages were high enough to attract pursuers, and the country entered its post-LTP pursued stage. As shown in Figure 3.9, Japanese wages stopped growing in 1997 and then stagnated or fell.

Although these three Asian countries were also chasing the West, the shock to Japan was greater because it was the first time the country had been pursued since it opened itself up to the world in the 1868 Meiji Restoration. All of Japan's institutions, ranging from education to employment, were optimized for catching up with the West, not fending off competitors from the East. Meanwhile, the Europeans and Americans who had experienced the Japanese onslaught 25 years earlier had already made adjustments to their economies and were therefore less disturbed by China's emergence.

FIGURE 3.10 Demand from Labor Surges Once Lewis Turning Point Is Passed (2): South Korea

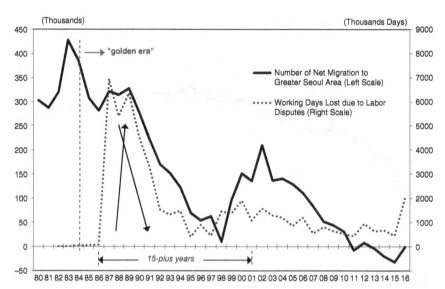

*Note:* Greater Seoul Area consists of Seoul City, Incheon City, and Gyeonggi-do.

*Sources:* Ministry of Employment and Labor, *Strikes Statistics*, Statistics Korea, *Internal Migration Statistics*, and *Korea Statistical Year Book*

Today the Japanese are worried about income inequality as highly paid manufacturing jobs have migrated to lower-cost countries. They are also concerned about the emergence of the so-called "working poor," who were once employed in manufacturing but have now been forced to take low-end service jobs. Some estimate that as many as 20 million out of a total population of 130 million are now living in poverty[3]. Their suffering, however, has been eased somewhat by a flood of inexpensive imports that has substantially reduced the cost of living. This means that Japan has entered an import-led globalization phase and is reliving the West's experience when it was being chased by Japan.

Similar concerns are being voiced in Taiwan and South Korea as they experience the same migration of factories to China and other even lower-cost locations in Southeast Asia. These two countries passed their LTPs around 1985 and entered a golden age that lasted perhaps until 2005. The frequency of Korean labor disputes also shot up during this period (Figure 3.10) as

---

[3] *Nikkei Business* (2015) "Tokushu: Nisen Mannin-no Hinkon" ("20 million Japanese in poverty"), in Japanese, Tokyo: Nikkei BP, March 23, 2016, pp. 24–43.

FIGURE 3.11 Taiwanese Wages Peaked Around 2005 When Country Entered Post-LTP Pursued Stage

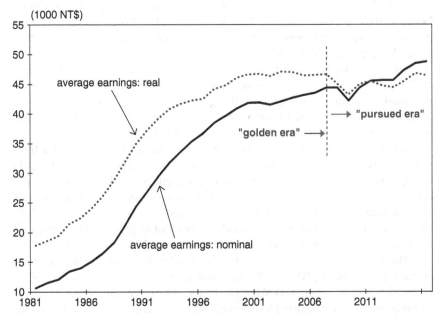

*Sources:* Nomura Research Institute, based on the data from Directorate General of Budget, Accounting and Statistics (DGBAS), the Executive Yuan, Taiwan, *Consumer Prices Indices*, and *Average Monthly Earnings*

workers gained bargaining power for the first time and won large wage concessions. In Taiwan, wages climbed sharply during the post-LTP golden era but peaked around 2005 and stagnated thereafter (Figure 3.11). Both countries are now feeling the pinch as China steadily takes over the industries that were responsible for so much of their past growth.

## Free Trade Accelerated Globalization While Rendering War Obsolete

This process of globalization, in which an ever-increasing number of countries joins the ranks of the pursuers, actually began with the free-trade regime introduced by the U.S. after 1945. Before then, a variety of constraints to trade hindered the process of industrialization—a lack of aggregate demand and difficulties in accessing foreign markets chief among them. In those days, most countries imposed high tariffs on imported products both to raise revenues and to protect domestic industries. If workers constituted the main source of consumption demand in the pre-LTP urbanizing world, they could not have provided enough demand for all the goods produced because their share of income was so low, while capitalists typically had a higher marginal propensity to save. As a result, aggregate supply often exceeded aggregate demand.

To overcome this constraint, European powers turned to colonialism and imperialism in a bid to acquire both sources of raw materials and captive markets where they could sell the goods they produced. Indeed, it was believed for centuries that national economies could not grow without territorial expansion. That led to centuries of wars and killings.

When World War II ended, the victorious Americans introduced a free-trade regime known as the General Agreement on Tariffs and Trade (GATT) that essentially allowed any country with competitive products to sell to any other country. Although the concept and practice of free trade were not new, the U.S. took the lead by opening its vast domestic market to the world. With the U.S. economy accounting for nearly 30 percent of global GDP at the end of World War II, the impact of this game-changing decision was huge.

The U.S. was partly motivated by the need to fend off the Soviet threat by rapidly rebuilding Western Europe and Japan, but the free-trade regime allowed not only Japan and West Germany but also many other countries to prosper without the need for expanding their territories. Indeed, it is difficult to find a country that grew rapidly in the post-1945 world that did not benefit from the U.S. market.

The advent of free trade actually made obsolete the whole notion that territorial expansion was a necessary condition for economic growth and prosperity. After World War II the victorious allies found themselves busy fighting indigenous independence movements in their colonies at enormous expense. Meanwhile, Japan and West Germany—which had lost all of their overseas and some of their domestic territories—quickly grew to become the world's second- and third-largest economies. In other words, postwar Japan and Germany proved that economic growth requires markets and investment opportunities, not territories. Economic growth will accelerate if markets can be accessed without the expense of acquiring overseas territories.

The relative infrequency of wars after 1945 is often attributed to the Cold War and the deterrent of Mutually Assured Destruction ("MAD"), but the drastic reduction in conflicts between countries that had been fighting since history began may also be due to the fact that territorial expansion was no longer viewed as a necessary or sufficient condition for economic prosperity. Colonies actually became more of a liability than an asset for economic growth under the free-trade regime. Today, thanks to the fabulous track record of economic growth made possible by the American-led move to free trade, almost no one sees territorial expansion as a prerequisite for economic prosperity, a development that should be seen as one of the greatest achievements of human civilization. How this regime may fall apart under Donald Trump is discussed in Chapter 9.

In Asia, it was the Japanese who discovered in the 1950s that their economy could still grow and prosper by producing high-quality products for the U.S. market. They then put their best and brightest to the task while leaving complicated diplomatic and national security issues to be decided by the Americans. Indeed, many high-end products made in Japan during the 1950s and 1960s, such as TEAC audio gear, were only sold in the U.S. because Japanese consumers were still too poor to afford them.

Japan's spectacular success then prompted Taiwan, South Korea and eventually the rest of Asia to follow the same export-oriented growth formula in a process dubbed the "flying geese" pattern of industrialization. These countries' golden eras then became synonymous with export-led globalization.

## China Now in Post-LTP Maturing Stage of Industrialization

The biggest beneficiary of the U.S.-led free-trade regime was China, which succeeded in transforming a dirt-poor agrarian society of over a billion people into the world's second-largest economy in just 30 years. The three decades after Deng Xiaoping opened the Chinese economy in 1978 probably qualify as the fastest and greatest economic growth story in history, with per capita GDP for over a billion people increasing from a little over $300 to more than $8,000 in 2016. China wasted no time in integrating itself with the global economy and attracted huge quantities of foreign direct investment, not just from the West and Japan but also from Asian tigers such as Taiwan, Hong Kong, Singapore, and South Korea. Indeed, it was Taiwanese and Hong Kong businessmen in the 1980s who taught the Communist Chinese how to run a market-based economy.

More precisely, China's fantastic economic growth was made possible by the U.S.-led free-trade system, which allowed businesses (both Chinese and foreign) to sell their products anywhere in the world. It was that access to the global market that prompted so many businesses from around the world to build factories in China. Were it not for the markets provided under the U.S.-led free-trade regime, it probably would have taken China many more decades to achieve the growth it did.

Businesses in the West and elsewhere that were able to capitalize on the situation in China found almost unlimited investment opportunities and operated like the capitalists in their own countries' pre-LTP eras. Those investments added massively to China's economic growth and transformed the country into "the world's factory."

But workers in Asia and the West who had to compete with Chinese workers have experienced flat or even negative income growth. Foreign businesses expanding rapidly in China are also likely to invest less at home, which has a depressing effect on domestic growth and productivity. Indeed, slow productivity growth in the advanced economies is the flip side of the rapid productivity and income growth in China and other emerging markets that was made possible by investments made by businesses from developed nations.

Those in the advanced economies who still wonder where the earlier enthusiasm for fixed-capital investment has gone need only get a window seat on a flight from Hong Kong to Beijing (or vice versa) on a nice day. They will see below them an endless landscape of factories stretching in all directions. Most of those plants were started with foreign capital because when Deng Xiaoping opened up the economy in 1978, there were no capitalists left in China: they had all been killed or driven into exile by the Communist revolution in 1949 and Mao's Cultural Revolution in the 1960s.

At the beginning, only foreign capital, mainly from Taiwan and Hong Kong, was available to jump-start China's industrialization. And capitalists from Taiwan and Hong Kong came in only because they realized they could sell whatever they produced in China to the rest of the world. After their pioneering efforts, they were joined by others from the West and Japan, who realized that the return on capital investment in China was far higher than what was available at home—*assuming that the goods produced there could be sold around the world.*

The point is that businesses are still investing to meet shareholders' demand for greater profits, but not necessarily in their home countries. And that is because businesses in advanced countries are finding that the return on capital is higher abroad, especially for manufacturing processes requiring large labor inputs. This has also led to a social backlash in advanced countries as represented by Trump and others who question the merits of free trade as practiced since 1945. This issue is discussed further in Chapter 9.

## Post-LTP China Faces "Middle-Income Trap"

China is also subject to the same laws of urbanization, industrialization, and globalization as other countries. China actually passed the LTP around 2012 and is now experiencing sharp increases in wages. This means the country is now in its golden era, or post-LTP maturing phase. However, because the Chinese government is wary of strikes, labor disputes, or other public disturbances of any kind, it is trying to pre-empt such conflict by administering significant wage increases each year, with businesses required to raise wages under directives issued by local governments. In some regions,

FIGURE 3.12  China May Grow Old Before It Grows Rich: Working-Age Population* Has Started to Contract

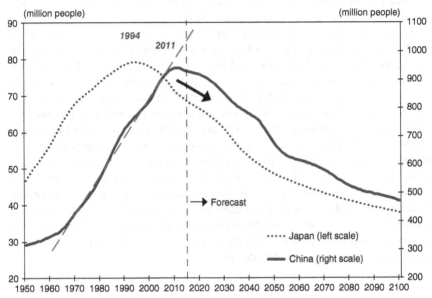

**The Working Age Population (15-59) in China and Japan, Actual and Forecast**

*Note:* The Chinese National Statistical Office defines the working-age population as the people from 15 to 59.

*Sources:* United Nations, Department of Economic and Social Affairs, Population Division (2015) *World Population Prospects: The 2015 Revision*, custom data acquired from website.

wages had risen at double-digit rates in a bid to prevent labor disputes. It remains to be seen whether such top-down actions can substitute for a process in which employers and employees learn through confrontation what can reasonably be expected from the other party.

Just as China was passing the LTP, its working-age population—defined as those aged 15 to 59[4]—started shrinking in 2012. From a demographic perspective, it is highly unusual for the entire labor supply curve to begin shifting to the left just as a country reaches the LTP. Japan, Taiwan, and South Korea all enjoyed about 30 years of workforce growth after reaching their LTPs. The huge demographic bonus China enjoyed until 2012 is not only exhausted, but has now reversed, as shown in Figure 3.12. That means

---

[4] In most countries, the working age population is defined as those aged 15 to 64.

China that will not be able to maintain the rapid pace of economic growth seen in the past, and in fact growth has already slowed sharply.

Higher wages in China are now leading both Chinese and foreign businesses to move factories to lower-wage countries such as Vietnam and Bangladesh, prompting fears that China will become stuck in the so-called "middle-income trap". This trap arises from the fact that once a country loses its distinction as the lowest-cost producer, many factories may leave for lower-cost destinations, resulting in less investment and less growth. In effect, the laws of globalization and free trade that benefited China when it was the lowest-cost producer are now posing real challenges for the country.

Although the sudden slowdown in the Chinese economy since late 2014 has been attributed partly to the unexpected rise in the exchange rate (this point is discussed further in Chapter 6), the easy part of China's economic growth story is now over. If it hopes to maintain economic growth in the face of rising wages and a shrinking workforce, China needs to begin investing more to raise the productivity of domestic workers at a time when businesses are discovering that in certain industries the return on capital is higher abroad, i.e., that it is easier to make money by simply moving factories to lower-cost locations overseas. That is precisely the challenge advanced countries faced when they were pursued by China and other emerging economies in earlier decades.

## Growth, Happiness, and Maturity of Nations

The discussion above regarding the stages of economic growth is summarized in Figure 3.13. Here, "industrialization with urbanization" refers to the pre-LTP urbanization phase, "golden era" to the post-LTP maturing phase, and "pursued by __" to the post-LTP pursued phase. The bold arrows indicate the direction of pursuit.

Countries appear to be reaching their "golden eras" sooner owing to accelerated globalization, which has been made possible by free trade and rapid advances in information technology. However, the golden eras themselves are also becoming shorter as more countries join the globalization bandwagon. For example, the golden era for the U.S. and Western Europe probably lasted for about 40 years until the mid-1970s, while Japan's ended after around 30 years in the mid-1990s. The golden era for Asian NICs like Taiwan and Korea was only about 20 years long, coming to an end around 2005. It will be interesting to see how long the golden era lasts in China, where policymakers are already worried about the middle-income trap.

FIGURE 3.13 Growth, Happiness, and Maturity of Nations

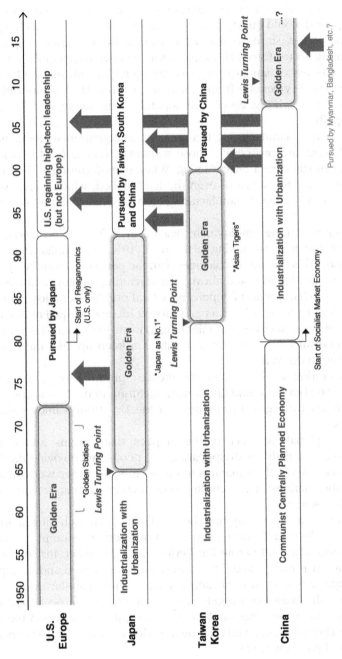

*Note:* A ⇔ B = A pursuing B.

*Source:* Nomura Research Institute

If a nation's happiness can be measured by (1) how quickly inequality is disappearing and (2) how fast the economy is growing, then the post-LTP maturing period would qualify as the period when a nation is at its happiest. During this period, strong demand for workers from a rapidly expanding manufacturing sector forces all other sectors to offer comparable wages to retain workers. Since manufacturing jobs do not require advanced education, the whole of society benefits from economic growth led by manufacturing as wages rise for everybody. People are hopeful for the future, and inequality shrinks rapidly.

In this sense manufacturing is a great social equalizer: when manufacturing industries are prospering, those without advanced (and expensive) education can still earn a decent living. When manufacturing is driving job creation, it raises the wages of even the least skilled, which affects wages in all other sectors even if manufacturing's share of the economy is not that large.

U.S. manufacturing employment peaked in 1979 at 19.6 million, with the bulk of the increase taking place from 1946 (12.7 million) to 1969 (18.8 million). This timeframe coincides with the period of shrinking income inequality in the U.S. as noted above. Manufacturing employment has now fallen to 12.4 million, or just 8.5 percent of total non-farm employment. The corresponding figure in 1946 was 32 percent. Income inequality begins to worsen once manufacturers start migrating to lower-cost countries, and only those with advanced educations and skills can keep up with the changes and continue to do well.

Manufacturing is also where the greatest productivity gains can be expected. The above rise and fall of manufacturing in the U.S. is consistent with the productivity growth numbers for the U.S. from Stanley Fisher as noted earlier.

From a global perspective, this implies that nations are at their happiest—i.e., inequality is disappearing and people are enjoying the fruits of their labor—when their manufacturing sectors are either well ahead of those in other nations or are chasing other economies but are not being pursued themselves.

The West was at its happiest before Japan started chasing it in the 1970s because its manufacturing was ahead of all other economies. It was a French person who said before the Berlin Wall came down that the world would be a much nicer place if there were no Soviet Union and no Japan.

The Japanese were at their happiest when their manufacturing sector was chasing the West but nobody was chasing them. Those happy days ended when the Asian Tigers and China began pursuing Japan in the mid-1990s. The Tigers then enjoyed their own golden era for about 20 years until China started pursuing them.

The concept of the post-LTP pursued phase and the "post-industrial society," popularized by authors such as Daniel Bell, both refer to the same period in history. When the latter concept was introduced in the 1970s, people were excited about the prospect of societies becoming cleaner and more humane as knowledge-based industries became increasingly dominant in the economy. This was in contrast to the age of industrialization, which forced people to work long hours on dirty, oily factory floors.

Today, most advanced countries enjoy cleaner air with fewer factories operating inside their borders. But for a large part of the population, the rosy, humane scenario promised by the proponents of a post-industrial society never materialized. Instead, many feel less secure and hopeful today than they felt in the earlier era.

The overly optimistic post-industrialization scenarios never came to pass because they require knowledge-based industries to be expanding so rapidly and paying so well that they draw workers away from the manufacturing sector. Manufacturers will then be forced to leave the country because they cannot compete for workers when knowledge-based businesses are offering such high wages.

What actually happened, however, was that advanced countries were forced into a process of de-industrialization because the return on capital was higher abroad than at home. Society suffered from slower wage and productivity growth coupled with widening income inequality, since only those with special abilities or advanced degrees did well for themselves.

Although knowledge-based businesses are expanding in most societies, their growth is far from sufficient to offset the loss of jobs and big-ticket expenditures on plant and equipment needed to drive capacity- and productivity-enhancing investments in the manufacturing sector. Since slower wage growth and rising inequality are not positive developments for most of the population, the author chose the term "pursued phase" to convey the sense of urgency with which the problems resulting from low returns on capital at home must be addressed.

Now that most advanced countries are in the post-LTP pursued phase, the key issue for policymakers should be how to reorganize society to maximize the economy's growth potential in this new phase. Unfortunately, there has been virtually no macroeconomic theories or models on policy implications of capital earning higher returns abroad than at home, and very little of the policy debate in advanced countries is couched in these terms.

Instead, the slogans used by presidential and prime ministerial hopefuls all suggest a longing for the return of the golden era. But politicians will not be able to improve the lives of ordinary people until they fully appreciate the current economic reality in a global context. These points are discussed in greater detail in the next two chapters.

## Rise and Fall of Communism

The preceding description of how inequality increases and decreases before and after the LTP also explains why so many people have found Communism appealing at a certain juncture in history. Marx and Engels, who lived in pre-LTP industrializing Europe, were appalled by the horrendous inequality around them and the miserable working and living conditions for ordinary people. As noted above, it was not uncommon for people to work 16 hours a day in dirty, dangerous industrial environments while capitalists rapidly grew rich. Any intellectual with a heart would have found it difficult to turn a blind eye to the social and economic inequality of the time.

Marx responded by proposing the concept of Communism, which called for capital to be owned and shared by the laborers. He argued that if capital were owned by the workers, the exploitation of labor would end and workers would enjoy a greater share of the output. Many "exploited" workers who had been working long hours in dreadful conditions embraced the new theory enthusiastically because it appeared to offer the hope of a better life with little to lose. In that sense, the birth of Communism may itself have been a historical imperative of sorts.

Marx and Engels' greatest mistake, however, was to assume the extreme inequality they witnessed (points G and H in Figure 3.1) would continue forever without a Communist revolution. In reality, it marked just one inevitable step on the path toward industrialization. If capitalists are earning large profits in the pre-LTP period, they will probably continue to invest in the hope of making even more money. It is that drive for more profits that eventually pushes the economy to reach and pass the LTP, when a totally different labor-market dynamic emerges.

As soon as the economy reaches the LTP and wages start rising rapidly, the appeal of Communism wanes as workers begin to realize they can get what they want within the existing framework. The early years of the golden era, however, are typically characterized by frequent strikes and labor disputes as workers start to utilize their newfound bargaining power for the first time. While scenes of workers marching under red Communist banners may give the impression that a Communist takeover is just around the corner, their success in winning higher wages ends up undermining the movement's appeal.

After 15 or 20 years of such struggles, employers and employees alike begin to understand what can be reasonably expected from the other side, and a new political order is established based on that understanding. The result is the prevalence of center-right and center-left political parties seen in advanced countries today.

Although this political arrangement served advanced countries well in their post-LTP golden eras, it remains to be seen whether it is the most appropriate arrangement under the very different labor dynamic of the post-LTP pursued phase. The rise of far-right political parties in the West opposed to free trade and globalization, for example, presents a major challenge to the established political order. These issues are discussed further in Chapter 9.

Ironically, countries that adopted Communism before reaching their LTPs, such as pre-1979 China and pre-1986 Vietnam, ended up stagnating because the profit motive needed to promote investment and push the economy beyond the LTP was lost.

Interestingly, the economy also ends up stagnating when labor becomes too powerful and expensive before the country reaches the LTP, for both economic and political reasons. First, the economy stops growing and becomes stuck in the pre-LTP phase because the protected workers are too expensive for capitalists to expand production. Second, unionized and privileged workers end up creating a two-tier labor market with a permanent underclass that is denied meaningful employment because the economy is not growing (or at least not growing fast enough). This leads to political problems that slow the economy even further, as seen in many Latin American countries since the 1950s.

The discussion above suggests that inclusive social and political reforms are mostly possible only after a country passes the LTP. Even in the advanced countries, the majority of inclusive reforms, such as the Civil Rights movement in the U.S., took place in the post-LTP era. This means sequencing matters, and those in emerging countries seeking more inclusive social and political reforms might first need to grow their economies beyond the LTP if they want to avoid the pitfalls noted above.

Although the above suggests that all countries are going through the same development process, there has also been a general progress toward a more agreeable working conditions in all countries. For instance, European workers in pre-LTP urbanizing phase were working as long as 16 hours a day, whereas post-1978 Chinese workers have been working not much more than 8 hours a day even before the country reached its LTP. This suggests that the progress made elsewhere in the world is reflected in the working conditions of at least some parts of emerging economies today.

## Real Source of Thomas Piketty's Inequality

Income inequality has become one of the hottest and most controversial issues in economics, not only in the developed world but also in China and elsewhere as well as. Many are growing increasingly uncomfortable with the divide between the haves and the have-nots, especially after Thomas Piketty's *Capital in the 21st Century* sparked a fresh debate on the optimal distribution of wealth, an issue that had been largely overlooked by the economics profession.

Although the author cannot claim to have understood the full implications of Piketty's enormous contributions, the analysis presented here contradicts one of the key historical points he makes. Namely, he claims that the extreme inequality that existed prior to World War I was corrected by the wealth destruction of two world wars and the Great Depression. He then goes on to argue that the retreat of progressive taxation in the developed world starting in the late 1970s ended up creating a level of inequality that approaches that seen prior to World War I.

Although he has ample data to back his assertions, his pre-World War I results may also be due to the fact that those countries were all in the pre-LTP industrialization stage, which is characterized by a rapid increase in inequality. His post-World War I findings may also be attributable to the West's entering the post-LTP maturing phase or "golden era" of industrialization, where everyone enjoys the fruits of economic growth and inequality shrinks. Piketty attributes this to the destruction of wealth brought about by two world wars and the introduction of progressive income taxes, but this period was also characterized by an end to rapid urbanization in most of these countries. Furthermore, the four decades through 1970 marked a golden era for Western economies as they were ahead of everyone else and were being chased by no one.

Finally, Piketty's post-1970 results may be due to the fact that Western economies entered their post-LTP pursued phase as Japan and other countries began chasing them. For Western capitalists able to utilize Asian resources, this was a golden money-making opportunity. But it was not a welcome development for Western factory workers who had to compete with competitively priced imports from Asia.

This also suggests that the favorable income distributions observed by Piketty in the West before 1970 and in Japan until 1990 were transitory phenomena. These countries enjoyed a golden era of growing incomes and shrinking inequality not because they had the right kind of tax regime but because it was a time when manufacturing prospered. And manufacturing prospered because the global economic environment was one in which these countries were either ahead of everyone else or chasing others but were not being pursued, i.e., the return on capital was highest at home.

Just because such a desirable state of affairs was observed once does not mean it can be maintained or replicated. Any attempt to preserve that equality in the face of fierce international competition would have required massive and continuous investment in both human and physical capital, something that most countries are not ready to implement.

It is not even certain whether such investments constitute the best use of resources, since businesses may still find that the return on capital is higher elsewhere. To the extent that businesses are under pressure from shareholders to invest in countries offering the highest returns, forcing them to invest at home is no easy task. This means a more extreme form of protectionism than that proposed by President Donald Trump may be needed to keep cheaper foreign goods out and force businesses to invest at home. What is certain, however, is that a completely different mindset is needed to secure economic growth in the pursued countries. This topic is discussed in the next chapter.

# CHAPTER 4

# Macroeconomic Policy During the Three Stages of Economic Development

In order to understand the unique policy challenge faced by pursued economies, it is useful to see how various sectors of the economy change as they go through the different stages of economic development. It was already noted that when the economy is in the pre-Lewis Turning Point (LTP) urbanizing phase, capitalists can take advantage of workers because there are so many of them in rural areas who are willing to work for the going wage in urban factories. Workers also have no bargaining power prior to reaching the LTP. During this phase, the limited opportunities for education and vocational training in rural areas mean most workers are neither well-educated nor highly skilled when they migrate to the cities. And with so many of them competing for a limited number of urban jobs, there is little job security.

Once the economy passes the LTP, the tables are turned completely in favor of the workers. The supply of surplus workers in rural areas is exhausted and the labor supply curve takes on a significant positive slope. As long as some businesses seek to increase their workforce, all businesses will be forced to pay ever-higher wages. At this stage, businesses also have plenty of reasons to expand because workers' purchasing power is growing rapidly. Expansion here means domestic expansion: firms have little of the experience or know-how needed for overseas production, and domestic wages, although rising, are still likely to be competitive.

To satisfy increasing demand while paying ever-higher wages, businesses invest in both productivity- and capacity-enhancing equipment. Strong domestic demand for both types of machinery during this phase manifests itself in the form of robust demand for funds to finance capital investments. This means the economy is firmly in Case 1. Investments in additional equipment effectively raise the productivity of employees even if the workers themselves are no more skilled or educated than before the country reached its LTP.

With wages rising rapidly, job security for workers also improves significantly as businesses try to hold on to their employees. Lifetime employment and seniority-based remuneration systems become more common. Working conditions improve as businesses offer safer, cleaner working environments to attract and retain workers. The emerging power of unions also forces employers to enhance job security. In contrast to the pre-LTP period, when businesses were effectively exploiting workers because there were so many of them, businesses in the post-LTP maturing period "pamper" their employees with productivity-enhancing equipment so they can afford to pay them more. With everyone enjoying the fruits of economic growth, this period is remembered as the nation's "golden era."

At some point, however, wages reach point EQ in Figure 3.1, and businesses are forced to look for alternative production sites abroad because domestic manufacturing is no longer competitive. It is at this point that firms realize that capital invested abroad earns higher returns than capital invested at home.

Producing abroad, however, requires that management possesses foreign language competency and other specialized skills, and that takes time. If the process appears too daunting, which is often the case for small and medium-sized firms, they may simply give up the business altogether or outsource all production to foreign firms. The transition from golden era to pursued era may therefore take many years. Once the know-how to produce abroad is acquired, however, the firm will start considering the entire emerging world when it looks for possible locations for production facilities. The process of investing overseas will therefore become increasingly irreversible. Although different industries may reach this point at different times, a country can be said to have entered its post-LTP pursued phase when a meaningful number of industries have reached this point.

## Workers Are on Their Own in Pursued Phase

The way businesses perceive workers changes once again in the new pursued phase because they now have the option of tapping overseas labor resources. With capital going much further abroad than when invested at home in labor-saving equipment, businesses have fewer incentives to undertake domestic investment. Fixed-capital investment, which was such a large driver of economic growth during the post-LTP golden era, begins to slow. As investment slows, growth in labor productivity, which shot up during the golden era, also starts to decelerate, a trend that has been observed for some time now in most advanced countries. And with slower productivity growth, wages begin to stagnate.

It is at this point that the ability of individual workers begins to matter for the first time, because only those able to do things that overseas workers cannot will continue to prosper. This stands in sharp contrast to the previous two stages, where wages were determined largely by macro factors such as labor supply/demand and institutional factors such as union membership, both of which had little to do with individual skills. Once the supply constraint is removed by the option of producing abroad or engaging in outright outsourcing, the only reason a company will pay a higher wage at home is because a particular employee can do something that cannot be easily replicated by a cheaper foreign worker.

If workers were "exploited" during the pre-LTP urbanization stage and "pampered" during the post-LTP maturing stage, they are entirely "on their own" in the post-LTP pursued stage because businesses are much less willing to invest in labor-saving equipment to increase the productivity of the domestic workforce. Workers must invest in themselves to enhance their productivity and marketability.

In this pursued phase, job security and seniority-based wages become increasingly rare in industries that must become more agile and flexible to fend off pursuers. It is no accident that lifetime employment and seniority-based wages, which were common in the U.S. until the 1970s, disappeared once Japanese competition appeared. The same thing happened to the Japanese labor market with an increased use of "non-regular" workers after China emerged as a competitor in the mid-1990s. Achieving a more flexible labor market has also been a major issue in Europe.

Workers who take the time and effort to acquire skills that are in demand will continue to do well, while those without such skills will end up earning close to minimum wage. Those who benefited from union membership during the post-LTP golden era will find the benefits of membership in the new pursued era are not what they used to be. Income inequality will increase again, even though when adjusted for skill levels it may not change all that much.

Workers who want to maintain or improve their living standards in a post-LTP pursued economy must therefore think hard about their individual prospects and the skills they should acquire in the new environment. To the extent that the answer to this question differs for each individual, workers are truly on their own. The "good old days," when businesses invested to increase worker productivity so they could pay employees more, are gone for good. In some sense this is only fair, since it means workers who put in the time and effort to improve their productivity will be rewarded more generously than those who do not.

## Consumers' Progression During Three Stages of Economic Development

Workers are also consumers, and their consumption behavior changes along with the stages of economic development. During the pre-LTP industrialization phase, most workers are paid very little. Their limited share of output serves as a constraint on consumption, and their low incomes prevent them from saving much. Most of the saving and investing is therefore done by the capitalist class, which typically has a higher marginal propensity to save. Because capitalists in this era have a high share of output but also a high propensity to save, domestic supply often exceeds domestic demand, which tends to keep prices depressed.

Once the economy passes the LTP and wages began to rise rapidly, consumers' mindset changes. With the future looking bright, they begin demanding high-quality products and luxury goods that they could only dream of during the pre-LTP period. Many begin to compete with each other on the basis of their possessions, a phenomenon dubbed "keeping up with the Joneses" in the U.S. Businesses strive to ensure they have a line of products capable of attracting these upwardly mobile consumers.

In the automobile industry, for example, General Motors had the Chevrolet marque at the entry level, Pontiac as an upgrade, Buick and Oldsmobile further up the ladder, and Cadillac at the top. Ford had Ford at the bottom, Mercury in the middle, and Lincoln at the top, while the order for Chrysler was Plymouth, Dodge, and Chrysler. And within each brand, different grades of cars were offered to keep customers always desiring a better automobile.

Consumers in those days were willing to buy a new car every two years not only to feel good but also to keep up with their neighbors and friends. Automakers' efforts to capture this upwardly mobile consumer every two years from beginning to end was called "full-line marketing."

In Japan, similar behavior was observed once the economy entered the post-LTP golden age where households began to compete with each other on the basis of their possessions. When a family bought a piano so that its children could take piano lessons, others in the neighborhood felt pressured to buy some sort of musical instrument so that their children could also have music lessons. This sort of peer pressure became so intense in the early 1990s that women of high school age and older felt they had to have at least one Louis Vuitton bag, resulting in a huge proportion of the nation's female population carrying such bags to school and work every day. Such competition to own better things or to keep up with the Joneses provided a significant positive feedback loop to the economy, and both consumption and GDP grew rapidly.

Once an economy enters the post-LTP pursued phase and the prospect of unlimited income growth disappears, however, consumers are forced to reorient their priorities. With incomes growing slowly or not at all, consumers are forced to ask whether they are receiving value for their money. At the same time, a huge inflow of inexpensive foreign goods, a key feature of post-LTP pursued economies, creates shopping options that did not exist before.

During this reorientation, the "keeping up with the Joneses" mentality is thrown out the window, and most consumers stop buying a new car every other year. Instead, they begin checking consumer websites like Consumer Reports to ensure that they get good value for money regardless of what make the product is, where it is sold, or where it is made.

In the U.S., this resulted in the growth of large discount retailers such as Walmart and Costco. The reduced importance of brand hierarchies also prompted the disappearance of venerable brands such as Oldsmobile and Plymouth.

In Japan, this reorientation led to the explosive growth of so-called "100 yen shops", where everything from electronic calculators to kitchenware can be purchased for 100 yen. Indeed, most new household formations in Japan now start with a shopping spree at a 100 yen shop because of the impressive quality and selection of goods offered. They then go to other stores to buy goods that cannot be found at the 100 yen shops.

When Poundland, which sells everything from scientific calculators to snacks for one British pound, first opened its doors, many UK consumers said they did not want to be seen in one. Apparently, they were not yet ready to shed their "keeping up with the Joneses" mentality. More recently, however, such resistance is said to have diminished as British consumers begin demanding more value for money.

In retrospect, this evolution of consumer behavior is perfectly reasonable: it was ridiculous for people to buy a new car every other year when the cars themselves are made to last much longer, or for a large proportion of the female population to be walking around with a Louis Vuitton bag. Just as workers are "on their own" in the post-LTP pursued phase, consumers are forced to become smarter and more independent in the post-LTP pursued phase, in the sense that they are no longer easily swayed by silly fads and fashions. Many simply cannot afford that sort of behavior any more.

# Different Inflationary Trends During Three Stages of Economic Development

These changes in the behavior of businesses, workers, and consumers during the various stages of economic development have profound implications for monetary and fiscal policy via their impact on economic growth and inflation.

In terms of monetary policy, workers are paid very low wages during the pre-LTP urbanization period, meaning that wage- or consumption-led price growth is very limited. Low wages mean workers are not likely to be great contributors to the nation's savings pool, either. The financial markets, as intermediators of savings and investment, are therefore relevant only for the top echelon of society. Although those at the top are likely to have a higher propensity to save, the availability of those savings effectively limits the investment that can take place during this period.

When many workers cannot afford to buy the products they are making, over-supply and deflation are likely to result unless exports are robust. If domestic demand is insufficient to absorb domestic production, the authorities may be forced to keep exchange rates low in order to promote exports. In other words, inflation is not likely to be a major problem during this period.

When the economy enters the post-LTP golden era, however, wage increases become so common as to become ingrained in the system. This leads to rapid increases in both the total wage bill and final demand from consumers. Consumers with ever-increasing incomes are also more willing to accept higher prices during this phase if those prices give them higher-quality goods or greater prestige in their social circles.

Businesses facing rising wages and increasing domestic demand must undertake substantial investment in productivity- and capacity-enhancing equipment, and one of the key characteristics of the post-LTP golden era is a high level of capital expenditure and correspondingly strong demand for funds to finance those investments.

Strong consumption demand from consumers and strong investment demand from businesses are likely to push prices steadily higher, and inflation becomes a real threat to economic growth. Strong demand for funds from businesses also means the money multiplier is pushed to its maximum value[1]. This means that economic conditions are fundamentally inflationary, but monetary policy is also at its most effective.

Indeed, private-sector demand for funds can increase dramatically during this period unless the central bank makes sustained efforts to keep it in check by adjusting interest rates and the supply of reserves. In other words, the central bank has to make sure that higher interest rates and the availability of reserves are the binding constraint on money supply and credit growth during this era. By doing so, it will be able to control the inflation rate.

During the golden era, therefore, central banks have their hands full fighting inflationary pressures. It is no coincidence that central banks are given ever-greater powers and independence during this phase of economic development.

---

[1] This point is explained in Chapter 8.

Milton Friedman's argument that inflation is everywhere and always a monetary phenomenon is actually valid during the golden era, when private-sector demand for funds is strong and the money multiplier is stable at its maximum value. As domestic inflationary pressures grow, a stronger exchange rate also becomes more desirable.

When the economy enters the post-LTP pursued phase, however, both incomes and wages are growing slowly, resulting in more moderate growth in consumption. Businesses' demand for capacity- and productivity-enhancing equipment also slows during this phase as they find higher returns on capital abroad. Weak or non-existent income growth leads to the emergence of more fastidious, value-conscious consumers, making it more difficult for businesses to raise prices. Rapid growth in inexpensive imports also has a depressing effect on domestic prices. All in all, inflation becomes much less of a problem than in the post-LTP golden era.

The fall in domestic demand for funds due to businesses' reduced domestic investment also makes monetary policy less effective. This can be seen from the lost correlation between the Fed's monetary policy actions and the movement in financial condition index starting in the 1990s. Financial condition index measures the difficulty borrower face in procuring funds.

As Figure 4.1 indicates, the index was moving more or less in line with the Fed's policy actions until the end of 1980s. In other words, when the Fed was raising interest rates to make it more costly for the borrowers to borrow, the financial index was also moving higher, indicating that the financial condition has tightened.

Starting in the 90s, however, this linkage was broken. There were four major monetary tightening cycles since then (circled areas in Figure 4.1), but in all cases, the financial condition index failed to respond to the Fed actions and stayed at very favorable levels for the borrowers. In the most recent episode starting in 2015, the financial condition index actually improved despite the Fed raising interest rates four times.

This loss of effectiveness of monetary policy is matched by the shrinkage in demand for funds from the U.S. non-financial corporate sector starting around 1990. Figure 4.2 shows the flow of funds data for the sector going back to 1971. It indicates that, until 1990, U.S. non-financial corporate sector was squarely in financial deficit, i.e., it was a large net borrower of funds as suggested by economic textbooks. Starting in 1990, however, the sector has become more or less neutral, i.e., it has stopped borrowing money. It is probably no coincidence that the effectiveness of monetary policy fell as non-financial corporations, the traditional borrower of funds, stopped borrowing money.

In short, both the importance and effectiveness of monetary policy change as the economy develops. Inflation is not a big problem for the monetary authorities during the pre-LTP phase with its depressed wages.

FIGURE 4.1  U.S. Monetary Policy Has Grown Less Effective Starting in 1990s

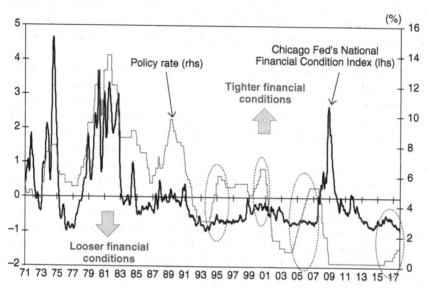

*Note:* In the Chicago Fed's national financial conditions index (NFCI), 0 represents the average from 1971 to the present. Prior to 1987, when the Fed began targeting fed funds rate, the policy rate in the graph refers to the official discount rate. Since the Fed began targeting a corridor of values for fed funds, the graph shows the top end of the Fed's target range.

*Source:* Board of Governors of the Federal Reserve System, The Federal Reserve Bank of Chicago, "National Financial Conditions Index"

During the post-LTP golden age, inflation becomes a major issue, and the central bank must be extremely vigilant, employing monetary restraint to keep higher wages and stronger domestic consumption and investment demand from pushing prices higher. Monetary policy is also very effective during this period because strong demand for funds keeps the money multiplier stable at its maximum value.

Once the economy enters the post-LTP pursued state, inflation becomes less of a problem amid slower wage growth, a surge of imports, weaker consumption, and reduced demand for fixed capital investment. Hence there is less need for the central bank to exercise monetary restraint. Monetary policy also becomes much less effective during this phase because of the reduced demand for borrowings to fund capital expenditures reduces the money multiplier. With an increasing number of jobs lost to oversees, and reduced inflationary pressure at home, the monetary authorities may also come under pressure to bring exchange rates down.

This also means that the neutral rate of interest—the level of interest that does not add to or subtract from economic activity—stays low

FIGURE 4.2 U.S. Nonfinancial Companies' Demand for Funds Shrunk after 1990

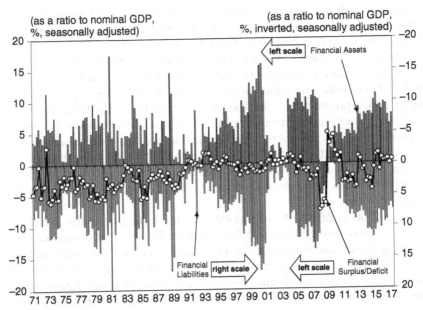

*Notes:* Latest figures are for 2017 Q2.

*Sources:* Nomura Research Institute, based on flow of funds data from FRB and U.S. Department of Commerce

during the pre-LTP phase, goes up significantly during the golden age, and comes down again when the economy enters the post-LTP pursued phase. One must therefore be careful when using elasticities and multipliers for monetary policy tools obtained in an earlier era, because they may no longer be relevant in the current period.

## Fiscal Policy Challenges in Three Stages of Economic Development

The importance and effectiveness of fiscal policy, or government borrowing and spending, also change with the stage of economic development. In the pre-LTP urbanization phase, fiscal policy is not only effective but is often crucial in providing essential infrastructure so that private-sector investments can come in and flourish. The social rate of return on infrastructure investments is therefore very high during this phase.

When the economy is in the golden era, however, fiscal policy has limited ability to stimulate the economy except during balance sheet recessions because of its tendency to "crowd out" private sector investment in productivity- and capacity-enhancing equipment. It is no coincidence that economists tend to disparage fiscal stimulus during this period because the government will be competing with private businesses for limited private-sector savings. This also suggests that the social rate of return on public works projects is often far below the yield on government bonds.

Once the economy enters the pursued phase, however, fiscal policy is less likely to cause crowding out since private-sector demand for funds is weaker. Fiscal policy therefore becomes more effective than in the golden era. Indeed, if private-sector demand for funds falls below the level of private savings even at very low interest rates, the economy is effectively in Case 3 and fiscal policy becomes absolutely essential in keeping the economy going.

At the same time, the absence of private-sector borrowers means borrowing costs for the government, sometimes the only borrower left, drop to very low levels. Many public works projects therefore become wholly or nearly self-financing.

The 2008 collapse of asset price bubbles exacerbated this trend of shrinking private-sector demand for funds in the pursued economies by throwing these economies into balance sheet recessions. As indicated in Figure 1.1, private-sector demand for funds is now negative in virtually all the pursued economies despite zero interest rates. That has further reinforced the tendency for monetary policy to grow less effective and fiscal

FIGURE 4.3 Effectiveness of Monetary and Fiscal Policies in Three Stages of Economic Development

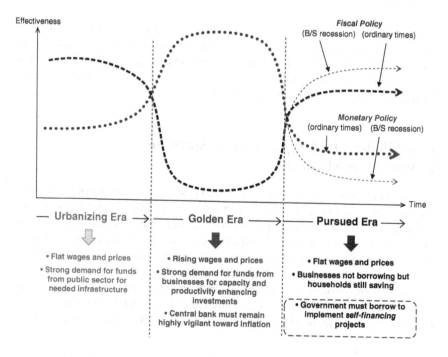

policy more so. Even if these countries were not in balance sheet recessions, fiscal policy would most likely have become more effective than during the golden era, with the reverse being true for monetary policy.

These changes in the effectiveness of fiscal and monetary policy are illustrated in Figure 4.3. Here there are two lines each for the pursued phase because most economies in this phase today are also suffering from balance sheet recessions or their aftermath. The point here is that the presence of balance sheet problems made fiscal policy even more effective than usual and monetary policy even less so. It also means that monetary policy in advanced countries will *not* regain its golden-era effectiveness even after the balance sheet problems are resolved, because these countries are already in the pursued phase.

The golden era is the era of monetary policy, with limited opportunities for fiscal policy to serve a useful role. But in the pursued phase these roles are essentially reversed.

## Policymakers Unable to Shake off Memories of Golden Age

In spite of the fact that all of the advanced economies are now in the pursued phase, the policy debate in these countries has yet to shake off the cobwebs of the golden era, a period that ended more than 20 years ago. The mentality of the golden era is still very much with us for at least two reasons.

First, it was a great time when incomes were growing for everyone. Everyone wants to return to that era because it defined what is possible for an economy. For many, in fact, this era defined the economy's "trend growth."

Second, it was the era when the discipline of macroeconomics was founded. Big names such as Paul Samuelson and Milton Friedman all wrote against the backdrop of the golden era. Most theories and models taught in economics are based on the assumption that the private sector is maximizing profits because that was largely true during this era.

But once the golden era ends and the economy starts to be pursued by foreign competitors, private-sector capital investment and demand for funds both fall markedly. Inflation slows as wages stop rising, imports increase sharply, and consumers grow more cautious. The implication is that monetary policy has a much smaller role to play (as inflation fighter) and is much less effective than during the golden era, while the reverse is true for fiscal policy.

The problem is that the policy debate in most countries has yet to acknowledge that these inevitable and fundamental changes have taken place and that these changes are attributable to changes in the stage of economic development. In all advanced countries, for example, a huge group of economists continues to claim that monetary policy is the right tool for addressing economic fluctuations and that fiscal policy should be

discouraged because of its tendency to crowd out private-sector investment—even though governments' borrowing costs have dropped to record
low levels in most countries. Both the media and market participants are
also intently focused on changes in central bank monetary policy as mentioned in Chapter 2, even though such policies largely lost their effectiveness once the countries entered the pursued phase.

The low fiscal multiplier of which they speak is something observed
almost exclusively during the golden era or periods including the golden
era, i.e., when the economy was in Case 1 or 2. During those periods, the
low fiscal multiplier argument is valid because governments running budget
deficits are in fact competing with private-sector borrowers for a limited
amount of savings. That leads to higher interest rates, the crowding out of
private-sector investments, and the frequent misallocation of resources, all
of which result in a low fiscal multiplier.

But the assumption of a low fiscal multiplier is totally inappropriate for
a world in which most advanced economies are in Case 3 or 4. If Figure 2.1
is any guide, for example, the fiscal multiplier in post-1990 Japan has been 4
to 5 if correctly measured based on the counter-factual GDP that would have
resulted in the absence of fiscal stimulus. This is easily double or triple the
typical multiplier observed during the golden era. In other words, fiscal multipliers measured during the golden era should *not* be used in the policy debate
when an economy is in the pursued era and/or in a balance sheet recession.

Unfortunately, those (like the author) who studied economics during the
golden era or used textbooks written during that era have had it hammered
into their heads that fiscal policy has a low multiplier effect. Some cite fiscal and monetary multipliers that were obtained using *only* those data from
earlier periods because those are what they are familiar with. Hence there
is always a danger that they will subconsciously base policy recommendations on those outdated multipliers and elasticities. Even though a low fiscal
multiplier was "common sense" three decades ago, the global environment
surrounding advanced economies has changed dramatically since then.

# Fundamental Macro-Policy Challenges Facing Pursued Countries

Based on the changes that economies go through, it appears that the most
fundamental macroeconomic challenge for all pursued countries is that (1)
households are still saving for an uncertain future as they always have,
but (2) businesses are unable to absorb all of those savings because they
cannot find sufficient domestic investment opportunities, even at very low
interest rates. But if someone is saving money, someone else must borrow
and spend that money to keep the income cycle and the economy going.

To maintain macroeconomic stability when households are saving but businesses are not borrowing even at very low interest rates, either net exports must be increased or the government must borrow and spend those savings without sacrificing its fiscal future. When the former is an unrealistic option in the short to medium run (in part because all countries cannot increase net exports at the same time), the government has no choice but to administer fiscal stimulus. The fact that pursued phase can go on for decades makes this a truly monumental challenge at a time when the public debt of most advanced countries has already reached alarming levels.

This is the same challenge that economies in balance sheet recessions confront, as discussed in Chapter 2. In a balance sheet recession, it is the millions of underwater balance sheets that lead to the disappearance of private-sector borrowers, whereas in pursued economies, it is the lack of attractive domestic investment opportunities that produces the same outcome. In the former case, the lack of private-sector demand for funds will not be corrected until private-sector balance sheets are repaired, while in the latter case, the lack of demand for funds will not be corrected until sufficient domestic investment opportunities present themselves. In the meantime, both economies will face a deflationary pressure unless someone outside the private sector returns the private sector's excess savings to the economy's income stream.

Faced with this challenge, those with a golden-era mindset would argue that the use of fiscal stimulus is out of the question because public debt in the advanced countries has already reached its limits. They might also add that, while fiscal stimulus may be acceptable during balance sheet recessions (since the need for stimulus will end once private-sector balance sheets recover), there is no obvious end to the need for fiscal stimulus in a pursued economy. With public debt already at very high levels, they would argue that unleashing fiscal stimulus with no end in sight is nothing short of madness.

Instead, they say, with the population ageing, the public and private sectors should be working to cap the growth of debt, if not actually reduce it. Indeed, the amount of debt has become a much-discussed topic among economists not only in the advanced countries but also in places like China.

## Debt Limit Argument Ignores the Fact That Debt Is Flip Side of Savings

The problem with this argument is that debt is simply the flip side of savings. Somebody has to be saving for debt to grow, and it is bound to increase as long as someone in the economy continues to save. Moreover, if someone is saving but debt levels fail to grow (i.e., if no one borrows and spends the

saved funds), the economy will fall into the $1,000–$900–$810–$730 deflationary spiral described in Chapter 1, with highly unpleasant consequences.
Growth in debt (excluding debt financed by the central bank) is merely a
reflection of the fact that the private sector has continued to save.

If debt is growing faster than actual savings, it simply means there is
double counting somewhere, i.e., somebody has borrowed the money but
instead of using it himself, he lent it to someone else, possibly with a different
maturity structure (maturity transfer) or interest rates (fixed to floating or vice
versa). With the prevalence of carry trades and structured financial products
involving multiple counterparties, debt numbers may grow rapidly on the
surface, but the actual debt can never be greater than the actual savings.

Furthermore, the level of debt anyone can carry also depends on the
level of interest rates and the quality of projects financed with the debt.
If the projects earn enough to pay back both borrowing costs and principal,
then no one should care about the debt load, no matter how large, because
it does not represent a future burden on anyone. Similarly, no matter how
great the national debt, if the funds are invested in public works projects
capable of generating returns high enough to pay back both interest and
principal, the projects will be self-financing and will not increase the burden
on future taxpayers.

## Making the Mistake of Communist Central Planners

Another problem with the debt limit argument is that it looks only at the
quantity of debt and ignores the price, the same mistake Communist central
planners made, and one which invariably ended in tears. By looking only
at debt levels, these people are ignoring messages from the bond market,
i.e., the price of government bonds, in deciding whether fiscal stimulus is
good or bad for the economy. Whether or not fiscal policy has reached its
limits should be decided by the bond market, not by some economist using
arbitrarily chosen criteria.

During the golden era, when the private sector has strong demand
for funds to finance productivity- and capacity-enhancing investments,
fiscal stimulus will have a minimal if not negative impact on the economy
because of the crowding-out effect. The bond market during this era correctly assigns very low prices (high yields) to government bonds, indicating
that such stimulus is not welcome.

During the pursued era or during balance sheet recessions, however,
private-sector demand for funds is minimal if not negative. At such times,
fiscal stimulus is not only essential, but it has maximum positive impact
on the economy because there is no danger of crowding out. During this

period, the bond market correctly sets very high prices (low yields) for government bonds, indicating that they are welcome.

They are welcome because for economies in Cases 3 and 4, the only destination for surplus private-sector savings that cannot take too much foreign exchange risk or principal risk is debt issued by the sole remaining domestic borrower—the government. The yields on government debt therefore fall precipitously. Low bond yields, in turn, provide the government with the fiscal space it needs to offset deflationary pressures from excess private-sector savings. This self-corrective mechanism of economies in Cases 3 and 4 as represented by super-low government bond yields has already been observed in most pursued countries in recent years, including those not suffering from balance sheet recessions.

The fact that economies collapsed when the Japanese government ignored the bond market and tried to reduce the deficit in 1997 and when European governments tried to do the same in 2010 suggests that it is dangerous to ignore the bond market's warnings (the reason why government bond yields skyrocketed in Eurozone peripheral countries in 2010 is discussed in detail in Chapter 7). In the above Japanese case, the fiscal deficit actually *increased* 72 percent as a result of fiscal austerity, as mentioned in Chapter 2. The bond market, via ultra-low yields, has been telling policymakers that this is no time to cut deficits, since 1995 for Japan and 2008 for the West.

## Fundamental Solution to Fundamental Problem

Ultra-low bond yields in economies in Cases 3 and 4 are also a signal to the government to look for public works projects capable of producing a social rate of return in excess of those rates. If such projects can be found, fiscal stimulus centered on them will ultimately place no added burden on future taxpayers.

The most important macroeconomic challenge for policymakers in pursued countries, therefore, is to *find* infrastructure projects capable of earning social rates of return in excess of these ultra-low government bond yields. As long as projects are self-financing, the government can implement them without worrying about the size of the deficit or hitting some hypothetical "upper limit" on the public debt because those projects do not constitute a burden on future taxpayers. As long as such projects can be found and implemented, the economy will continue to function even though it is being pursued. Economies in Cases 3 and 4 should therefore mobilize their best and brightest to find and implement such projects instead of wasting time worrying about the size of the public debt.

On the other hand, few public works projects are "self-financing" when the economy is in Case 1 or 2, with strong private-sector demand for funds keeping interest rates high. This means the option of finding self-financing public works is largely unavailable. It also means there *is* an upper limit on the amount of debt a government can accumulate in Cases 1 and 2.

The above also explains why it has been difficult for economists to specify the upper limit on public debt. The correct answer depends on the amount of public debt that is self-financing, and that, in turn, depends on the quality of the public works projects selected and the prevailing level of government bond yields. Government bond yields, in turn, will vary depending on whether the economy is in Cases 1 and 2 or Cases 3 and 4.

Some may argue that if such self-financing projects exist, they should be undertaken by the private sector instead of the government. There are two reasons why that may not work. First, private-sector businesses are under pressure from shareholders to maximize their return on capital. That means that even if there are self-financing projects at home, they must invest abroad if higher returns are available. Since the government has no mandate to maximize its return on capital but *is* expected to keep the economy out of a deflationary spiral, it can and should implement public works projects to keep the economy going.

Second, and more importantly, the rate of return that is relevant here is the *social* rate of return with all the externalities which the private-sector operators may not be able to capture fully. In other words, there may be projects which do not have high enough return as private ventures but make sense as public ventures because of their positive externalities on the larger society.

Traditional economists often made the mistake of focusing entirely on one side of the balance sheet while ignoring the other. As noted earlier with regard to Figure 2.13, economists who looked only at money supply growth from 1933 to 1936 concluded that the U.S. economy emerged from the Great Depression because of the Fed's monetary accommodation. In fact, however, it was government borrowing that increased the asset side of banks' balance sheets and thereby allowed the money supply, the liability of the banking system, to grow.

The same problem applies to the recent emphasis on debt levels. While it has become popular to decry the size of the private- or public-sector debt, debt is increasing only because savings continue to grow. Since it is difficult to tell people *not* to save, policymakers need to make sure those savings are borrowed and invested wisely in projects that will earn returns in excess of the borrowing costs. That is where the debate should focus. Simply discussing the *size* of the debt is a meaningless waste of time.

During the textbook world of Cases 1 and 2 when domestic investment opportunities are plentiful, economists rightfully focus on strengthening monetary policy's ability to rein in inflation while disparaging profligate fiscal policy. Interest rates are also relatively high, which makes it difficult to find public projects capable of earning equal or higher rates of return.

Now most advanced countries find themselves in Cases 3 and 4, where the private sector becomes a large net saver. This means economists and policymakers must reorient their focus from monetary policy to finding viable infrastructure projects so that the government can, in good conscience, continue in its crucial role as borrower of last resort. And that task of finding viable projects has become much easier with government bond yields at record lows.

## Independent Commission Needed to Select and Oversee Projects

To make this reorientation happen, the country will need an independent commission comprising highly trained experts who can judge whether projects are likely to produce a social rate of return in excess of government bond yields. These calculations are not at all easy or straightforward, since a typical public works project involves many externalities that are hard to quantify but that will have to be considered before making a final judgment.

Some techniques have been developed to this end by institutions such as the World Bank, but because the quality of the decisions made has huge implications for the country's future when the government is the only entity borrowing and investing for the future, the existing methodologies might have to be reviewed and refined. If the projects selected turn out to be not self-financing, they can literally extinguish the nation's economic future by burdening taxpayers with costly white elephants and a massive debt load. In theory at least, these projects are not limited to brick and mortar construction types either. In tourism-dependent economies such as Spain, targeted English language training program may have a social rate of return that is higher than the government's bond yield.

Here, a politically independent commission staffed with the nation's best and brightest is essential to ensure the proposed projects are actually self-financing. It has to be independent because politicians will naturally try to win projects for their constituencies, and governments in general have a poor reputation for their ability to select good projects.

The importance of this commission's independence cannot be overemphasized: its independence is no less important in a pursued economy than the independence of the central bank in a golden-era economy. Just like the independence of central banks, the legal status of the independent commission will have to be very strong because it will need to reject projects proposed by democratically elected representatives of the people.

When the U.S. was closing military bases after the end of the Cold War, an independent commission was set up to decide which bases to shut down. The process went reasonably smoothly, although there were some complaints from politicians in affected districts. What a country in Cases 3 and 4 needs is a similar set-up where projects may be proposed by elected representatives, but the commission is charged with ranking them so that those that are self-financing are given the highest priority.

The commission must also make sure that the selected projects are designed and implemented correctly. Such continued scrutiny is essential to prevent cost overruns and the inclusion of unnecessary features, and the construction contracts should be given to reliable contractors offering the lowest price. This watchdog function of the commission is crucial to ensure that the projects remain self-financing.

It may also take years to develop and refine proper techniques and guidelines for assessing projects and training people to use them. If the number of projects increases with the government taking a leading role as borrower of last resort, the number of trained staff employed by the commission will have to increase as well. Inasmuch as pursued economies are likely to remain in that state for an extended period of time, there is no time to waste in developing the human capital needed for the independent commission.

## When Waiting for Good Projects Is a Bad Idea

The creation of an independent commission to select self-financing public works projects is the fundamental solution for all countries in Cases 3 and 4. However, many countries in balance sheet recessions today may be unable to wait for such a commission. Many need fiscal stimulus right now to stave off the $1,000–$900–$810–$730 deflationary spiral.

Since the cost of recovery from a depression, the end result of an unattended deflationary spiral, is so high these countries should implement whatever projects, that are "shovel-ready" now, without waiting for the ideal self-financing projects. The GDP and jobs so saved by *not* waiting for ideal projects will greatly exceed any savings the latter might have yielded.

This can be seen by comparing the U.S. after 1929 with Japan after 1990. In the U.S., President Herbert Hoover and Treasury Secretary Andrew Mellon allowed the U.S. economy to find its own bottom by taking no fiscal action until 1932, three years after the bubble burst. That decision resulted in a 46 percent contraction of nominal GNP (Figure 2.1) and skyrocketing unemployment. The U.S. economy then required the truly astronomical fiscal stimulus of World

War II to achieve a recovery. In 1944, at the height of the war, the U.S. budget deficit *alone* was more than 30 percent of the nation's GDP.

In contrast, post-1990 Japan was able to keep its GDP from falling below the bubble peak because it implemented fiscal stimulus from the outset without waiting for the best projects. Although some of this investment did attract criticism, the post-bubble Japanese unemployment rate never exceeded 5.5 percent even though Japan suffered balance sheet damage three times larger as a percentage of GDP than what the U.S. incurred after 1929.

Some commentators have also argued that using fiscal policy to keep GDP at bubble-era levels is wrong and unsustainable. But the examples of the post-1929 U.S. and post-1990 Japan demonstrate that the option of letting the economy find its "contractionary equilibrium" at a depression-level GDP is no option at all. This also means that waiting for good public works project is no option either.

Once macroeconomic stability is achieved, countries should shift fiscal stimulus to self-financing projects or those that are close to self-financing as they become available. When the patient is in intensive care and every second counts, doctors should not be wandering around for hours in a search for the most cost-effective medicine. They should do so only after the patient is out of intensive care and in a stable condition.

Fiscal stimulus should continue until the private sector is ready to borrow again. When it is, the public sector should reduce its investments by the amount of new private-sector demand for funds. The financial markets should be warning the government with higher interest rates that the private sector has resumed borrowing. If no private-sector demand for funds is forthcoming, the independent commission will have to continue finding self-financing projects or those that are nearly so to keep the economy functioning.

## Old (and Costly) Beliefs Die Hard

In spite of strong and consistent messages from the bond market for the last 27 years, Japanese Ministry of Finance (MOF) officials with a golden era mindset have continued to warn that the huge public debt and massive fiscal deficits would soon push the yields on Japanese government bonds (JGBs) sky-high and trigger a fiscal crisis. Fiscal hawks in the U.S., including members of the Tea Party, have also warned that the large public debt will eventually cripple the U.S. economy. The German government has been making similar arguments in Europe since 2008.

All those who listened to the warning of an imminent fiscal crisis, including U.S. hedge funds that shorted JGBs, lost their shirts as government bond prices continued to rise for 27 years. The yield on 10-year Japanese government bonds fell below two percent in 1998, long before the Bank of Japan embarked on quantitative easing (QE). By then, the public debt had already reached 118 percent of GDP, and the government was running a budget deficit amounting to 10.2 percent of GDP. The 10-year bond yield then fell to 0.7 percent on the eve of Governor Kuroda's QE even though the public debt had by then climbed to 240 percent of GDP, all because of the self-corrective mechanism of economies in balance sheet recessions.

It was fortunate that Japanese pension fund managers did not act on the warnings from the MOF. If they had followed its advice and shorted JGBs over the last 27 years like some U.S. hedge funds, they would have lost every yen of their retirees' money by now.

The 10-year U.S. Treasury bond yield also slipped below 3 percent in 2009 even as the federal deficit skyrocketed from 2.4 percent of GDP in 2007 to 10.8 percent in 2009. The yield then went as low as 1.5 percent in 2016 after the Fed had stopped buying bonds with its QE program. Bond yields in pursued countries that are not in balance sheet recessions, including Canada, Taiwan, and Korea, have also dropped to unusually low levels.

Such developments, where a massive expansion of the public debt is associated with sharply lower government bond yields, are unthinkable for textbook economies in Cases 1 or 2, but are perfectly understandable for economies in Cases 3 and 4 where the private-sector is not only not borrowing money but is actually increasing savings and government is the only borrower remaining. Those who were taught economics when the economy was in Case 1 or 2, however, are still unable to grasp the huge changes that have taken place since then.

## Is Two Percent Inflation Target Appropriate for Pursued Economies?

Much like the golden-age aversion to fiscal policy, the golden-age obsession with monetary policy is dying hard. In particular, the two percent inflation target adopted by many advanced countries today is not only inappropriate for a post-LTP pursued economy but has the potential to cause huge problems later on.

The two percent target was proposed by economists who studied the experiences of many countries over an extended period of time. The problem is that this period mainly covers a time when the economies were in their post-LTP golden era. The Reserve Bank of Australia was one of the earliest central banks to adapt a two percent inflation target, in 1992. According to Glenn Stevens, then deputy governor, it did so in order to emulate the success of Germany's Bundesbank in the 1970s when it was fighting rapid increases in German wages[2]. But that world of rapidly increasing wages no longer exists.

In the golden era, ever-rising wages and ever-increasing domestic demand created a fundamental tendency toward higher inflation. Businesses were also investing heavily at home to increase both capacity and productivity to meet that demand. Nor were consumers particularly fastidious about value when wages were rising year after year.

Indeed, many if not most of the recessions during the golden era were caused when the central bank tightened monetary policy to bring inflation back to a more acceptable level. And frequent tightening was necessary because golden-era economies are fundamentally inflationary. It was therefore understandable that economists sought an inflation target that the central bank should try to maintain *preemptively* so it would not be forced to engage in the periodic but belated tightening that was costly in terms of both uncertainty and output lost.

When the economy entered the pursued phase, however, the majority of the factors that fueled inflation during the previous era disappeared. Instead, huge inflows of cheap imports, stagnant wages, and price-conscious consumers made it very difficult for businesses to raise prices. At the same time, corporate demand for funds decreased as attractive investment opportunities at home shrank while the household sector continued to save, producing a fundamentally deflationary environment. Even without a balance sheet recession, which adds another layer of deflationary pressures not seen during normal times, economies in the pursued phase are far less inflationary than in the golden era.

The question then becomes whether it is advisable for central banks to stick with a two percent inflation target that was designed to keep inflation rates from *accelerating* during the golden era. If the same target is used to keep inflation rates from *decelerating* below two percent in the pursued era, the expectation must be that this level of inflation will prompt businesses and consumers to behave as if they were in the golden era.

But far too many things have changed during the last 30 years to expect businesses and consumers to return to the old and, in retrospect, somewhat crazy ways. For example, it is difficult to expect consumers to resume buying a new car every other year, or to choose their purchases based on social pressure just because inflation is running at two percent. Stores like Costco

[2] Stevens, Glenn (2003) "Inflation Targeting: A Decade of Australian Experience," address to South Australian Centre for Economic Studies, April 2003, Economic Briefings, on April 10, 2003. www.rba.gov.au/speeches/2003/sp-dg-100403.html.

in the U.S., Japan's 100 yen shops, and Poundland in the UK are not going to disappear just because the inflation rate has risen to two percent: consumers are much wiser now.

Businesses in pursued countries are also under pressure from shareholders to be constantly watching for overseas opportunities to ensure that their capital is invested where the return is highest. They also have plenty of experience producing abroad, which was not the case during the golden era, when their focus was largely domestic. In this environment, higher inflation rates, and especially rising wages, may actually discourage businesses from investing at home for competitive reasons.

In spite of this, two percent has become *the* inflation target for many central banks around the world, and they have injected huge amounts of liquidity into the system in an attempt to achieve it. Those pushing for this target argue that it is necessary to realign the public's inflationary expectations in order to lower their expected real interest rates.

But borrowers have absented themselves not because real interest rates are too high, but because either (1) they cannot find attractive investment opportunities at home or (2) their balance sheets are still not presentable. Few businesses in this condition will be impressed by central bankers' two percent inflation targets.

Perhaps even more importantly, the general level of prices is irrelevant for most businesses: it is the prices of their products that matter. And they know from their own daily struggle in the fiercely competitive post-LTP pursued economy that it is not easy to raise prices. They understand as well as anyone that today's consumers are very different from those of the golden era.

Furthermore, companies invest when they encounter capacity constraints or when they find opportunities to enhance productivity or move into new businesses. They do not invest just because the inflation rate has recovered to two percent.

The excess liquidity injected by central banks in pursuit of the two percent target has created mini-bubbles in various asset classes via the portfolio rebalancing effect. In the post-2008 West, there have been mini-bubbles in emerging market debt, commodities, equities and now commercial real estate. Although these bubbles do have some positive impact on the real economy via the wealth effect, it is usually short-lived and will be more than reversed when the bubble invariably bursts. Furthermore, there are significant costs to removing the excess reserves now in the system. This is discussed in detail in Chapter 6.

In view of the above, it is hoped that monetary authorities will re-examine the relevance of the two percent inflation target in post-LTP pursued economies that are also suffering from balance sheet recessions. Instead of mindlessly adding excess reserves—which are useless when the economy is in Cases 3 and 4 but can cause huge problems later on when the economy returns to Cases 1 and 2—central banks should be directing governments to borrow the private sector's excess savings and invest the funds in viable public works projects because that is the correct way to avoid deflation by supporting both the money supply and the GDP from contracting.

## Recovery in Private Investment Would Not Bring Back Golden Era

An improvement in private-sector balance sheets after almost a decade of deleveraging since 2008 would almost certainly bring about some rebound in private-sector demand for funds. There is also a non-negligible probability that the emergence of major technological innovations will lead to substantial growth in private-sector investment and demand for funds. Although discoveries and innovations are notoriously difficult to predict, among recent innovations, the widespread adoption of self-driving cars and fuel cells has the potential to elicit substantial public and private investment.

If that were to happen, central bank monetary policy would once again have a bigger role to play—just as it did during the golden era—while fiscal policy would have to be reined in to prevent the crowding out of private investment. In that sense, one cannot rule out the future emergence of a world resembling the golden era, given big enough technological breakthroughs.

If that happens, the central banks that created massive excess reserves via QE during the balance sheet recession will have to drain those funds quickly, before private-sector fund demand recovers. Otherwise inflation will go through the roof. This challenge is discussed in Chapter 6.

However, the chances of pursued economies returning to a *real* golden era in which all members of society are able to benefit from economic growth do not seem very high. During the golden era, it was the manufacturing sector that offered an ever-expanding number of well-paying jobs, thereby forcing service-sector firms to offer comparable wages to keep their workers. Because manufacturing jobs did not require a great deal of education, the entire population was able to benefit from manufacturing-led economic growth. In other words, manufacturing was helping the economy from the bottom.

In the future, it is difficult to envision an innovation that will create a huge number of well-paying jobs for those without higher education. If anything, the current trend in innovation is for reducing headcount via automation, robotics, and artificial intelligence. In other words, technological innovation may bring back investment opportunities, but not jobs.

In summary, just as there are proper ways to run an economy in a golden era, there are proper ways to run an economy in the pursued era. The single most important macroeconomic policy for the government is to create an independent commission to identify and undertake public works projects that promise a social rate of return in excess of ultra-low government bond yields. This is an entirely new challenge for fiscal authorities in the pursued era, just as fighting inflation was a new challenge for central banks during the golden era.

The best and the brightest, many of whom headed for independent central banks during the golden era, are now needed in an as-yet-to-be-created independent fiscal commission to identify and implement public works projects that are self-financing or close to it. It is hoped that the economics profession has the courage to jettison inflation targets, the aversion to fiscal stimulus, and other legacies of the golden era and take up the task of identifying the self-financing public works projects that economies in the pursued era desperately need.

# CHAPTER 5

# Challenges of Remaining an Advanced Country

Instead of trying to return to a lost golden era, an advanced country in the pursued phase should undertake self-financing fiscal projects to maintain macroeconomic stability along with microeconomic policies designed to increase return on capital at home and fend off pursuers so it can remain an advanced economy. To fend off pursuers, the government needs to implement structural reforms in at least two areas. First, it must maximize the innovative potential of its people so that the country can remain at the forefront of the latest technological developments. Second, it must increase the economy's flexibility so that it can take "evasive action" when chased from behind. These are unique challenges for countries in the pursued state.

## How U.S. Dealt with Challenge of Japan

On both issues, the U.S. experience in fending off Japan is instructive because it is the story of a country that lost its high-tech leadership and then regained it two decades later. When the U.S. began losing industries left and right to Japanese competition starting in the mid-1970s, as described in Chapter 3, it pursued a two-pronged approach in which it tried to keep Japanese imports from coming in too fast while simultaneously shoring up the competitiveness of domestic industries.

The U.S. utilized every means available to prevent Japanese imports from flooding the market. These included accusations of dumping, Super 301 clauses, various "gentlemen's agreements," and currency devaluation via the Plaza Accord of 1985. The struggle was neither easy nor pleasant.

As a resident of Japan who had worked for the Federal Reserve as an economist and also held American citizenship, the author was frequently asked by the U.S. Embassy in Tokyo to explain the U.S. trade position to Japanese TV audiences at the height of U.S.-Japan trade frictions, as he was a frequent guest on those programs. After receiving extensive briefings from embassy staff, the author would make the case for U.S. exporters in those televised debates with Japanese economists and pundits. In all of those encounters, the author, in addition to discussing individual trade cases, also argued that if Japan continued to resist pressures to open its market while at the same time running huge trade surpluses with the U.S., the trade imbalances would eventually push the yen sky-high and force Japan's best industries to leave the country, a prediction that unfortunately came true in 1995 when the yen appreciate as high as ¥79.75 to the dollar.

At the height of the trade friction debate, the author found an American car with right-hand-drive on the streets of Sydney, Australia and imported it to Japan both to find out what sort of non-tariff trade barriers there really were, and to stop Japanese Ministry of International Trade and Industry (MITI, now METI) officials from criticizing U.S. automakers for not producing right-hand-drive cars to match the Japanese market. Some of the exasperating non-tariff trade barriers the author encountered during the import process were mentioned by the U.S. Ambassador to Japan, Walter Mondale, in speeches at the time.

Although the author tried his best to explain to the Japanese public why it was in their own interest to find compromises with the U.S., he will never forget the intense mutual hostility that characterized the U.S.-Japan trade relationship from the mid-1980s to the mid-1990s. The author not only received his share of death threats, but the trade frictions ultimately began to resemble a racial confrontation.

Meanwhile, "Japanese management" was all the rage at U.S. business schools in the 1980s and 1990s. Harvard University professor Ezra Vogel's *Japan as Number One: Lessons for America*, published in 1979, was widely read by people on both sides of the Pacific. The schools also recruited a large number of Japanese students so they could discuss Japanese management styles in their classrooms. The challenge from seemingly unstoppable Japan, coupled with its defeat in the Vietnam War, sent U.S. confidence to an all-time low, while the consumption of sushi went up sharply.

After trying everything from protectionism and currency devaluation to learning "Japanese management," however, the U.S. seems to have concluded that when a country is being pursued from behind, the only real solution is to run faster—i.e., to stay ahead of the competition by continuously generating new ideas, products, and designs. In this regard, the U.S. was fortunate that the supply-side reforms of President Ronald Reagan—who cut taxes and deregulated the economy drastically starting in the early 1980s—had the effect of raising the return on capital at home by making the economy more flexible and encouraging innovators and entrepreneurs to come up with new ideas and products.

Reaganomics itself was a response to the stagflation of the 1970s, which was characterized by frequent strikes, high inflation rates, sub-standard manufacturing quality, and mediocrity all around. It was a reaction against labor, which was still trying to extend gains made during the post-Lewis Turning Point (LTP) golden era without realizing the U.S. had already entered the post-LTP pursued phase in the 1970s with the arrival of Japanese competition. The fact that the U.S. was losing so many industries and good jobs to Japan also created a sense that a break from the past was urgently needed.

People with ideas and drive began to take notice when President Reagan lowered taxes and deregulated the economy. These people then began pushing the technological envelope in Information Technology (IT), eventually enabling the U.S. to regain the lead it lost to the Japanese in many high-tech areas. Few Americans in the 1980s thought the nation would ever win back high-tech leadership from Japanese companies such as Sony, Panasonic, and Toshiba, yet today, even the Tokyo offices of Japanese companies are full of products from U.S. brands such as Apple, Dell, and HP. In other words, the U.S. learned how to run *faster*.

The U.S. was also fortunate to have had a long tradition of liberal arts education that encouraged students to think independently and challenge the status quo, since such thinkers are essential to the development of new products and services.

More specifically, deregulation and lower taxes helped improve the return on capital by improving the allocation of resources, especially of human capital, within the U.S. economy. By channeling both money and the best minds toward promising high-tech areas, the U.S. was able to acquire a new engine for growth.

Reagan also pushed for greater labor-market flexibility by firing all civilian air-traffic controllers who had gone on strike in defiance of Federal regulations and replacing them with military controllers. This bold action, widely supported by the public, finally broke the back of the labor unions that were still trying to extend gains made during the golden era.

The need for labor-market flexibility became increasingly obvious as the country entered the pursued era. In the golden era, when a country is ahead of everyone else or is chasing somebody without being chased by anyone else, there is typically no need to take evasive action. With the road ahead looking promising and no one visible in the rear-view mirror, businesses take a forward-looking approach and emphasize finding good employees and keeping them for the long term. Consequently, seniority-based wages and lifetime employment are typical features of the golden era, especially at successful companies, since such measures help maintain a stable and reliable work force. In the U.S., IBM and other top companies did in fact have lifetime employment systems during the golden era.

Once the country enters the pursued phase, however, businesses must become more flexible and take evasive action to fend off pursuers from behind. Foreign competitors may show up from anywhere, often with a very different cost structure. When faced with such competition, businesses must downsize or abandon product lines that are no longer profitable and shift resources to areas that remain profitable. These tough decisions— which must be made without delay—make it difficult for firms to maintain seniority-based wages and lifetime employment because both programs effectively turn labor expense into a fixed cost and undermine management's flexibility and ability to take evasive action.

Reagan's deregulation and anti-labor-union moves enhanced the flexibility U.S. businesses needed to fend off competitors from behind. Even though those measures hurt labor and increased income inequality in some quarters, chances are high that without them the post-1990 U.S. resurgence might have been much weaker or faltered altogether.

## Structural Reforms Need Time to Produce Results

Although the U.S. success in regaining the high-tech lead from Japan was a spectacular achievement, it took nearly 15 years. Reagan's concepts were implemented in the early 1980s, but it was not until Bill Clinton became president that those ideas actually bore fruit. The U.S. economy continued to struggle during Reagan's two terms and the single term of George H.W. Bush, who had served as vice president under Reagan.

The senior Bush achieved a number of monumental diplomatic successes, including the end of the Cold War, the collapse of the Soviet Union, and victory in the first Gulf War. Yet he lost his re-election campaign to a young governor from Arkansas named Bill Clinton who had only one campaign slogan: "It's the economy, stupid!" Bush's election loss suggests the economy was still far from satisfactory in the eyes of most Americans 12 years after Reaganomics was launched.

Once Clinton took over, however, the U.S. economy began to pick up—even though few today can remember his administration's economic policies. Things were going so well that, by Clinton's second term, the Federal government was running budget surpluses. The conclusion to be drawn here is that while supply-side reforms are essential in a pursued economy, it will take many years for such measures to produce macroeconomic results that the public can recognize and appreciate. The time needed for structural reforms to bear fruit also means they are no substitute for fiscal stimulus for economies in Cases 3 and 4.

## The Challenge of Finding and Encouraging Innovators

The problem is that not everyone in a society is capable of coming up with new ideas or products. And it is not always the same group that generates new ideas. It also takes an enormous amount of effort and perseverance to bring new products to market. But without innovators willing to persevere to create new products and industries, the economy will stagnate or worse. The most important human-capital consideration for countries being pursued, therefore, is how to maximize the number of people capable of generating new ideas and products and how to incentivize them to focus on their creative efforts.

On the first point, only a limited number of people in any society are capable of coming up with new ideas. Often they are outside the mainstream, because those in the mainstream have few incentives to think differently from the rest, and only those with a different, independent perspective can create something new. Some may also show little interest in educational achievement in the ordinary sense of the word. Indeed, many successful start-ups have been founded by college dropouts. Many innovators may actually infuriate and alienate the establishment with their "crazy" ideas. If sufficiently discouraged by the orthodoxy, they may withdraw altogether from their creative activities. Consequently, finding these people and encouraging them to focus on their creative pursuits is no easy task.

In this regard, the West's tradition of liberal arts education served it well. In particular, the notion that students must think for themselves and substantiate their thinking with logic and evidence instead of just absorbing and regurgitating what they have been taught is crucial in training people who can think differently and independently. At some top universities in the U.S., students who simply repeat what the professor said in her lectures may only get a B; an A requires that they go beyond the lectures and add something of their own. This training encourages them to challenge the status quo, which is the only way to come up with new ideas and products.

Liberal arts education has a long tradition in the West, starting with the Renaissance and Enlightenment, when the value of the human intellect was finally recognized after being suppressed for centuries by the Catholic Church. This long struggle to free the intellect from church authorities was not an easy one—many brilliant thinkers were burned at the stake. Societies that went through this long and bloody struggle therefore tend to cherish the liberal arts tradition.

Societies that did *not* experience such struggles, however, may have to guard against the tendency of the educational hierarchy to worship "authorities" to the detriment of independent thinkers. Once such a hierarchy is established, it becomes very difficult for new thinkers to gain an audience, especially when their ideas challenge the orthodoxy. The implication here is that citizens' creativity may not be fully utilized in societies where the educational establishment and other authorities continue to act like the Catholic inquisitors of the past.

One problem, however, is that a true liberal arts education is expensive. It requires first-rate teachers to guide and motivate students, and teachers with such abilities are usually in strong demand elsewhere. Tuition at some of the top U.S. universities has reached almost obscene levels as a result. Furthermore, the ability to think independently does not guarantee that students will immediately find work upon graduation. As such, this type of education is usually reserved for those who can afford it, which exacerbates the already widening income inequality in post-LTP pursued economies.

## Need for the Right Kind of Education

In contrast, the cookbook approach to education, where students simply absorb what teachers tell them, is cheaper and more practical in the sense that students at least leave school knowing how to cook. The vast majority of the population is exposed only to this type of education, where there is limited room to express creative ideas or challenge established concepts. Creative minds may be buried and forgotten in such establishments, like the proverbial diamonds in the rough.

In pursued economies, therefore, teachers in all schools should be asked to keep an eye out for students who seem likely to come up with something new and interesting. Once found, those students should be placed in a program that encourages them to pursue their creative passions.

The U.S. always had an excellent system of liberal arts education that encouraged students to challenge the status quo. As such, it was able to maintain the lead in scientific breakthroughs and new product development even as it fell behind the Japanese and others in manufacturing those new products at competitive prices.

In contrast, many countries in catch-up mode adopted a cookbook-style approach to education, which can prepare the maximum number of people for industrial employment in the shortest possible time. When a country is in catch-up mode, this type of system is often sufficient and is also more practical because the hard work of inventing and developing something new is already being done by someone else in the developed world.

However, these countries will have to come up with new products and services themselves once they exhaust the low-hanging investment opportunities related to industrialization and urbanization. The question then is whether they can alter their educational systems to produce the independent and innovative thinkers needed for sustained economic growth in the pursued era. This can be a major challenge if society has discouraged people from thinking outside the box for too long, since both teachers and students may be unable to cope with the new task of producing independent thinkers.

Although people in most societies can recall the names of famous native innovators, the issue for economic policymakers is whether there are enough innovators and businesses to pull the entire nation forward. Often that is not the case, which means policymakers must work harder to create an environment that will allow innovators to flourish. A country with a large population may also need a large number of innovators.

## The Challenge of Keeping Students in School

In many countries, education starts with the challenge of keeping students in school long enough to learn something useful. Janet Yellen, the Fed Chair, noted in a speech on June 21, 2016 that the median U.S. income is $85,000 for Asian-Americans, $67,000 for whites, and $40,000 for African-Americans[1]. From the author's own experience with the Japanese and American educational systems, the reasons for this gap are not difficult to understand.

It is not that Asians are any smarter than the rest. It is simply that many, if not most, Asian youth are brainwashed to such an extent that the option of *not* studying hard no longer exists in their minds. The default option for students is to spend most of their waking hours studying. When the author attended a Japanese elementary school as a boy, his school happened to have no classes on Saturdays when virtually all other schools in the country had classes on Saturday mornings. When the author would go outside on Saturday mornings, he was frequently stopped by adults asking him why he was not in school, as though he were some kind of delinquent. And each time he had to explain that his school had no classes on Saturdays. This shows just how much social pressure there was on each student to be in school studying five and a half days a week.

When the author moved to the U.S. at the age of 13 and enrolled in a public junior high school, he was shocked to find that many students there had no intention of studying at all. It came as a surprise because the idea that a student could get away with *not* studying was unthinkable for someone from Asia. And he envied them because they seemed to enjoy their teenage lives and freedom so much more than him.

---

[1] Board of Governors of the Federal Reserve System (2016) *Monetary Policy Report*, submitted on June 21, 2016, p. 7. www.federalreserve.gov/monetarypolicy/files/20160621_mprfullreport.pdf.

Fifty years later, some of those who neglected their studies might regret their decisions back then. But fifty years ago, during the "Golden Sixties," many of them probably thought they could make a decent living without an advanced degree. In this golden era, it was quite possible for someone without an advanced degree to buy a three-bedroom house and a car with a V-8 engine, automatic transmission, and power steering.

Many of them saw their parents, who also lacked advanced degrees, still doing relatively well and assumed that the good life was within easy reach. Little did they know that the well-paying manufacturing jobs their parents had would be disappearing to pursuing economies and that their lack of education would prevent them from moving higher up on the jobs ladder.

In retrospect, it could be said that the good life experienced during the golden age, when everyone benefited from economic growth, created a false sense of security for many who came to believe the good life would continue forever. They were then caught totally off guard when the U.S. entered the post-LTP pursued phase.

Had they grown up in a country where they could see what happens to workers when a country enters the post-LTP pursued phase, the chances are they would have been more diligent students. But there was no example for them to follow in the U.S. and Western Europe because they were the first ones in history to experience this phase of economic development. In a sense, those who did not apply themselves to their studies constitute a lost generation, since it is now too late for many of them to go back to school.

These frustrated people blame their plight on visible targets such as immigrants and imports, but that does change the fact that they themselves do not have the skills that businesses need. Although their frustrations are understandable and some social safety net must be provided, at the end of the day people must realize that they need to acquire skills that are in demand, since the clock cannot be turned back.

Many Asian-Americans, on the other hand, are the offspring of recent immigrants or are first-generation immigrants themselves. For centuries, China (starting in 598 A.D.) had an imperial examination system that assured upward mobility for the educated regardless of the person's background. In Japan, the emphasis on education was such that the largest building in most villages, towns, and cities a century ago was often the public school rather than city hall or mansions for the well-to-do. With so much emphasis on education, the cultural imprinting to study hard still affects many of their offspring in the U.S. Because of this cultural straitjacket on the matter of educational achievement, even the dimmest Asian student ends up studying and acquiring some useful skills.

They may not be the most creative or articulate within their respective fields, and aspirations and talents that fell outside the confines of formal education may have been suppressed to the detriment of their self-actualization and true happiness. Indeed, an OECD survey of "life satisfaction" among 15-year-olds in 2015 indicated that Japan ranked 42 out of 47 countries, followed by South Korea, Taiwan, Macau, Hong Kong, and Turkey[2]. This stands in sharp contrast to the latest scientific literacy tests, where the same East Asian countries were all in the top 10. These results suggest that the cultural differences regarding education the author felt 50 years ago still hold today, i.e., high educational achievement in Asia does not come without a cost. But those who study manage to earn a decent living, which pushes up the average income for the group. This cultural imprinting of Asians in the U.S. is likely to wane as subsequent generations become more fully integrated into the American mainstream.

For the other two groups, which do not have such a pervasive cultural straitjacket, much depends on the particular family or environment where the child grew up. This is because the pay-off of education takes 15 years or more to realize. At a time when it is said that American corporate executives can only see as far as the next quarterly earnings report, it is a tall order for a child to commit to educating himself or herself when the economic pay-off of such effort is 12, 16, even 20 years away. In other words, most students will need a great deal of outside support to continue their long educational journey.

Those from families with a strong commitment to education will naturally go further than those who do not enjoy such support. Even in households where parents are often absent or too busy to help, studying and "being a nerd" is not so painful if the student is surrounded by hard-working friends and classmates. But studying can be very painful for youths who do not receive sufficient support and encouragement to stay in school when others like them seem to be having so much fun outside school.

It is these youths that need help, because their eventual inability to contribute to the economy will be a loss to the entire society. They must also be made aware that they are now effectively competing with youths in the emerging world who are studying and working hard to achieve the living standards of those in the developed world.

An advanced degree is not for everyone, of course, but all students need to know what they are good at and what they enjoy doing so they can make appropriate choices given their personal circumstances. The emphasis on personal strengths and circumstances is important because workers in the post-LTP pursued phase are really on their own, and the chances are high that they will not do well in a field they do not enjoy.

This means counselors advising students at regular intervals might have just as big an impact on the student's final educational outcome as

---

[2] OECD (2017) *PISA 2015 Results (Volume III): Students' Well-Being*, Paris: OECD Publishing, p. 71.

teachers and parents. In addition to supporting students who need outside encouragement to further their education, these counselors can help students discover what they are good at and what they enjoy doing so they can be directed to areas where they are likely to succeed. If at all possible, these counselors should also be trained to spot independent thinkers and encourage them to pursue their ideas further.

## Importance of Proper Tax and Regulatory Environment

Countries in the pursued phase must also revamp their tax and regulatory regimes not only to increase return on capital at home, but also to maximize people's creative potential. In this regard, it must be stressed that to create something out of nothing and actually bring it to market often requires so much effort that "any rational person will give up," in the words of Steve Jobs. In a similar vein, Thomas Edison famously claimed a new invention is 1 percent inspiration and 99 percent perspiration.

Although some individuals are so driven that they require no external support, most mortals find outside encouragement important during the long, risky, and difficult journey of producing something the world has never seen before. Financial, regulatory, and tax regimes should therefore do everything possible to encourage such individuals and businesses to pursue their pioneering efforts.

Piketty cited the retreat of progressive tax rates as the cause of widening inequality in the post-1970 developed world[3]. But the U.S., which led the reduction in tax rates, has regained its high-tech leadership while Europe and Japan, which did not go as far as the U.S., have stagnated. This comparison suggests that tax and regulatory changes might have to be drastic enough for people to take notice. The gradualist approach preferred by the traditional societies of Europe and Japan may not work well when the economic surroundings change so dramatically between the golden era and the pursued phase. This outcome also suggests that a tax regime that was reasonable when a country is not being pursued may no longer be appropriate when it is.

## Difficulty of Achieving a Public Consensus

Unfortunately for many countries, these sorts of measures are often derided as "favoring the rich" and rejected out of hand by those with a golden-era mindset. When an economy is in a golden era with a surfeit of investment

---

[3] Piketty, Thomas (2014), op. cit.

opportunities, this may not lead to a noticeable economic slowdown. But in a pursued economy that needs to outrun its chasers, a country's inability to fully utilize the creative and innovative potential of its people can have devastating consequences. Its future growth may well depend on how quickly it can achieve a social consensus on developing growth-friendly infrastructure, such as a liberal arts education system and innovator-friendly financial, regulatory and tax regimes to maximize the population's innovative capacity.

This may require a new consensus in which those who are unable to think outside the box understand and appreciate the fact that their well-being depends on those who can. Indeed, the whole of society must understand that such thinkers are essential to generating the new investment opportunities at home that will keep the economy out of prolonged stagnation.

This is far from easy, however. As Thomas Piketty noted, inequality in the West began increasing in the 1970s and is reaching alarming levels in some countries. This increasingly unequal distribution of income is prompting many developed countries to raise taxes on the rich. But such actions, which often represent the opposite of supply-side reforms, could easily backfire by discouraging innovation and risk taking, the most important drivers of economic growth in a pursued country.

To make matters worse, most advanced economies plunged into balance sheet recessions when their housing bubbles burst in 2008. This exacerbated the shortage of borrowers that began in the 1970s when these countries entered their post-LTP pursued phases. Because fiscal stimulus was needed to fight the recession, these countries will be saddled with a huge public debt when they finally emerge from their balance sheet recessions.

Faced with a large national debt, the natural tendency of economists and policymakers with a golden-era mindset is to raise taxes wherever possible. But such wanton tax hikes may discourage businesses from investing aggressively in new innovation, thus prolonging the period of sub-par economic growth. This means that economies currently emerging from balance sheet recessions need to resist the temptation to raise taxes that may thwart innovation. Only in this way can they gain the escape velocity needed to fend off pursuers. This is particularly important in Japan, where debt levels are high and an orthodox (i.e., golden era), tax-raising mindset still dominates the bureaucracy, academia, and the media.

Most advanced countries today are fighting two wars: one because they are in balance sheet recessions and one because they are being pursued by increasingly sophisticated emerging economies offering attractive returns on capital. This means they are squarely in the other-half of macroeconomics, and the escape velocity needed for their economies to regain forward momentum is very high. The leaders of these countries therefore must realize that tremendous effort will be needed to reach that velocity.

Of all the post-LTP pursued economies, the U.S. probably comes closest to having achieved a consensus on the need for growth-friendly tax regime, which is why it attracts innovators from around the world. But with the rich growing ever richer while the remaining 80 percent of the population have seen little income growth for the last 20 years, the temptation to raise taxes on the wealthy is getting stronger even in the U.S. The anger of the 80 percent was also behind the support Donald Trump and Bernie Sanders received during the 2016 presidential campaign. The political challenge for pursued countries, therefore, is how to persuade voters to maintain and improve innovator-friendly tax regimes when the public debt is so large and the vast majority of the population has experienced no income growth for many years.

## Case Study in Bad Taxation: Japan's Inheritance Tax

If a pursued country with an aging or declining population is to sustain economic growth, it must maximize the productivity of those who are working, and especially of those who are able to create new products and transform them into viable businesses. This is because new, well-paying jobs are likely to come only from new businesses when a country is being pursued. If the country keeps on doing what it has always done, it is likely to be overtaken by emerging economies with lower wage costs. Each country in the post-LTP pursued state must therefore ask itself whether its tax and regulatory regimes are maximizing the productivity of the people capable of developing new products and services.

In Japan, the author has noted recently that many of those who took risks, worked hard, and succeeded are now spending much of their time worrying about their inheritance tax liabilities. It is really quite sad to see so many able people talking about such a backward topic when they could be spending their time expanding their businesses and chasing their dreams. They are worried because the top rate for this tax in Japan is 55 percent, and the tax-free ceiling was lowered drastically in 2015 to just $300,000 (at an exchange rate of $1 = ¥100). The tax rate starts at 10 percent for assets worth less than $100,000 but climbs rapidly to 40 percent at $1 million. The concerns of those who succeeded can be gleaned from the fact that Japanese bookstores today are full of books about this tax and how to minimize it. It is also common knowledge that a key reason for the boom in Japan's real estate market is that property offers a way to reduce inheritance tax obligations.

This represents a tremendous waste of human and physical resources that Japan, with its shrinking population, can ill-afford. People who should be expanding their businesses or developing iPS cells are instead wasting time and mental focus on managing rental properties, which is something that anyone could do, simply because of the inheritance tax. This represents a huge loss to the broader economy because so many capable people with a track record of success in generating new businesses are distracted by this tax.

The fact that the inheritance tax has fostered such a large real estate boom underscores just how distorted Japan's allocation of resources is. After all, this is a country where the population is shrinking and unoccupied homes are a major social problem.

A shrinking population also means the productivity of each and every worker must be raised to maintain the existing level of economic activity. To enhance productivity, resources must be allocated as efficiently as possible. But in Japan the opposite is happening, and the economy is stagnating as a result.

## Taiwan Slashed Inheritance Tax and Capital Gains Tax Rates to 10 Percent

What should be done about this issue? Taiwan's recent experiment may offer some clues. The administration of President Ma Ying-jeou implemented bold tax cuts in 2008, slashing the top inheritance and gift tax rates to 10 percent.

The Taiwanese authorities initially assumed the lower rates would reduce tax revenues substantially, but in the event tax receipts did not fall at all (Figure 5.1). Moreover, funds that had been fleeing Taiwan for decades because of concerns about taxes and military tensions with Communist China across the Taiwan Strait started returning, providing a major support for the Taiwanese economy in the immediate aftermath of the Lehman collapse.

Tax revenues did not fall because people who had been spending so much time and resources reducing their tax burden decided that at 10 percent it was no longer worth the effort. They just decided to pay the 10 percent so they could use their time and resources more productively elsewhere. The fact that tax revenues did not fall also means the lower tax rate did not reduce the amount of funds available for redistribution to the less fortunate.

From the perspective of the broader economy, the fact that the tax cuts eliminated distortions in the allocation of resources was far more important than any change in tax revenues. All the time and resources that had been devoted to avoiding taxes were now being channeled into more productive pursuits.

Like Japan, Taiwan is being chased by the emerging economies of China and Southeast Asia, and its working-age population began to shrink in 2015.

FIGURE 5.1  Taiwan's Inheritance and Gift Tax Cuts Enhanced Efficiency of Resource Allocation, and Tax Revenues Did Not Fall

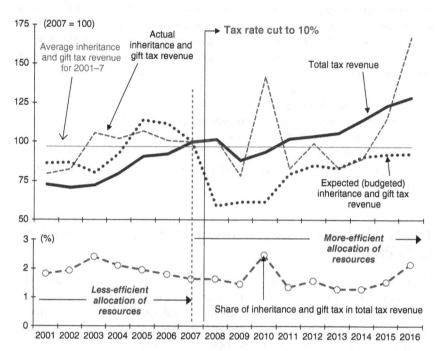

*Source:* Nomura Research Institute, based on the data from Ministry of Finance R.O.C.

With no language barrier between Taiwan and China, the challenges facing economic policymakers in Taiwan are substantial, which is precisely why they implemented the bold tax cuts noted above.

If Japan were to lower its highest inheritance and gift tax rates—which are currently 55 percent with a very low deduction—to 10 percent, a great deal of money and human resources that are either fleeing overseas or going to all the wrong places would come back to where they belong. Such a cut would also encourage the inter-generational transfer of assets in a country where wealth is concentrated in the hands of senior citizens who typically have a lower propensity to consume. Most importantly, the tremendous distortions in resource allocation that have resulted from efforts to avoid the inheritance tax would disappear as people decide that such efforts are simply not worth their time at a tax rate of 10 percent.

While it is difficult to say whether inheritance and gift tax revenues would increase or decrease relative to the current figure of around 2 trillion yen if a 10 percent rate were introduced, even a small decrease would be worth it if the change freed up increasingly precious human capital for forward-looking projects.

When the West was in its golden era lasting through the 1970s and had no competitors, and when Japan was in its golden era chasing the West but facing no competitors of its own, the entire population benefited from economic growth. With all the growth momentum that characterizes the golden era, efficiency losses from the income redistribution function of taxation were not large enough to derail growth. The fact that golden-era economies were inflationary in spite of not-so-growth-friendly tax rates shows just how strong the underlying growth momentum was.

But now that the West and Japan are being pursued instead of pursuing, they will find themselves in a serious predicament if they maintain their golden-era approach to taxation and regulation. The fact that pursued economies are all suffering from near-zero inflation rates in spite of astronomical monetary easing indicates just how weak the underlying growth momentum really is.

Tax and regulatory distortions are found in all countries, even though the source of the distortions may differ considerably. The ultimate goal of regulatory and tax reforms in pursued economies, therefore, should be to minimize the time people spend on tax avoidance and to maximize the time they spend on activities they are good at.

## How to Re-Organize Society for Post-LTP Pursued Phase Is an Open Question

How a society should reorganize itself for the post-LTP pursued phase is an open question. And the questions that need to be answered are many: what are the appropriate labor practices when so many workers are unhappy with wages that have been stagnant for the last two decades? What is the best kind of educational system when a true liberal arts education is so costly? How should society encourage innovators without appearing unfair to those who are not blessed with the ability to innovate? How should society help those who were caught off guard and are too old to go back to school? And finally, how should the society prepare young people to cope with this new environment that no one has seen before? All of these will be massive challenges for society and the political system.

There is also a mounting social backlash against measures to encourage innovators and increase the flexibility of the economy, particularly in the labor market. Even in Taiwan, the top inheritance tax rate was rolled back to 20 percent from the original 10 percent by the new government of President Tsai Ing-wen in 2017. Such setbacks indicate how difficult it is for social institutions to change to match the needs of the new pursued era. Many are also patiently waiting for a return of the golden era by pushing for a 2 percent inflation target even though the underlying realities have changed dramatically since then.

Not all the news is bad, however. Governments are finding the courage to expand infrastructure spending in Canada, Taiwan, and possibly even in the U.S. under President Trump. It is hoped that the projects selected by these governments will be self-financing or close enough to it so that this foray into fiscal activism is not short-lived.

For many traditional societies in Europe and Japan, some sort of shake-up may also be needed to open fields to new outside-the-box thinkers. In Japan, two decades of economic stagnation and the diminished appeal of established companies are prompting some college graduates to consider starting businesses for the first time in many decades. This is a welcome development in a country where tradition and authority still carry a great deal of weight. Some younger engineers in Japanese firms, for example, find it difficult to challenge the achievements of older engineers in the company because such actions can be viewed as a sign of disrespect. Such seniority-based rigidity has discouraged innovation in the country in no small way.

Some European designers are also migrating to the U.S. and Australia to free themselves from traditional constraints on how and where they can express their creative talents. Tradition-bound societies therefore desperately need new businesses that are open to new ideas and innovations.

If the domestic environment is not producing enough innovators, the government may also consider importing creative thinkers and innovators from abroad. The immigrant-friendly U.S. is full of foreign-born innovators competing with each other and with native innovators in universities and the business world. Singapore is also pushing hard to attract foreign talent by inviting not just well-known names but also their entire teams and families to undertake research in Singapore. Pursued countries should consider implementing and augmenting similar programs to acquire and retain people capable of creating new ideas and products. Generous tax treatment of stock options for innovating companies may also be useful. Since these incentives do not cost the government anything until the private sector actually succeeds, they are quite cost-effective as well.

If the tax and regulatory incentives are not sufficient, the government itself might have to function as *innovator of last resort* to develop new technologies or open up new fields of research. In this case, targeted spending on research by the government may encourage the private sector to follow by launching new businesses that might not have existed unless the government had taken the lead.

In this sense, pursued-era economies may be similar to pre-LTP industrializing economies in that infrastructure spending on new technology by the government can help create investment opportunities for the private sector. If the required self-financing projects turn out to be in areas where the government has to act as innovator of last resort, so much the better.

## Preparing Emerging Economies for the Future

Emerging countries that are now in the post-LTP golden era will eventually reach the pursued phase with all its challenges. How should they prepare themselves? What can they learn from the experiences of advanced countries today?

First, they should not assume that the rapid growth they are enjoying now will continue forever. There will almost certainly come a time when rising wages force businesses to look for higher returns on capital elsewhere. Wage inflation could be driven by both rising domestic wages and currency appreciation. And with so many countries joining the globalization bandwagon, those changes may arrive sooner rather than later. This means emerging countries should operate on the assumption that institutional arrangements such as tax codes and regulations are not permanent and may have to be modified as the economy moves from one stage to the next.

They should also operate on the assumption that the rapid growth in tax revenue typical of the golden era will also slow down in the future. This means those projects that have to be financed with taxes should be implemented while the economy is still in the golden era. People also like to "think big" during the golden era, which means those projects that require the population to think big should be implemented during the era. At the same time, policymakers must make sure that the generosity that is also typical of the golden era does not result in numerous white elephants.

They should also modify and refine their education system to ensure that it does not discourage out-of-the-box thinkers. Even though such people may appear to be of limited value when the economy is pursuing other countries, they will become the key drivers of growth when the economy enters the pursued stage. A system of liberal arts education should be introduced as early as possible to encourage students to think independently and allow them to challenge the status quo and come up with new ideas and products.

On the other hand, historical buildings and neighborhoods and monuments of cultural value should not be torn down in the name of modernization. The more rapidly the country develops, the more important this cultural heritage becomes, because people in a rapidly changing environment need to be able to put down psychological roots. They need psychological homes where they can reaffirm who they are and whence they came. Historical neighborhoods and monuments also attract foreign tourists, which can help the country earn foreign exchange.

In this area, emerging countries should learn from Europe, which attracts a huge number of foreign tourists year after year because it kept its architectural heritage largely intact. Even though Europe's high-tech industry has fallen behind those of America and Asia in some areas, the European tourist industry draws millions of American and Asian visitors every year. And income from a nation's architectural heritage is far more stable and reliable than income from volatile and extremely competitive high-tech industries.

At the same time, developing countries should be aware that there is a social backlash against free trade in the developed world from those in the "lost generation" mentioned earlier. The emergence of the "America First" Trump administration and similar groups elsewhere makes it less easy for emerging countries to take advantage of markets in the U.S. and other pursued economies. This means they will have to accept changes to their own economies, such as lower tariffs on imports from advanced countries, *sooner* than otherwise if they want to enjoy continued access to the markets of pursued economies. This point is discussed further in Chapter 9.

## Economic Destiny of Human Progress

In 5,000 years of civilization, the human race has made tremendous progress in according respect to individuals regardless of their background, creed, sex or sexual orientation, or skin color. Although the process is far from complete and there are unfortunately areas where the progress is going backwards, it is far ahead of where it was just 100 years ago, and much of it has taken place after countries entered their post-LTP golden eras. What, then, is the *economic* destiny of human progress? What is the end game for all the chasing and being chased described in Figure 3.13?

The economic destiny of human progress would seem to be a world in which the opportunity for economic advancement is available equally to everyone on the planet regardless of where they were born or raised. It is a world in which a person born in Somalia or Uruguay will have the same opportunity to advance themselves economically as someone born in the U.S. or Germany. Today, unfortunately, the world remains far from that destination.

A person born in Somalia today would have to study and work exceptionally hard to attain the economic well-being of even the less-diligent people born in the U.S. or Germany. During the golden age of the U.S. in the 1950s and 1960s, even those with minimal skills could afford a nice house and a big car and enjoy a comfortable living that was unthinkable for people on other continents. It is this geographic *inequality* that is being corrected by the process of industrialization and globalization described above.

During the last three decades, this process of globalization received a huge boost from developments in the IT industry that have dramatically lowered the cost of communication. As a result, any job that can be performed outside an office can now be performed anywhere in the world. IT has also lowered the stock advantage advanced countries used to enjoy vis-à-vis emerging nations. For example, it was not too long ago that the quality of a university was judged by the number of books its library held. Today, however, the vast majority of the material needed for research in many fields is available on the web. And this material is accessible from anywhere in the world with an internet connection.

This means the easy days are over for those in the advanced countries who do not study or work hard. Their real wages are likely to stagnate or fall if they do not upgrade their skillsets to match and stay ahead of current demand. The educational system must also be upgraded so that it is not only producing independent thinkers but also raising the general level of education to allow the whole society and not just businesses to take evasive actions to fend off pursuers from behind. This means Reagan's supply-side reforms would have worked better had he also increased spending on education at the same time (unfortunately, he did the opposite.) If governments in pursued countries rely on protectionism to preserve jobs for those with limited skills, the nation itself may fall off the list of advanced countries as its industries lose their ability to compete with the rest of the world.

These developments also lower the cost of starting a company or doing business in both the developed and the developing world. As a result, opportunities in both the developed and the developing world are expanding rapidly for those willing to put in the effort.

An advanced economy that is being pursued must run faster if it hopes to remain an advanced economy. And it is the outside-the-box thinkers who will create the innovations and breakthroughs that enable these countries to remain at the forefront of progress. The first and foremost microeconomic policy priority for a country in the post-LTP pursued phase, therefore, should be to implement tax incentives and other measures to maximize innovation and domestic investment opportunities.

# CHAPTER 6

# Helicopter Money and the QE Trap

O ld beliefs die hard. Even though fiscal policy is the most effective remedy in addressing the problems caused by a lack of borrowers (Cases 3 and 4), orthodox economists who never considered the possibility that the private sector may shift to minimizing debt continue to rely on monetary policy, which was designed to address problems caused by a lack of *lenders* (Cases 1 and 2). Since the key assumption of Cases 1 and 2 is that there are willing private-sector borrowers, the appropriate policy response in their minds is to reduce budget deficits, thereby ending the phenomenon of crowding-out, while easing monetary policy. And that is exactly what the three central bankers mentioned in Chapter 2 did.

With the Japanese and European economies having difficulty reaching their inflation targets even after implementing negative interest rates and massive quantitative easing, some people are now discussing the possibility of helicopter money. This probably marks the end of the road for believers in the omnipotence of monetary policy, who have continued to press for further accommodation in spite of the fact that such policies simply cannot work during a balance sheet recession.

In spite of all post-2008 evidence to the contrary (Figures 2.9 to 2.14), these true believers have implemented a variety of policies that go beyond zero interest rates—among them quantitative easing, negative interest rates, forward guidance, and inflation targeting—and each has failed to produce the expected results. Now they have reached the end of the line, and the signpost reads "Last stop: helicopter money."

In some sense, it is the belief that the economy will invariably pick up if only money is dropped from the sky that provided the psychological foundation for these economists' confidence in the efficacy of monetary policy. For example, Waseda University professor Masazumi Wakatabe, one of the most ardent proponents of monetary easing in Japan, declared without irony that "the question of how to increase nominal GDP always has an answer: helicopter money."[1] It is their belief that, since dropping money from helicopters will always revive the economy, slightly less extreme policies, such as quantitative easing and inflation targeting, will also help stimulate it.

## Four Versions of Helicopter Money: (1) Dropping Money from the Sky

An overview of the helicopter money debate shows that the actual policies being discussed can be classified into four main types. The first is helicopter money in the literal sense of dropping money from helicopters. Would this work?

In Japan, at least, it would be yet another complete failure. This is because when the typical Japanese finds a 10,000-yen note lying on the ground, she will turn it in at the nearest police station rather than spend it. A helicopter money policy can work only if people in the country have little sense of right and wrong.

A more fundamental defect in the argument that helicopter money will always resuscitate the economy is that it focuses exclusively on the logic of buyers while totally ignoring the logic of sellers. Unethical people may try to go shopping with money that has fallen from the sky, but there is no reason for sellers to accept such money. No seller would exchange products and services for money that fell from the sky

Sellers are willing to take money in exchange for goods and services only because they believe the supply of money is strictly controlled by the central bank. If money starts falling from the sky, sellers will refuse to accept it as payment for their products. If the authorities actually began dropping money from helicopters, shops would either close their doors or demand payment in foreign currency or gold, and the economy would quickly collapse. There is no economy so wretched as one that no longer has a national currency the people trust.

It is astonishing that economists arguing in favor of helicopter money have never considered the perspective of the sellers of goods and services. Once sellers realize what is going on, there is no reason for them to accept money falling from the sky. The argument that monetary policy is effective because helicopter money, the ultimate form of monetary accommodation, always works is complete nonsense that ignores the other half of the economy: the sellers. Taking monetary accommodation to such extremes will lead to the economy's collapse, not its recovery. There is no case in recorded history of an economy without a credible national currency outperforming an economy that has one.

---

[1] Wakatabe, Masazumi (2016), Herikopta Mane to wa Nanika (3) ("What Constitutes Helicopter Money?"), *Nikkei*, June 20, 2016.

## Four Versions of Helicopter Money: (2) Direct Financing of Government Deficits

Some proponents of helicopter money would say that the helicopter money policies now being discussed do not actually involve dropping money from the sky but rather call for direct financing of government fiscal expenditures by the central bank. The argument here is that since fiscal expenditures help the economy, direct central bank financing of the government should help the economy even more.

There are two problems with this view. First, as noted in Chapter 2, the government does *not* need the central bank's help to finance fiscal stimulus when the economy is in Case 3 or 4. The funds needed to finance the stimulus are sitting in the financial market in the form of unborrowed private-sector savings. And the fund managers of financial institutions (outside the Eurozone, at least) are more than happy to lend to the government because it is the only borrower left. That, in turn, takes government bond yields down to very low levels.

Second, the reason why this kind of helicopter money will not work is no different from the reason why quantitative easing failed to deliver the inflation expected by the three central bankers mentioned in Chapter 2. Fiscal stimulus itself will provide a large boost to the economy and is absolutely essential when the economy is in Case 3 or 4. But the "direct" part of direct financing of fiscal stimulus by the central bank cannot stimulate the economy or raise inflation any more than the "non-direct" quantitative easing (QE).

While direct financing by the central bank will increase reserves in the banking system, those reserves will become trapped in the system in exactly the same way that QE-supplied reserves are trapped when no one in the private sector is willing to borrow the money from the banks and inject it into the real economy. In other words, how the central bank acquired the government bonds is irrelevant. Both growth and inflation have remained at depressed levels in Japan (since 1990) and the West (since 2008) regardless of how accommodative monetary policy is because the private sector, facing a huge debt overhang, stopped borrowing after the bubble burst.

## Four Versions of Helicopter Money: (3) Handing Cash Directly to Consumers

A third version of helicopter money involves handing out money directly to consumers without requiring it to pass through financial institutions. This approach at least acknowledges the difficulty noted for the second version of helicopter money when the economy is in Case 3 or 4, namely, that liquidity injected by the central bank cannot leave the financial sector and enter the real economy without the help of private-sector borrowers.

In this scenario, a consumer might open her mailbox one morning to find an envelope from the central bank containing thousands of dollars in cash. While that discovery may bring momentary joy, she may feel a chill down her spine once she realizes that everyone around her has received similar envelopes. Unless the amount involved is very small, the entire country would quickly fall into a state of panic as people lose confidence in the central bank and no longer know the value of their national currency. Regardless of what recipients of such cash might wish to do, sellers of goods and services would be forced to protect themselves, with stores putting up signs requiring payment in either foreign currency or gold. This is no different from the nightmare scenario in which money is actually dropped from helicopters.

## Four Versions of Helicopter Money: (4) Government Scrip and Perpetual Zero-Coupon Bonds

A fourth version of helicopter money involves government (instead of central bank) printing of money or the replacement of the government bonds held by the central bank with perpetual zero-coupon bonds. The people proposing these policies hope that fiscal stimulus financed by government scrip or perpetual zero-coupon bonds, which are not viewed as government liabilities, will elicit spending from people who are currently saving because of concerns about the size of the fiscal deficit and the likelihood of future tax increases.

Economists refer to the public's reluctance to spend because of worries about future tax hikes as the Ricardian equivalence. "Equivalence" here refers to the possibility that deficit spending or tax cuts will have only a limited stimulative impact on the economy because the public will begin saving more to prepare for the future tax increases needed to pay for the spending and tax cuts.

If this equivalence holds, however, it also implies that consumption will *increase* each time the government raises taxes since higher taxes mean lower deficits in the future. The fact that this phenomenon has never been observed in the real world suggests it is nothing more than an empty conjecture. The author himself has not met a single person who would refrain from purchasing something because of the fear that taxes will eventually go up in response to increased government fiscal stimulus today. Even economists who talk endlessly about Ricardian equivalence do not practice it themselves. This means only a very small number of people would be enticed to spend money simply because the government is using scrip or zero-coupon perpetual bonds (instead of conventional bonds) to finance its expenditures.

## Question of How to Mop Up Excess Liquidity Has Not Been Answered

The biggest problem by far for both QE and all versions of helicopter money is the difficulty the central bank will eventually face in unwinding these policies when the economy recovers. Although this may be two steps ahead of the current discussion on how to beat deflation, the private sector will sooner or later complete its balance sheet repairs and resume borrowing.

Borrowings will not recover to the level of the golden era, because advanced countries are now in the pursued phase. However, they could still be significantly more than at present inasmuch as the private sector now suffers from both balance sheet problems and a lack of domestic investment opportunities. When the balance sheet part of the problem goes away and demand for funds turns positive, inflation could accelerate significantly unless the central bank drains the excess liquidity it pumped into the economy under QE or helicopter money policies.

For example, excess reserves created by the Fed via QE currently amount to some 12.5 times the level of statutory reserves (Figure 6.1). That implies that if businesses and households were to resume borrowing in earnest, the U.S. money supply could balloon to 12.5 times its current size, sending inflation as high as 1,250 percent. The corresponding ratios are 32.5 times for Japan, 30.5 times for Switzerland, 9.6 times for the Eurozone, and 15.3 times for the UK. The only reason these countries have not faced such inflation rates is because their private sectors are not borrowing money—in fact, they are saving money or paying down debt despite near-zero interest rates.

Because these economies are no longer in the golden era, money supply growth and inflation rates are not likely to approach anywhere near their potential maximum values even after borrowers return. But if money supply and credit growth are even one-tenth the potential maximum, i.e., 125 percent growth instead of 1,250 percent growth, inflation rates could still rise to unpleasant levels.

Since the Fed has already created some $2.1 trillion in excess reserves under quantitative easing and the BOJ has supplied about ¥305 trillion, central banks will have to slash excess reserves to a fraction of current levels once private-sector demand for loans recovers. But that sort of

FIGURE 6.1  QE Far Easier to Begin than End: Central Banks Must Reduce Reserves Massively to Avoid Credit Explosion

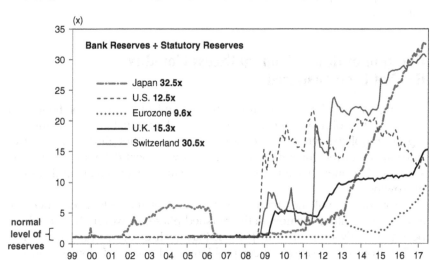

*Notes:* The Bank of England has suspended reserve requirement in March 2009. The post-March 2009 figures are based on the assumption that the original reserve requirement is still applicable.

*Source:* Nomura Research Institute, based on BOJ, FRB, ECB, BOE, and SNB data

extreme reduction in reserves will require the central bank to unload the bonds it holds, which would be a nightmare for the economy and the bond market.

Figure 6.2 shows what would be needed to normalize monetary policy in the U.S. It indicates that both interest rates and the monetary base will have to be normalized, a task that has never been successfully attempted in the past. Alan Greenspan, who brought interest rates down to 1 percent after the dotcom bubble collapsed, did succeed in normalizing interest rates by raising the policy rate seventeen times starting in 2004. But he was simultaneously allowing the monetary base to grow, albeit slowly. In other words, at the same time as he was tightening monetary policy by raising interest rates, he was also easing policy by allowing the monetary base to grow.

Janet Yellen and her successor will have to both raise interest rates and shrink the monetary base at the same time. The difficulty inherent in the latter task is one of the costs of QE, something traditional central bankers never had to face.

FIGURE 6.2 Monetary Policy Normalization Requires Both Rate Hikes and Shrinkage of Monetary Base

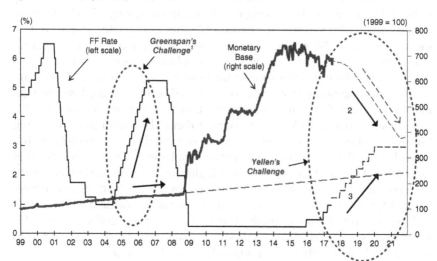

*Notes:* 1. Last two rate hikes were made under Bernanke. 2. Supposed to take 45 months according to schedule. 3. Supposed to take "several years."

*Sources:* Nomura Research Institute, Board of Governors of the Federal Reserve System

## Need for Shock Absorber

The tremendous difficulty and uncertainty surrounding the task of normalizing the monetary base was acknowledged by the Fed when it reversed the order of monetary policy normalization in September 2014. Prior to this date, the Fed's official position on unwinding QE was that it would normalize its balance sheet (i.e., shrink the monetary base) first, and only then set about normalizing interest rates. But as the difficulty and uncertainty surrounding the task of normalizing the monetary base became clearer, the order was reversed for the following reason.

First, the bond market has never seen the Fed unload trillions of dollars in government bonds, but it has plenty of experience with rate hikes. By raising interest rates first and normalizing its balance sheet only after rates have recovered to sufficiently high levels, the Fed buys itself a shock absorber in case the balance sheet normalization process triggers a collapse of the bond market. In other words, if balance sheet normalization causes bond prices to tumble, the Fed can lower interest rates to absorb the shock.

Raising interest rates when the private sector is not borrowing money is a tricky business. Indeed, some financial condition indexes have actually indicated an easing of borrowing conditions in the spring of 2017, as mentioned earlier with Figure 4.1, in spite of higher policy rates engineered by the Fed. But that did not stop the Fed from raising interest rates, because one of the key reasons for doing so was to obtain a shock absorber.

Although the lack of private-sector borrowers also suggests there is no need to rush the normalization process, central banks that implemented QE must move much faster than those that did not. This is because bond yields can surge (as bond holders try to protect themselves from inflation) if the borrowers return and the market starts to believe that the central bank has fallen behind the curve on inflation after supplying so many funds. Sharply higher bond yields, in turn, will have highly unpleasant consequences for the economy. To avoid such a disruption, central banks that have implemented QE must start normalizing before private-sector demand for funds picks up in earnest if the normalization process is to proceed smoothly. This is because bond yields can go up only so much, even if the Fed started to unload the bonds, if there are no private-sector borrowers.

## Fed More Concerned About Real Estate Market Than Stock Market

Another reason for the Fed to normalize monetary policy quickly was the emergence of asset price bubbles in certain sectors, and especially in the U.S. commercial real estate market. As mentioned in Chapter 2, mini-bubbles are possible even in balance sheet recessions because the disappearance of traditional borrowers forces fund managers to seek whatever assets that go up in value. But for central bankers, such bubbles are most unwelcome: after all, it was the collapse of the real estate bubble in 2008 that triggered the Western world's worst postwar recession.

While the media tend to focus on the stock market's reaction to Fed policy changes, the Fed is probably more concerned about commercial real estate prices, which are now 26 percent higher than at the peak of the bubble in 2007. While house prices are still slightly below their 2006 peak at the time of this writing, they, too, have exceeded the bubble peak in such markets as San Francisco, which has benefited from its proximity to the booming Silicon Valley (Figure 6.3).

With asset price bubbles already evident in these markets, it would hardly be surprising if monetary authorities felt pressured to act quickly to avoid a repeat of the last decade's bubble and its aftermath. The surge in commercial real estate prices alone is enough to make the argument that the Fed is already behind the curve on asset prices. St. Louis Fed President

**FIGURE 6.3** Asset Price Increases Also Prompting Fed to Normalize Monetary Policy

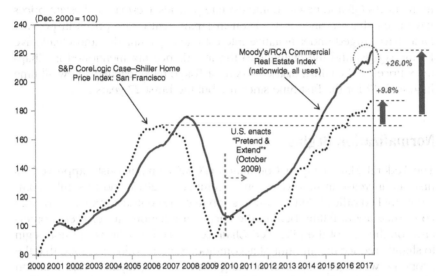

*Note:* "Policy Statement on Prudent Commercial Real Estate Loan Workouts" (October 30, 2009).

*Sources:* Nomura Research Institute, based on the data from Real Capital Analytics; "Moody's/REAL CPPI," and S&P Dow Jones Indices; "S&P CoreLogic Case-Shiller Home Price Indices"

James Bullard has cited the need to curb this rise in asset prices as one of the key reasons for tightening policy early.

Whether or not the Fed will be able to handle the collapse of mini-bubbles on the path to normalization depends on the amount of private-sector leverage in the system. If parts of the private sector are highly leveraged, a burst bubble could lead to a bigger mess, while if the leverage is modest, any resulting correction should be manageable.

A look at the U.S. economy from the standpoint of private-sector leverage shows that the household sector, the trigger of the last crisis, has steadily reduced its leverage (Figure 2.16). Even in places like San Francisco where house prices are in bubble territory, most of the high-priced deals are said to involve all-cash offers.

Unfortunately, that is not the case with commercial real estate, where most deals are done with borrowed money. Few businesses buy commercial properties with cash. Fed officials are therefore rightfully concerned about this market and have already imposed strong macro-prudential measures to clamp down on real estate lending since 2016. Some of the flattening in credit growth seen since the second half of 2016 in Figure 2.9 may reflect this macro-prudential policy action by U.S. monetary authorities.

The emergence of real estate bubbles is not only a U.S. problem. Thanks to the ECB's QE and negative-interest-rate policies, German real estate prices have risen sharply since 2015. Even in Japan, real estate prices in popular areas have surged under negative interest rates, Quantitative and Qualitative Easing (QQE) and the changes to the inheritance tax mentioned in Chapter 5. Prices in the Ginza district in central Tokyo have reached a new all-time high in 2017 for the first time since the bubble burst 27 years ago.

## Normalization Begins

The Federal Market Open Committee (FOMC) unanimously approved its first rate increase in nine years on December 16, 2015, and post-hike comments by Fed officials left the impression that the central bank was seriously concerned about falling behind the curve on inflation. At her press conference on the day of the hike, Fed Chair Yellen said that "if we do not begin to slightly reduce the amount of accommodation, the odds are good that the economy would end up overshooting both our employment and inflation objectives."[2] She also said that if the Fed were to postpone the normalization process for too long, it "would likely end up having to tighten policy relatively abruptly at some point," thereby increasing the risk of recession.

In a January 6, 2016 interview with CNBC, Vice-Chairman of the Fed Stanley Fischer declared that market expectations for the pace of tightening were "too low," which suggested the Fed was confident in its ability to raise rates as many as four times in 2016 along the path indicated in its dot plot[3]. He also said the Fed needed to proceed with normalization in order to "head off excessively high asset prices," referring to mini-bubbles in both stocks and commercial real estate. Mr. Fischer warned that such high asset prices would be "creating big messes in the markets," which is probably a shorthand for the eventual need to raise interest rates rapidly triggering a plunge in the value of stocks, bonds, and other assets.

These comments by Fed officials suggest that they are fully cognizant of the danger of waiting until the two percent inflation target is reached, when the private sector is likely to have resumed borrowing. A Fed attempt to tighten when the private sector is already borrowing again could push

---

[2] Board of Governors of Federal Reserve System (2015) "Transcript of Chair Yellen's Press Conference, December 16, 2015," p. 10. www.federalreserve.gov/media-center/files/FOMCpresconf20151216.pdf.

[3] CNBC (2016) "Fed's Fischer: Markets Missing Mark on Future Rates," January 6, 2016. www.cnbc.com/2016/01/06/feds-fischer-uncertainty-has-risen-in-markets-unsure-of-n-korea-news-impact.html.

interest rates sharply higher in what Yellen referred to as an "abrupt tightening" scenario. That in turn may result in what Stanley Fischer called a "big mess" scenario of collapsing asset values and the economy, an outcome the Federal Reserve would like to avoid at all costs.

## Cycle of Conflict Between Authorities and Markets Seen Continuing for Now

Even with the above precautions, however, the first rate hike in nine years sparked tremendous volatility in early 2016 when the Fed indicated that it was willing to raise rates as many as four times within the year. The market's reaction forced the Fed to postpone the later rate hikes. Volatility picked up not only because many market participants had gotten used to easy money but also because the Fed would have been tightening when the inflation rate was still well below target. But the Fed's determination not to fall behind the curve on both asset prices and the general level of prices can be seen from the fact that, as soon as its decision not to hike at the March 2016 FOMC meeting helped stabilize the markets, senior Fed officials resumed talking about another rate hike as early as the late April 2016 FOMC meeting.

For example, Atlanta Fed President Dennis Lockhart and San Francisco Fed President John Williams both suggested in late March 2016 that an April rate hike might be in order. Williams said the 30 percent decline in share prices on Black Monday in October 1987 had had little impact on the real economy. He also made a point of citing economist Paul Samuelson's quip that the stock market has predicted "nine out of the last five recessions" in an attempt to emphasize that the stock market and the real economy are not the same thing[4]. Vice-Chairman Fischer also noted that the U.S. economy was largely unaffected by large swings in equity prices in 2011.

The fact that these remarks came out as soon as markets regained their composure underscores the sense of urgency at the Fed regarding the normalization of monetary policy and suggests that it was hard at work on managing expectations of further rate hikes. Moreover, the hints at a possible April rate hike indicated that, for some Fed officials, even the severe market turmoil experienced in early 2016 was only enough to delay a hike by one FOMC meeting, or about six weeks.

---

[4] Williams, John C. (2016) "The Right Profile: Economic Drivers and the Outlook," a presentation to Town Hall Los Angeles, February 18, 2016. www.frbsf.org/our-district/files/Williams-Speech-The-Right-Profile_Economic-Drivers-and-the-Outlook.pdf.

## First Iteration of "QE Trap"

This is the first iteration of what the author dubbed the "QE trap" in his previous book[5]—a cycle of conflict between investors and the authorities in which market turmoil prompts the Fed to take a step back, but only until markets regain their balance, at which point it resumes its drive to normalize monetary policy. A fall in the stock market triggered by monetary tightening, like that seen in January 2016, will force the central bank to pause, but it must move forward again as soon as the market regains its composure because the road to normalization is such a long one. That, in turn, prompts another round of volatility. Given the amount of excess reserves in the banking system, this sort of back-and-forth iteration of conflict between the markets and the authorities could come to surface many times until monetary policy has been normalized.

Figure 6.4 illustrates the possible behavior of long-term interest rates in two scenarios: one in which the central bank has engaged in quantitative easing (thick line) and one in which it has not (thin line). When a central bank takes interest rates to zero after a bubble bursts but does not engage in QE, long-term government bond yields will still fall sharply because the government is the only borrower issuing fixed-income assets denominated in the local currency. This fall in government bond yields is the self-corrective mechanism of economies in balance sheet recessions noted in Chapter 2.

Once the economy begins to show signs of life after a few years, bond yields will be rising gradually in line with the recovery in both the economy and private-sector loan demand. At this point, people will be happy and relaxed because the recovery finally came, and the central bank will be raising short-term rates at a pace it deems appropriate for the extent of the economic recovery and inflation. This is the usual pattern of monetary policy and bond yields in an economic recovery.

A central bank that has implemented QE or helicopter money, meanwhile, faces a very different set of circumstances. In this case, long-term rates will fall further and faster than in the non-QE case because the central bank is also buying huge quantities of government bonds. Such low rates are likely to support asset prices via the portfolio rebalancing effect and bring economic recovery a little sooner $(t_1)$ than in the economy where there was no QE $(t_2)$.

Once the recovery begins, however, the market starts to gird for trouble as rate hikes and a mop-up of excess liquidity appear increasingly likely. Market participants must brace themselves because the amount of long-term bonds the central bank must unload to drain the excess reserves is truly huge. If the Fed has to sell those bonds, bond prices will fall and yields will go up. If the Fed holds on to the bonds until maturity, the

---

[5] Koo, Richard (2015) *The Escape from Balance Sheet Recession and the QE Trap*, Singapore: John Wiley & Sons, Chapter 6.

FIGURE 6.4 QE "Trap" (1): Long-term Interest Rates or Exchange Rates Could Go Sharply Higher When QE Is Unwound

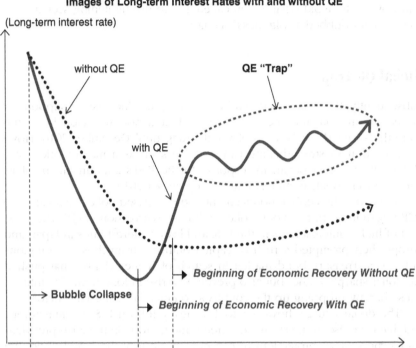

**Images of Long-term Interest Rates with and without QE**

(Long-term interest rate)

without QE

QE "Trap"

with QE

Beginning of Economic Recovery Without QE

Bubble Collapse

Beginning of Economic Recovery With QE

$t_0$    $t_1$    $t_2$    (Time)

Treasury will have to sell an equivalent amount of bonds on the Fed's behalf to absorb the excess liquidity (this point is discussed further below). And if the Fed wants to postpone the normalization of its balance sheet, it will have to raise interest rates that much faster to stay ahead of the curve.

To the extent that market participants have become addicted to monetary easing, the reverse portfolio rebalancing effect (= negative wealth effect) brought about by the central bank's normalization of monetary policy would be equivalent to going through painful withdrawal symptoms. From the standpoint of the policy authorities, however, withdrawal symptoms alone are not cause enough to discontinue treatment of the patient. While the treatment may be paused temporarily if the symptoms become too severe, it will need to resume as soon as the market stabilizes lest the central bank fall behind the curve.

The Fed's first rate hike in nine years took place on December 16, 2015. That, and the market turmoil that followed in January 2016, signaled the start of the economy's long journey through the QE trap. The point is that the Fed has been raising interest rates in spite of increased market volatility because it not only needs a shock absorber for when it winds down QE, but it also wants to avoid what Yellen called an "abrupt tightening scenario" or what Fischer dubbed a "big mess" scenario

## Global QE Trap

Subsequently, the rising dollar and the consequent increase in support for protectionism from then-Republican presidential nominee Donald Trump and others forced the Fed to delay tightening until December 2016. However, the dollar's strengthening can itself be seen as a manifestation of a global QE trap that began in response to the Fed's announcement of its intention to normalize interest rates in September 2014.

Soon after the Fed's announcement, the BOJ eased policy again and the ECB began indicating it would follow with its own version of QE. The prospect of higher interest rates in the U.S. and lower interest rates in Japan and Europe then prompted a rush of capital outflows from those two regions to the U.S. Treasury bond market in search of higher yields. That pushed the dollar sharply higher but also prevented a rise in long-term U.S. interest rates, thereby propping up the country's commercial real estate sector.

The dollar's surge, however, took a heavy toll on U.S. manufacturers, and that gave rise to the strong anti-free-trade rhetoric in the 2016 presidential election. Since protectionism can quickly destroy the world trade, the Fed had to postpone rate hikes in order to keep the dollar from strengthening even further.

Although the dollar rose only around 20 percent against the yen and euro starting in the summer of 2014, it had climbed as much as 48 percent against the Mexican peso and as much as 37 percent against the Canadian dollar (Figures 6.5 and 6.6) by the beginning of 2016. Not only are both countries key U.S. trading partners, but many U.S. companies have factories in one or both. U.S. workers who must compete with factories in these countries were therefore rightfully worried about such a substantial appreciation of the U.S. currency.

Presidential candidates Donald Trump and Bernie Sanders capitalized on this situation. Their stances against free trade have proved very popular among the blue-collar workers who have suffered as the dollar has risen. Trump has even proposed levying a 35 percent duty on some imports from Mexico to help U.S. workers and companies fighting imports from that country.

Calls for protectionism became so loud that even Hillary Clinton was forced to declare her opposition to the current form of the Trans-Pacific

**FIGURE 6.5** U.S. Dollar Skyrocketed Against Mexican Peso After Fed's Normalization Announcement[1]

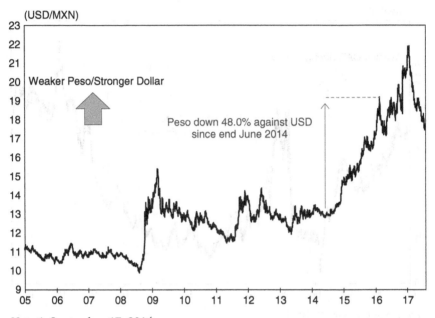

*Note 1:* September 17, 2014
*Source:* FRB

Partnership (TPP), an agreement she herself had helped negotiate. Her uncharacteristic shift can be attributed to the fact that the U.S. dollar's substantial appreciation against not only the yen and the euro but also against the Canadian dollar and Mexican peso have made the free-trade argument a difficult one to sell in the U.S. Indeed, when she accepted the Democratic Party's nomination for President in 2016, the whole convention arena was filled with signs saying "No to TPP!"

U.S. authorities, having seen the political and economic repercussions of the strong dollar at home and abroad (discussed below), decided their only option was to curb the rise in the U.S. currency that was causing these problems. After all, allowing the free-trade naysayers free run could have severe consequences for the global economy. Both Treasury Secretary Jack Lew and Fed Chair Janet Yellen had to ask themselves whether something could be done to slow the dollar's ascent. In this round of the QE trap, therefore, it was the surging dollar rather than falling stock prices or rising bond yields that forced the Fed to slow down. Because the rise in the dollar was fueled by the anticipation of Fed rate hikes, U.S. monetary authorities had to curb their rate hikes until the Presidential election was over.

FIGURE 6.6 U.S. Dollar Skyrocketed Against Canadian Dollar After Fed's Normalization Announcement[1]

*Note 1:* September 17, 2014
*Source:* FRB

## RMB's Sharp Rise Against USD Triggered Chinese Slowdown

The QE trap—in the form of a strong dollar—also created huge headaches for policymakers in China. Indeed, the Chinese predicament, together with explosive increase in support for protectionism in the U.S. fueled by the strong dollar, created a global QE trap that delayed the Fed's normalization plans in the second half of 2016. Although many have blamed China for the market turmoil in August 2015 and again in January 2016, the causes of both episodes can actually be traced to Washington, D.C., and specifically to the *reverse* portfolio rebalancing effect stemming from the dollar's rise in response to the expected normalization of U.S. monetary policy.

A great deal of attention has focused on the sharp deceleration in China's economy since 2015. Chinese policymakers had of course anticipated a certain slowdown given the decline in the nation's working-age population since 2012 (Figure 3.12), but the severity of the downturn was unexpected. The key contributing factor was the Chinese currency's sharp rise—along with that of the U.S. dollar—against most of the world's major currencies starting in September 2014 (circled area in Figure 6.7).

The RMB climbed as much as 35 percent against the dollar between 2005 and mid-2014, but the nominal effective rate rose only about 30 percent

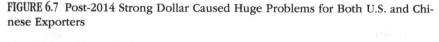

**FIGURE 6.7** Post-2014 Strong Dollar Caused Huge Problems for Both U.S. and Chinese Exporters

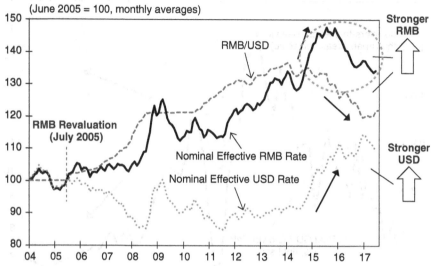

*Source:* Nomura Research Institute, based on the data from FRB and BIS

because this happened at a time of relative dollar weakness. An appreciation of this magnitude over a ten-year period was also modest enough for the fast-growing Chinese economy to overcome.

But the U.S. dollar took off in September 2014 with the Fed's announcement of a normalization of monetary policy, sending the U.S. currency nearly 20 percent higher on a nominal effective basis (bottom graph of Figure 6.7). Since China had effectively pegged its currency to the dollar, the RMB was taken along for the ride, and the currency appreciated another 15 percent on top of the aforementioned 30 percent on a nominal effective basis. This was a major reason for the sharp slowdown in China's economy that began in 2015.

The strong dollar struck a heavy blow to U.S. manufacturers, agricultural producers, and other exporters, but exports represent only 9 percent of U.S. GDP. The stronger currency had much more serious implications in China, where exports account for nearly 23 percent of the economy (figures for both countries based on 2014 trade statistics).

The job-to-applicants ratio, which had been rising for many years, suddenly fell below its historical trend line in mid-2015, alarming Chinese economic policymakers (circled area in Figure 6.8). The fact that this indicator had been rising until 2014 in spite of the slowdown in China's economy suggests that the country was close to full employment and that there were no more surplus workers in the countryside. Knowing that the nation was near full employment, Chinese authorities also refused to implement fiscal stimulus in spite of the economic slowdown until the job-to-applicants ratio began to fall in 2015.

FIGURE 6.8 Job-to-Applicants Ratio Started Falling After RMB-USD Appreciation

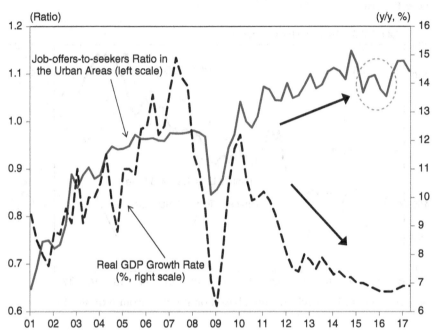

*Sources:* National Bureau of Statistics of China, Ministry of Human Resources and Social Security, PRC, and CEIC Data

## RMB's Costly Decoupling from USD

The sudden slowdown in China's economy and labor market then led the authorities to decouple the RMB from the dollar in August 2015, an event that not only roiled global markets but also elicited a decline in other Asian currencies. Because other Asian currencies had weakened further than the RMB, this decoupling worked only against the dollar and left the Chinese currency still trading at relatively high levels on a nominal effective basis (Figure 6.7).

Moreover, the decoupling prompted hot money that had previously flowed into China on expectations of continued RMB gains to flee the country suddenly, forcing Chinese authorities to intervene in support of their currency. As the RMB climbed more than 30 percent on a nominal effective basis over the ten years prior to 2014, China experienced massive capital inflows from speculators anticipating further appreciation. These inflows also played a significant role in pushing the Chinese currency higher prior to August 2015.

When the authorities cut the link between the RMB and the dollar in August 2015, however, speculators realized the RMB could also go down. That realization then led to significant capital flight, and those outflows have weighed on Chinese stock markets.

Previously, the People's Bank of China (PBOC) had intervened in the foreign exchange market to prevent speculative capital inflows from causing excessive appreciation of the RMB. That led to the accumulation of huge foreign reserves. Since 2015, the central bank has been using those reserves to manage the currency's decline as speculative money tries to leave the country.

The PBOC's pre-August 2015 interventions expanded the monetary base and therefore had the potential to spark inflation. But the authorities prevented a corresponding increase in the money supply by repeatedly raising reserve requirements for the banks.

The PBOC's post-August 2015 interventions to stem the RMB's decline, on the other hand, have reduced the growth in the monetary base and are potentially deflationary. The Chinese authorities therefore began lowering their reserve requirements in 2015 in an attempt to prevent the contraction in base money from causing the money supply to shrink. The stability of post-2015 money supply and credit growth in Figure 6.9 suggests that they have been quite successful so far.

These foreign exchange interventions are justified inasmuch as they are designed to prevent short-term portfolio capital inflows and outflows from upsetting the stability of China's economy and exchange rate. U.S. Treasury Secretary Jack Lew understood the Chinese predicament when he poked fun at those clamoring about China. He noted that, at a time when China's foreign reserves were much smaller than they are now ($3.15trn at the end of June 2017), those same individuals had argued that the reserves were too large, whereas now they say they are insufficient.

The Obama administration was also concerned about the global economic slowdown starting in China. Administration officials had not forgotten that it was China and other emerging markets (EMs) that supported the global economy in the darkest years after the global financial crisis, which had originated in the U.S. In their view, any set of policies that ignored those countries would not lead to broader economic growth and recovery.

In effect, China's policy has been to (1) hold onto foreign reserves accumulated in currency interventions undertaken in response to speculative capital inflows and (2) subsequently use those reserves to stabilize the exchange rate when those speculative funds leave the country. This can serve as a model for the many emerging economies that have been roiled by inflows and outflows of speculative capital, some of which were triggered by wanton use of QE in the developed world. Had China not adopted this long-term approach, the RMB probably would have risen much further

FIGURE 6.9 China's Monetary Aggregates Are Decoupling Because of Intervention to Support RMB

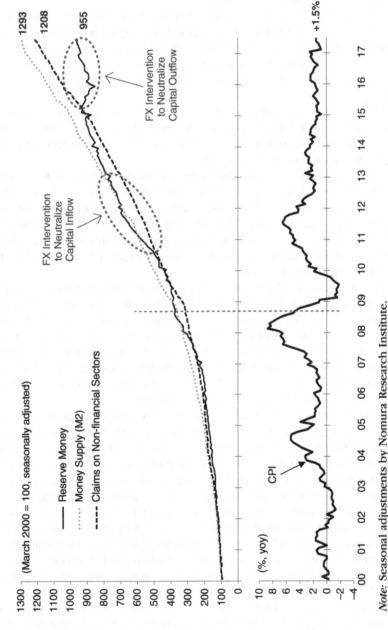

*Note:* Seasonal adjustments by Nomura Research Institute.

*Source:* Nomura Research Institute, based on the data from CEIC Data and People's Bank of China

when capital was flowing in and fallen much more sharply now that those funds are fleeing the country.

The proper policy response for emerging markets experiencing an influx of speculative capital is therefore to intervene on the currency market and raise reserve requirements to keep currency appreciation in check and prevent asset bubbles from forming. When capital starts to leave the country, authorities should then lower reserve requirements to curb deflationary pressures while intervening on the foreign exchange market to support the currency. This combination of currency intervention and reserve ratio adjustments should be proactively used by countries affected by the wanton use of QE by advanced economies. Exchange rate problems created by capital flows are discussed further in Chapter 9.

The stock market's surprisingly strong reaction to the Trump victory in November 2016 gave the Fed a window of opportunity to raise interest rates three times, thereby making up for time lost during the election campaign. That gave the Fed the shock absorber it needed to embark on the real event, i.e., the normalization of its balance sheet and the monetary base.

## Difficulty of Normalizing Central Bank's Balance Sheet

If normalizing interest rates with QE is difficult, normalizing the central bank's balance sheet is no easier. Some have argued that this process should be relatively straightforward since banks have the excess reserves supplied under QE to buy the bonds being unloaded by the central bank, but there is an asymmetry involved here.

When the central bank was acquiring the bonds under QE in a crisis, there was no private-sector demand for funds. This means that interest rates were low and bond prices were high. But when the time comes for the central bank to sell the bonds, both the economy and private-sector demand for funds have presumably recovered. This means that interest rates will be higher and bond prices lower. The fact that the central bank is selling bonds at a time when the private sector also wants to borrow means that interest rates could go much higher than when the central bank was a buyer. Indeed, rates can go sharply higher if the central bank is not careful. This is also why the Fed wants to undo QE before the return of private-sector borrowers when the asymmetry problem is minimal.

Many in the market, however, became complacent after Bernanke assured them that the Fed would hold the bonds until maturity. He indicated that instead of selling the bonds to absorb excess liquidity, the Fed will absorb the liquidity by not reinvesting the proceeds of maturing bonds in its possession. Hearing this, many in the market assumed that nothing terrible would happen even if the Fed normalized its balance sheet as long as it did not sell the bonds. This complacency of market participants, however, is not without problems.

When a government bond matures, the government usually issues a refunding bond to obtain funds from the private sector to pay the holder of the maturing security. Because of the huge quantity of government bonds issued in the past, the market for refunding bonds in both Japan and the U.S. is three to four times the size of that for newly issued debt to finance government expenditures.

Ordinarily the issuance of refunding bonds is not thought to produce significant upward pressure on interest rates because the proceeds will be paid to private-sector holders of maturing government debt who are likely to reinvest those funds in government debt. In contrast, market participants grow tense when a new-money bond is issued because fresh private-sector savings will have to be found to absorb the bond—this money, after all, will be used to build roads and bridges and will not be coming back to the bond market. Bond market participants therefore relax when they hear that the Treasury is issuing refunding bonds as opposed to new-money bonds, because they know those bonds have a largely neutral impact on the market.

If the maturing government debt is held by the central bank, however, redemption funds raised from the private sector by the Treasury via the issuance of refunding bonds do not flow back to the bond market. Instead, the funds go to the central bank, where they disappear. Their disappearance, of course, represents the absorption of excess liquidity by the Fed. This means that those refunding bonds—despite their name—are no different from new-money bonds issued to finance budget deficits in terms of their upward pressure on interest rates. In other words, they have the same negative impact on supply/demand as if the central bank had sold its bond holdings directly on the market.

## Fed Tackling QE Exit Problem Head-On

On June 14, 2017, the Fed decided to tackle this difficult issue of unwinding QE head-on by presenting a concrete plan. Under this plan, the Fed will initially stop reinvesting $6bn a month in Treasury securities and $4bn a month in mortgage-backed securities (MBS), raising those amounts by $6bn and $4bn, respectively, every three months until they reach $30bn and $20bn. This process will continue until the excess reserves in the banking system have been brought down to a desirable level.

Figure 6.10 shows a projection for the amount of reserves remaining in the market under the Fed's proposed schedule. In making this projection, it was assumed that currency in circulation (the shaded areas in the

FIGURE 6.10 Balance Sheet Normalization Process Envisioned by Fed

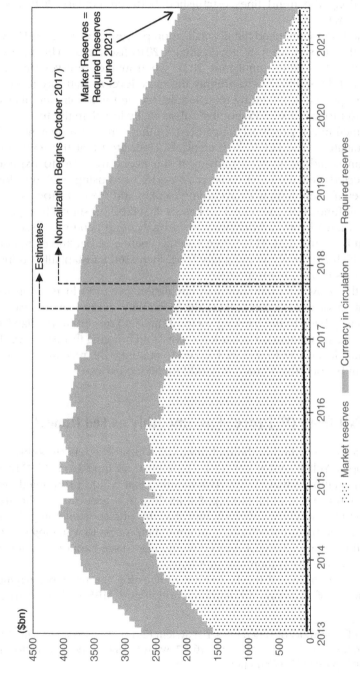

*Notes:* Reserve balances, currency in circulation and required reserves will continue trends observed from January 2015 to May 2017.

*Source:* Nomura Research Institute, based on Fed data; estimates by Nomura Research Institute

graph) and required reserves (the heavy black line) would continue to grow along the trend lines established between January 2015 and the present (May 2017).

The Fed commenced the normalization process in October 2017, which marks the start of the U.S. government's 2018 fiscal year. This means the program will continue until June 2021, when market reserves (the dotted portion of the graph) fall to roughly the same level as statutory reserves. If the plan proceeds according to schedule, the Fed will complete its exit in just under four years or 45 months, substantially less than the five- to eight-year timeframe it previously suggested. In that sense, it represents a fairly bold initiative. The FOMC statement also indicated that the reinvestment program could be revived midway if the economy were to experience unexpected weakness that could not be addressed using rate cuts alone.

Even if everything goes according to plan and the exit process is completed in June 2021, the monetary base will still be substantially larger than it would have been had the pre-crisis growth trend continued (see circled portion in Figure 6.2). This is because the volume of banknotes in circulation, which is part of the monetary base, increased substantially during the eight years of zero interest rates.

If the growth in banknotes in circulation occurred in reaction to the imposition of zero interest rates, the possibility exists that this cash will find its way back to the banking sector if interest rates are normalized. That would lead to an increase in bank reserves, and bringing those reserves back to normal levels would require the Fed to continue the recently announced program beyond the 45-month period mentioned above.

## Will Exit from QE Proceed as Smoothly as Fed Hopes?

The question is whether the exit from QE will proceed as smoothly as the Fed hopes. Yellen said at her press conference on June 14, 2017, "My hope and expectation is that . . . this is something that will just run quietly in the background over a number of years, leading to a reduction in the size of our balance sheet."[6] She quickly repeated the phrase "something that runs quietly in the background" and compared the process to watching paint dry. While this is naturally what the Fed would like to see happen, and it cannot be ruled out entirely, there are problems.

As noted above, if the Fed is not reinvesting the principal payments, the issuers of maturing Treasury securities and MBS will need to issue

---

[6] Board of Governors of Federal Reserve System (2017) "Transcript of Chair Yellen's Press Conference, June 14, 2017," pp. 16–17. www.federalreserve.gov/mediacenter/files/FOMCpresconf20170614.pdf.

new debt and sell it to the private sector in order to procure the funds to pay the Fed. The issuance of new debt, which will still be called "redemption bonds," is effectively "new money bonds" because it will have exactly the same economic effect as if the Fed had sold the bonds directly or if the Federal government had increased the fiscal deficit by an equal amount.

Moreover, the scale of the Fed's quantitative easing means the amounts involved are not trivial. Figure 6.11 shows the amount of additional private savings that would be required under the Fed's plan to discontinue its reinvestments. The savings required will amount to some $300bn in FY2018 and $600bn in both FY2019 and FY2020. The $600bn figure is roughly equal to the entire federal budget deficit for FY2016. In other words, removing the QE in those two years will have the same impact on interest rates as doubling the 2016 federal deficit.

It is hard to envision the massive hit to bond market supply/demand from an effective doubling of the fiscal deficit as "just running quietly in the background." Even with a shock absorber already in place, this process is likely to put some upward pressure on interest rates and may even lead to a steep drop in bond prices.

FIGURE 6.11 Additional Private Savings Required If Fed Stops Reinvesting in U.S. Treasuries (UST) and Mortgage-Backed Securities (MBS)

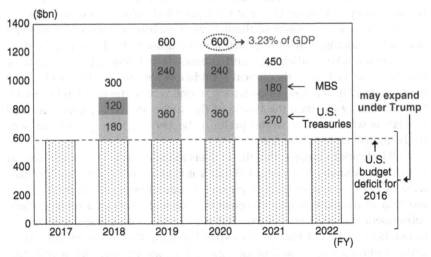

*Notes:* Assumes normalization will be conducted from October 2017 to June 2021. U.S. fiscal accounting year runs from October to following September. MBS = mortgage-backed securities.

*Source:* Nomura Research Institute

## So Why Is the Fed Intent on Winding down QE?

Some may question the Fed's decision to pursue such a risky path at a time when the U.S. inflation rate is significantly below the Fed's own target. However, as mentioned earlier, if the Fed waits until the economy is strong and growing and private-sector loan demand has recovered, winding down QE will have the same effect as doubling the fiscal deficit at a time of brisk private-sector demand for funds, which could send interest rates soaring.

To avoid this outcome, the Fed needs to begin winding down QE while private-sector loan demand remains weak. With no private-sector borrowers clamoring for funds, even a doubling of the fiscal deficit is likely to have a more modest impact on interest rates. The Fed will also want to let the bond market grow accustomed to the exit process while private-sector loan demand is still depressed.

## No Theoretical Consensus on Winding Down QE

Taking the discussion to a slightly more theoretical level, Professor Paul Krugman and many other economists encouraged central banks to adopt quantitative easing but have not provided any theoretical framework for how to wind down these policies. As a result, there is no consensus among academics, market participants or the authorities on what conditions should be satisfied before starting to unwind QE or at what pace it should be wound down.

The complete absence of theoretical consensus means when the Fed does start winding down the policy it will almost certainly be criticized by academics, market participants, and authorities as being either too early or too late. The lack of a theoretical foundation also means the decision of when to end QE is bound to be wrong in one way or the other in hindsight. With no theory to guide the timing of this move, the real question for Fed officials is whether they would prefer to be criticized *ten* years from now for being too early or too late.

All indications suggest that the Fed has already come to a conclusion on this matter. Namely, it has decided that if it is going to be criticized no matter what it does, it would rather err on the side of being too early. The loss function in this case is that a premature exit will result in a more gradual subsequent recovery, but an exit that is too late could cause the economy to overheat and asset bubbles to expand, forcing the Fed to engage in an abrupt tightening that could plunge the U.S. economy back into a 2008-like (balance sheet) recession.

This view that "too early" is better than "too late" is fully reflected in the Fed's 2013 decision to begin tapering of QE when inflation was running at just 1.1 percent and to carry out its first rate hike in 2015 when the inflation rate was only 1.3 percent. All three rate hikes to June 2017 were also implemented when inflation was less than 2 percent. These actions underscore just how afraid the Fed is of being too late and falling behind the curve.

In light of the above, there is little chance of the Fed hesitating to exit QE in response to a minor slowdown in the economy. The only case in which the Fed might reconsider is if the exit process itself were to trigger a bond market crash.

## Huge Exit Problems for Zero-Coupon Perpetuals and Government Scrip

This issue of mopping up reserves becomes even more complicated with the third and fourth versions of helicopter money. Perpetual zero-coupon bonds are absolutely worthless, which means the central bank cannot sell them to mop up the excess liquidity. With nothing worthwhile to sell, the only way for the central bank to drain the excess reserves created by the central bank purchases of perpetual zero-coupon bonds is to ask the government to issue an equivalent amount of conventional interest-bearing bonds.

The same would be true when trying to absorb reserves created by the issue of government scrip. Once this scrip starts circulating, it becomes part of the monetary base, and draining it from the system requires that the central bank either sell its bond holdings or ask the government to issue new bonds.

If the government were to issue bonds to mop up reserves created by zero-coupon perpetuals or government scrip, it has to do so with an understanding that it would not be able to spend the proceeds of the issuance. If it did spend them, the absorbed liquidity would flow back into the economy, defeating the whole purpose of draining the reserves—to keep inflation in check. Accordingly, when the bonds so issued to absorb the liquidity mature, the government will need to use the unused proceeds of the bonds noted above to redeem the bonds while issuing an equal amount of new bonds to quickly reabsorb the liquidity just released to the private sector via the redemption. Since this cumbersome process will have to go on forever, the government may just decide to issue perpetual (but not zero coupon) bonds to recover the liquidity for good.

Economists who recommend the issuance of government scrip or perpetual zero-coupon bonds say the key advantage of this approach is that it does not lead to an expansion of government liabilities. However, that is true only at the outset: these instruments will become the equivalent of government liabilities when the economy eventually recovers and will have to be absorbed by the bond-issuing government. The legal issues involved in a government issuing coupon-bearing bonds (on behalf of the central bank) to drain reserves when it cannot use the proceeds must also be resolved.

## "Ignorance Is Bliss" Scenario Exactly What Fed Wants

The next question is under what circumstances Yellen's preferred scenario of "running quietly in the background" might unfold. One possibility is that the size of the deflationary gap remains unchanged between the QE entry and the QE exit. In that case, there will be none of the asymmetry mentioned earlier. But that also implies that QE has had no impact on the real economy from the start.

If the liquidity injected under QE can be removed without any negative impact on asset prices, it means that the portfolio rebalancing effect was also minimal. This also implies that the U.S. economy was actually supported not by QE, but by President Obama's fiscal policies and Chairman Bernanke's warning about the fiscal cliff.

Another possibility is that the majority of market participants remain unaware that refunding bonds issued after the cessation of central bank reinvestments actually have the same (adverse) impact on supply/demand as new-money bonds issued to finance fiscal deficits.

For the past several years the author has made a point of mentioning this issue of refunding bonds when giving speeches or presentations to investors. The point was also made in the author's previous book, *The Escape from Balance Sheet Recession and the QE Trap*. The fact that many investors are still surprised by this point underscores how little-understood it is.

If most market participants remained unaware of this point and continued to act based on the view that refunding bonds issued after the cessation of reinvestments were no different from ordinary refunding bonds, the Fed chair's preferred scenario would become possible. Since the outcome of "running quietly in the background" is in the interest of many, including the Fed, few would want to disabuse the market of this notion—in this case, at least, ignorance would be bliss.

It should be remembered that Greek government bonds were trading at almost the same yields as their German equivalents up to 2009, with bond market participants believing that the government is within the Maastricht Treaty's 3 percent deficit cap. This is in spite of the fact that Greece had been running massive fiscal deficits for years in violation of the Treaty. This state of affairs ended only when the new government in Athens announced that October that the prior administration had been fudging the deficit data. After the announcement was made, however, the 10-year Greek bond yield skyrocketed to 33.7 percent in 2012 from about 5 percent before October 2008. This example suggests that the actual size of Greece's deficits was less important for bond market participants than their perception that the government was observing the Treaty.

As such, Ms. Yellen's "running quietly in the background" scenario would be possible even if the fiscal deficit were effectively doubled as long as the majority of bond market participants remained unaware of it.

## What If Other Central Banks Wound Down QE at Same Pace as Fed?

As of this writing, the BOE, ECB, and BOJ have not issued any comments about winding down QE, nor have they offered any indication how (or how fast) these policies would be wound down in the event they decide to do so. To provide a meaningful comparison of the challenges they will face in removing QE relative to those confronted by the Fed, the simulations below assume these central banks will follow the same unwinding schedule and procedure announced by the Fed on June 14, 2017.

For example, it was assumed that the three central banks would wind down QE over a 45-month period by gradually phasing in no-reinvestment policies that involve (1) increasing every three months the amount that will not be reinvested and (2) keeping this figure on hold after the fifth increase. All estimates assume that the three central banks will begin winding down QE in October 2017.

All of these simulations show the required amount of private-sector savings peaking in FY2019 and FY2020, just as in the U.S., although the figures before and after those two years differ by country and region. These differences are purely due to the use of different accounting years, which mean that the graphs would be shaped differently even if the other central banks began winding down QE in October 2017 and completed the process in June 2021, just like the Fed.

The private-sector savings required for an ECB exit from QE (Figure 6.12) would not be particularly large in 2017. In 2018, however, the process would require private-sector savings amounting to €227.5 billion, an amount substantially larger than the actual fiscal deficit of the entire Eurozone for 2016. In 2019 and 2020 the required funds would amount to €325.1 billion, or 1.96 times the size of the 2016 deficit. This implies that if the ECB begins winding down QE in October 2017 using the same proce- dure as the Fed, the Eurozone's fiscal deficit will effectively double in 2018 and triple in 2019 and 2020.

In contrast, the amount of private-sector savings required in the U.S. (Figure 6.11) will come to $600 billion at the peak in 2019 and 2020, roughly the same size as the FY2016 fiscal deficit. The Eurozone would therefore appear to face a greater challenge in relative terms. But this is only because the U.S. fiscal deficit was more than twice the size of the Eurozone deficit to begin with. The required savings in the Eurozone would peak at €325.1 billion, or $383.6 billion at an exchange rate of $1.18/euro, which is far less than the corresponding figure for the U.S. of $600 billion.

So when comparing the private-sector savings needed to wind down QE across different countries, it is important to look at the nominal amount as well as the percentage relative to GDP or to the fiscal deficit and not focus simply on the shape of the graph.

FIGURE 6.12 Additional Private Savings Required If ECB Begins Absorbing Excess Reserves

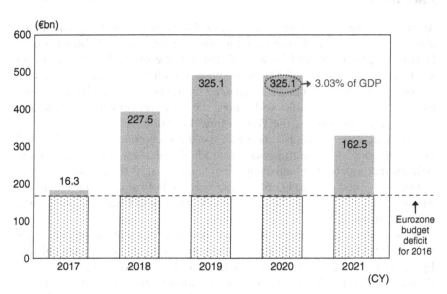

*Notes:* Assumes U.S.-style normalization will be conducted from October 2017 to June 2021. Fiscal deficit represents net borrowings of general government.

*Source:* Nomura Research Institute, based on ECB and Eurostat data

The UK would require private-sector savings of 126.5 billion pounds per year in FY2019–2020, several times the current fiscal deficit of 38.4 billion pounds. The effective quadrupling of the deficit would put substantial upward pressure on interest rates.

As a percentage of GDP, the required amount of private-sector savings will peak in FY2019–2020 at 3.23 percent in the U.S., 3.03 percent in the Eurozone, and 6.52 percent in the UK, suggesting the impact of the QE exit relative to the size of the overall economy will be roughly twice as great in the UK as in the Eurozone or the U.S.

Additionally, according to the latest flow-of-funds data, the UK's private sector has been running a financial *deficit* amounting to 2.97 percent of GDP[7]. Conditions are therefore very different from those in the U.S., where the private sector is running a financial surplus amounting to 4.12 percent of GDP, and the Eurozone, where the financial surplus is 4.62 percent of GDP. This means the asymmetry problem mentioned above is actually quite acute in the UK, i.e., it may experience more upward pressure on interest rates than the U.S. or the Eurozone because its private sector is now borrowing instead of saving.

---

[7] Four quarter moving average ending in Q1, 2017.

FIGURE 6.13 Additional Private Savings Required If BOE Begins Absorbing Excess Reserves

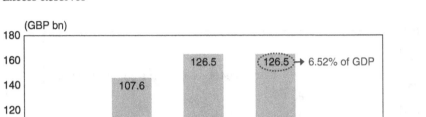

*Notes:* Assumes U.S.-style normalization will be conducted from Oct 2017 to Jun 2021. UK fiscal accounting year runs from April to following March. Fiscal deficit represents net borrowings of national government.

*Source:* Nomura Research Institute

## Japan Faces Massive Problems in Ending QE

Still, the scale of the problem in the UK is nothing compared with that in Japan. A look at current macroeconomic indicators shows that Japan has a lower unemployment rate than the U.S. and is also quite close to a state of full employment. Commercial real estate prices are rising sharply in central Tokyo and other areas, with data released early in July 2017 showing official land prices in Tokyo's Ginza district reaching new all-time highs for the first time in 27 years. If commercial real estate prices and unemployment rates give sufficient reason for the Fed to unwind QE, then the case for the BOJ to remove QE is even stronger.

Figure 6.14 provides an estimate of the private-sector savings required when the BOJ decides to wind down QE based on the same assumptions as those for the other central banks. It shows that Japan would need almost ¥95 trillion per year at the peak in FY2019 and FY2020, more than twice the size of FY2016's already large ¥38 trillion deficit. In other words, an exit

FIGURE 6.14 Additional Private Savings Required If BOJ Begins Absorbing Excess Reserves

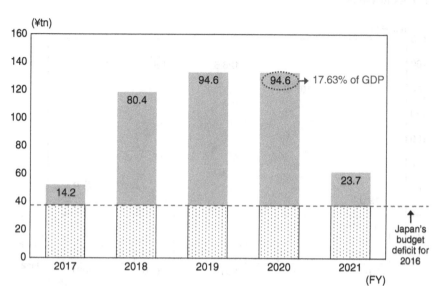

*Notes:* Assumes U.S.-style normalization will be conducted from October 2017 to June 2021. Japan's fiscal accounting year runs from April to following March.

*Source:* Nomura Research Institute, based on MOF and BOJ data

from QE would cause Japan's effective fiscal deficit to surge from ¥38 trillion at present to ¥118 trillion in FY2018 and to ¥133 trillion in FY2019 and FY2020, with corresponding upward pressure on interest rates. Required private-sector savings in Japan will amount to 17.63 percent of GDP in FY2019 and FY2020, nearly six times the corresponding ratios for the U.S. and Eurozone and about three times the figure for the UK.

Although the central banks are simply draining the liquidity they previously supplied to the market, winding down QE will naturally lead to higher interest rates if today's ultra-low interest rates are a result of this policy. The upward pressure on interest rates would also be more pronounced if the private sector was running a financial surplus when QE was being implemented but is running a financial deficit when the policy is removed, which is the case in the UK. Normalization is even more challenging for Japan because its central bank also bought ¥15 trillion in Japanese stocks via Exchange Traded Funds (ETFs). Unwinding these holdings would almost certainly have an adverse impact on the Japanese stock market.

The fact that the process of winding down QE will take years also means that the upward pressure on interest rates will continue. Moreover, this upward pressure will actually increase during the unwinding process as the amount that will not be reinvested by the central bank gradually rises.

Investors who understand this will naturally want to delay the purchase of bonds whose prices are almost certain to decline. Bond prices could crash if enough investors delayed their purchases or become active short sellers. But the central bank will be unable to buy the bonds these investors are selling if inflation is already running at two percent. This is because doing so will reinject reserves back into the banking system that could cause inflation to accelerate, triggering a further crash in bond prices.

The Fed understood this risk and worried that everything could collapse if the central bank was perceived by market participants as having fallen behind the curve on inflation. That is why it began tapering its asset purchases when inflation was running at just 1.1 percent and started raising rates when inflation was at just 1.3 percent.

BOJ Governor Haruhiko Kuroda, on the other hand, has shown absolutely no indication that he is concerned about this risk. Instead, he boldly declares that quantitative easing will continue until it is confirmed that prices are rising at a *sustained* rate of two percent a year.

## The Longer BOJ Waits, the Less Attractive JGBs Will Be

The BOJ also faces another difficult issue: given Kuroda's position, Japan is likely to be the last of the QE countries to wind down this policy. In contrast, the Federal Reserve is currently rushing to end QE while domestic loan demand remains weak and the other three central banks are still implementing their versions of this policy. This means the Fed will be able to count on increased demand for Treasury securities from overseas investors hungry for yield. The upward pressure on U.S. interest rates will be reduced if investors from Japan, the UK, and Europe absorb a significant portion of the increased supply of U.S. debt. In other words, the fact that the U.S. is the first to begin winding down QE means it may be able to complete the process with relatively little pain.

All of these factors will work against the BOJ, which will be the last of the major central banks to go down this road. When the time comes for Japan's central bank to wind down QE, government bond yields in other developed economies will be substantially higher, destroying any incentive for investors in Japan and elsewhere to buy JGBs. When the BOJ tries to wind down QE, therefore, the resultant rise in interest rates could be far greater than if it moved in tandem with its counterparts and opted to wind down the policy sooner.

The ultimate effect of removing QE on interest and exchange rates therefore hinges in part on when other countries decide to end the policy. In that sense, there may be approaches that will work for the U.S. as "first mover" but not for Japan, which will be bringing up the rear.

As the first country to normalize monetary policy, the U.S. will see the dollar rise against other currencies as normalization attracts capital inflows from abroad, but those inflows will also help limit the rise in domestic bond yields. As noted above, both phenomena have already been observed in the U.S.

Japan will benefit as other countries unwind QE because that will probably weaken the yen. But with the Trump Administration in the U.S. committed to reducing the U.S. trade deficit, the BOJ may not get very far with its wishes to weaken the yen. When the BOJ moves to wind down the policy, however, it will not be able to depend on foreign inflows to keep bond yields low. With Japan's public-sector debt already the largest in the world, some investors may question the ability of the government's finances to withstand higher JGB yields. Others may try to profit by short-selling JGBs. Such selling could develop into a massive fiscal crisis if not handled correctly.

## Total Cost of QE May Outweigh Its Benefits

The fact that the issuance of refunding bonds will raise interest and exchange rates that dampen economic activity means the total cost of QE, from implementation to unwinding, is likely to be much higher than anticipated by its supporters. Yet in all the debates over helicopter money and quantitative easing, the proponents of these policies have emphasized their initial benefits while ignoring the potentially high costs involved in mopping up the excess reserves later on. When the costs and benefits are examined over the course of the policy's lifetime, those initial benefits may well turn out to be small relative to the subsequent costs of unwinding the policy.

Ultimately, central banks that implemented QE will probably be forced to use all the tools at their disposal to either sterilize or drain excess reserves when borrowers return. Those tools would include tougher capital, liquidity and reserve requirements, and moral suasion to keep banks from lending to the private sector. The central bank is also likely to mobilize reverse repos, pay interest on reserves, and offer term deposits with higher interest rates so that commercial banks will have less incentive to lend to businesses and households. In effect, the central bank will be deliberately creating a Case 2 economy by reducing banks' ability to lend.

None of these remedies are pleasant or inexpensive. For example, if the Fed pays interest on reserves, $2.1 trillion in excess U.S. reserves at 3 percent (the FOMC's long-term goal for the Federal Funds rate) comes to $63 billion a year. If QE is not unwound, not only will the Fed have to pay

FIGURE 6.15 QE "Trap" (2): Stronger Currency and Higher Long-term Rates Could Weigh on Economic Recovery for Years

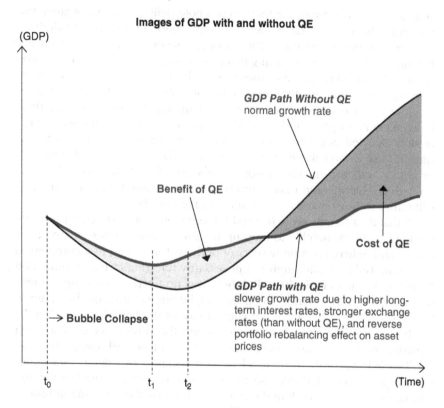

this amount every year, but the Federal government's fiscal deficit will also be $63 billion larger, in perpetuity, than it would have been otherwise. At some point, the interest income earned by the central bank on bonds purchased via QE will be fully offset by the accumulated interest costs.

In comparison to economies that did not implement QE, those that did may end up recovering much more slowly because of the higher interest and exchange rates they will face during the long journey out of the QE trap (Figure 6.15). Economies that did not resort to QE may even turn out to have greater cumulative GDP than those that did over the entire period, including the unwinding of QE. How to unwind trillions of dollars of QE without sending bond yields or exchange rates to damagingly high levels is the single most important challenge facing monetary authorities in the West and Japan today.

# Why Is Helicopter Money so Popular?

Why do so many pundits continue to promote policies like quantitative easing and helicopter money while completely ignoring the costs of draining the liquidity unleashed under these policies when the economy recovers? Perhaps economists are assuming that private-sector loan demand will *never* recover. If that were the case, there would be no need to drain the excess reserves, and consequently no need to worry about the attendant costs.

The massive excess reserves in the banking system could stay there indefinitely if people who had terrible experiences digging themselves out of debt decided never to borrow again. In this case, the economy would stay in Case 3, and the money multiplier at the margin would remain at or below zero indefinitely. History also shows that Americans who lived through the Depression never borrowed money again, and many Japanese still refuse to borrow today, 27 years after their bubble burst.

If this debt trauma were to persist, there would be no need for the central bank to move quickly to mop up the funds created under quantitative easing and helicopter money (except perhaps for reining in a commercial real estate bubble). Although not necessarily referring to this trauma, Ben Bernanke wrote in early 2017 that there was no need to speed up the normalization of Fed's balance sheet. Instead, he argued, it would be better to let the economy "grow into" the current size of the Fed's balance sheet[8].

It is extremely difficult to predict when the private sector will finish repairing its balance sheet, overcome its debt trauma, and resume borrowing. This is because there are few historical instances of a democratic country emerging from a balance sheet recession in peacetime. The fact that the advanced countries are all in the pursued phase for the first time in history makes this prediction even more difficult.

On the other hand, it is dangerous to keep quantitative easing and helicopter money policies in place based on the assumption that the current situation will continue forever. Figure 2.16 already indicated that some U.S. households have resumed borrowing after absenting themselves for about four years following the Lehman failure in 2008. The bottom chart of Figure 8.7 also indicates that some Japanese corporations are starting to borrow again. The bubbles in commercial real estate markets in the U.S. and elsewhere cannot be left to their own devices, either.

Indeed, the goal of all policies, including helicopter money, is to bring the economy back to Case 1, and that requires a recovery in private-sector demand for funds (even if not back to the level of the golden era). By ignoring

---

[8] Bernanke, Ben S. (2017) "Shrinking the Fed's Balance Sheet," from his blog at Brookings Institution, January 26, 2017. www.brookings.edu/blog/ben-bernanke/2017/01/26/shrinking-the-feds-balance-sheet/.

the cost of draining reserves, proponents of helicopter money and QE are essentially saying that private-sector demand for funds will never recover. But that is equivalent to admitting that these policies will never work, because a full recovery requires the return of private-sector borrowers.

## Fixation on Fiscal Limit Is Extremely Dangerous

Another reason why the focus of policy debate shifted to quantitative easing and helicopter money is the belief held by some economists that public debt levels in the advanced economies have reached "limits" that preclude the further use of fiscal policy. Policy options at the core of helicopter money, such as the issue of government scrip or perpetual zero-coupon bonds, were devised to overcome this "limit."

However, when the economy recovers and the liquidity created by scrip and perpetual zero-coupon bonds has to be drained from the system, the government must issue (interest-bearing perpetual) bonds to do so. This means that the use of scrip or zero-coupon perpetuals will eventually lead to an equal increase in government liabilities, as described above, and therefore does nothing to overcome this "limit."

Furthermore, as argued in Chapter 4, businesses and households in Japan, the U.S., and Europe are not only not borrowing but are actually saving money or paying down debt in spite of zero or negative interest rates. In other words, the funds to finance necessary fiscal stimulus during Cases 3 and 4 are sitting in the nation's financial sector in the form of unborrowed private-sector savings. If the government were to borrow those funds and spend them on self-financing infrastructure projects offering social rates of return equal to or higher than the ultra-low government bond yields typical of economies in Cases 3 and 4, there really is no "limit" to the size of the public debt because those deficits do not constitute a burden to future taxpayers.

## Deficit Spending as Bubble Prevention in Pursued Economies

If the government does not borrow these surplus savings when the economy is in Cases 3 and 4, those funds may end up chasing bubbles, which is by far the worst form of resource misallocation. This happens when fund managers are forced to consider other possibilities as traditional private-sector borrowers disappear. Desperate managers will eventually participate in bubbles, which offer great returns while they last. Even those who are cognizant they are in a bubble may join the party if they believe they can leave before the music stops playing. Of course if everybody thinks that way, no one will be able to leave when the crash comes because everybody will be sellers and nobody will be buyers of assets. This is another example of a fallacy-of-composition problem.

Indeed, the increased frequency of asset price bubbles during the last two decades may be attributable to governments not borrowing *enough* when economies are already in the pursued phase and demand for funds from the private sector is insufficient even with very low interest rates. Although this topic is outside the scope of this book, it may well be that pursued economies saddled with excess savings are susceptible to asset price bubbles because investors become desperate for higher yields.

Up to the end of pre-Lewis Turning Point (LTP) urbanization phase, financial sector was relevant only for the wealthy because most people were too poor to save any money. The wealthy, in turn, probably felt no pressure to lend if the return on lending appeared too low to justify risk. In other words, if interest rates fell below a certain level, lending simply ceased in what Keynes called the lender's liquidity preference. In other words, it made more sense for the rich money lender to just sit on cash rather than lend it at an interest rate that did not justly the risks involved. This may explain why recorded interest rates did not fall very much in historic times even when the economy was weak.

During the golden era, financial sector grows rapidly with millions of ordinary citizens joining the pool of savers. The sector also develops new and innovative products to meet the demand of increasingly influential institutional investors such as pension funds and insurance companies. At the same time, businesses have strong demand for funds to expand capacity and improve productivity. This means interest rates are quite high, and most saved funds are borrowed and spent by expanding businesses in a textbook fashion.

In the pursued phase, however, traditional demand for funds from corporate borrowers shrink while households continue to save for the uncertain future. This means interest rates will come down to very low levels as mentioned earlier, but unlike those wealthy lenders in the pre-LTP era who could simply sit on cash, a large number of today's fund managers working for financial institutions are under pressure to produce some returns at all times. Furthermore, many are now competing against market indexes. This means even if the absolute return of a fund manager is low, he will still be praised if his return was higher than that of the index. This means the notion of risk-adjusted-return is often pushed aside in order to beat the index in an environment of extremely low interest rates. These trends suggest that bubbles are easier to form in pursued economies than in two previous phases. Central banks implementing massive quantitative easing policies and zero or negative interest rates to reach golden era inflation targets are also reinforcing this trend.

If the pursued economies tend to encourage bubbles in the above sense, the governments of such countries may have to become more active borrowers in order to prevent their private sectors from squandering their precious savings on asset bubbles. Although governments sometimes produce white elephants, no government could ever hope to equal the misallocation of resources by the private sector during a nationwide asset bubble.

Once the bubble bursts, of course, the government must borrow and spend to keep the economy from entering the $1,000–$900–$810–$730 deflationary spiral. At that point, even white elephants are better than no elephants at all if they can keep the economy going.

Instead of wasting time talking about the "limits" of fiscal stimulus or public debt, policymakers in pursued economies should be setting up independent commissions to find public works projects offering a social rate of return that exceeds ultra-low government bond yields for the benefit of both present and future generations. If such projects also end up preventing bubbles from forming, so much the better.

## Economic Packages That Ignore Private-Sector Savings Surplus Cannot Succeed

Any economic stimulus package that does not take into account the fact that the private sectors in most advanced countries today are saving huge amounts of money in spite of zero or negative interest rates has little chance of achieving the expected results. Viewed from this perspective, there are only three examples of actual policies that were implemented since 2008 in the advanced countries that are based on a proper understanding of the situation.

One was the initial G20 fiscal package agreed to in November 2008—President Obama's $787 billion stimulus was part of this—which stopped these economies from falling into a deflationary spiral. The second was the warning sounded by former Fed Chairman Ben Bernanke and current Fed Chair Janet Yellen about the "fiscal cliff" (the dangers of premature fiscal consolidation), which saved the U.S. from a double-dip recession. The third was Japan's second "arrow" of Abenomics which was fiscal stimulus. All other policies, including the first arrow of Abenomics (= monetary easing), have failed to produce the expected results because they assumed economies in Case 1 or 2.

At the same time, many equity and foreign exchange market participants continue to operate based on the assumption of a textbook world, as noted in Chapter 2. Their actions in response to quantitative easing had a positive impact on the real economy, even though such moves were not justified by money supply or credit growth in any of these countries. It will be interesting to see how long this "ignorance is bliss" situation will last.

## Neither Monetary nor Fiscal Stimulus Is Cheap

Some may argue that while monetary accommodation via quantitative easing or helicopter money will leave excess reserves that must eventually be mopped up, a continuous reliance on fiscal stimulus will also generate public debt that must be paid back. Although the two outcomes sound similar, their impact on the economy will be very different.

First, fiscal stimulus works from day one in Case 3 or 4 by keeping both GDP and the money supply from shrinking. By preventing a decline in GDP, it gives the private sector the income (and jobs) it needs to repair damaged balance sheets. Government borrowing also keeps the money multiplier from turning negative in the face of private-sector deleveraging. That prevents the money supply from shrinking as it did during the Great Depression. Indeed, when the government is the only borrower, the effectiveness of monetary policy hinges on the size of its borrowings.

When GDP is prevented from falling, the damage to the banking system is also contained because those with income can still service their debts. Government borrowing also offers a destination for surplus savings, which in turn provides interest income to depositors, pensioners and financial institutions.

When the government is the only remaining borrower, government bond yields fall so low that many infrastructure projects become self-financing or nearly so if correctly chosen and executed. This means that even if the public debt is large, debt repayment problems may not arise if the projects themselves are generating enough income. Last but not least, undertaking necessary infrastructure spending when the economy is in Case 3 or 4, when interest rates are extremely low, provides massive cost savings for future taxpayers.

When the private sector regains its financial health and the economy recovers, the financial markets should be telling the government to change course via the signal of higher interest rates. At that point, the government should start raising taxes and cutting spending to match the increase in borrowings by the private sector. This is also likely to be a gradual process because the businesses and households who had to repair their balance sheets are not likely to resume borrowing quickly.

In contrast, monetary accommodation via quantitative easing, helicopter money or negative interest rates will have little impact on the real economy or jobs except via the actions of some misinformed foreign exchange and stock market participants who may push for a lower exchange rate and higher stock prices, believing that their economies are still in Case 1 or 2.

Lower exchange rates brought about by monetary easing, however, are a beggar-thy-neighbor policy at a time when many trading partners face the same problem. The U.S., which benefited from lower exchange rates when it became the first country to implement QE, is now suffering from a strong dollar and consequent bout of protectionism as other countries have undertaken their own versions of the policy.

Both President Draghi and Governor Kuroda have argued that the policy of negative interest rates is working because bond yields have fallen since it was introduced. In both cases, however, there has been virtually no pick-up in borrowing by the private sector, as shown in Figures 2.9 to 2.11 and Figure 2.14. And without an increase in borrowing, there is no reason to expect an expansion of economic activity from monetary easing.

The continued sluggishness in borrowing is to be expected—after all, if there were any borrowers left in the economy, they would have borrowed the money long before interest rates had come down to these levels. Unless one believes that the last 20 or 30 basis point decline in interest rates has somehow brought to an inflection point where a huge number of borrowers will suddenly line up to borrow money, it is difficult to argue convincingly that negative interest rates will bring about a recovery.

The fact that the central bank is crowding out private-sector *lending* to the only borrower left—the government—deprives pensioners, depositors, and financial institutions of interest income. Banks also suffer from the prolonged recession as more borrowers become unable to service their debts. The health of financial institutions and the livelihoods of pensioners are undermined even more by negative interest rates.

Precious time is also wasted when the entire policy debate is devoted to basically ineffective monetary policy. In the end, negative interest rates may only result in scared depositors, angry pensioners, and worried financial institutions without producing any of the growth in borrowing needed to lift the economy.

Under negative interest rates, some financial institutions may become so desperate for yield that they take risks they are ill-equipped to assume. Such investments are likely to end in tears for depositors and pensioners, if not for the institutions themselves. The benefits of monetary easing, therefore, are likely to be limited to a few mini-bubbles in certain asset classes (the so-called portfolio rebalancing effect) and their secondary effect on the real economy.

But if and when the economy recovers—for whatever reason—the central bank that has implemented these policies will face the massive task of selling bonds to drain the excess reserves (or having the government sell refunding bonds on its behalf) or sterilizing the reserves by paying interest on them. All of these would entail heavy costs for taxpayers. If either the central bank or the treasury sells bonds, yields are likely to go higher and become more volatile, which could adversely affect both financial markets and the recovery in the real economy.

Central banks that have implemented QE or helicopter money policies also cannot afford to be seen as falling behind the curve on inflation. That means they will have to start tightening much earlier than central banks that stayed away from these non-traditional easing measures.

The point here is that neither fiscal stimulus nor monetary stimulus is cheap, but a cost-benefit comparison shows fiscal stimulus to be far more desirable—if not absolutely essential—when the economy is in Case 3 or 4. This means when the economy is in the pursued phase or in a balance sheet recession, policymakers must mobilize the nation's best and brightest to identify and implement viable public works projects. Not only will this help the present generation, but it will also provide necessary infrastructure for future generations at the lowest possible cost. When the economy is in Case 1 or 2, of course, the opposite is true, and monetary policy should play a leading role in maximizing the economy's potential.

Harvard University professor Kenneth Rogoff recently argued that negative-interest-rate policies would work better if cash, or at least large denomination bills, were banned entirely[9]. But this is forcing people to undergo major inconvenience so that some economist's ill-conceived monetary policy remedy might work slightly better. Instead of forcing the public to endure such inconvenience—which could also hurt the economy through a loss of efficiency—economists should realize that (1) monetary policy worked well in the past because the advanced economies were all in a golden era characterized by strong private-sector demand for funds, but (2) it is not working now because these economies are all experiencing balance sheet recessions and are in the pursued phase of development with limited domestic investment opportunities.

It was Albert Einstein who said "stupidity is when you keep doing the same experiment but keep on hoping for a different outcome." Monetary easing policies such as zero interest rates, negative interest rates, quantitative easing, forward guidance, and inflation targets have all failed to produce results within the time frame indicated by their proponents. It is time for economists to question the fundamental assumptions behind these failed policies and to look for policies outside the monetary arena that may actually work.

---

[9] Rogoff, Kenneth S. (2016) *The Curse of Cash*, New Jersey: Princeton University Press.

# CHAPTER 7

# Europe Repeating Mistakes of 1930s

While some European economies have shown signs of life since the second half of 2016, the emergence of extreme-right political parties in many countries has been alarming. It is even more worrying to note that this is happening in economic circumstances very similar to those prevailing when similar groups appeared in the 1930s. It was already noted in Chapter 3 that Communism was a by-product of the extreme inequality created in the course of industrialization as an economy moves toward the Lewis Turning Point (LTP). In contrast, National Socialism or Nazism was a result of extreme economic hardship brought about by an inept policy response to a balance sheet recession. In other words, it was policymakers' inability to understand that their economies were in the other half of macroeconomics that led to that tragic outcome.

## The Failure of Economics in the 1930s and the Rise of National Socialism

When the New York stock market bubble burst in October 1929, all of those who had leveraged up during the bubble started paying down debt at the same time. This can be seen in the sharp fall in loans after 1929 in Figure 2.12. But since there was nobody on the other side to borrow and spend, the U.S. economy fell into the $1,000–$900–$810–$730 deflationary spiral and lost a full 46 percent of nominal GNP in just four years in what came to be known as the Great Depression. In 1933, the U.S. unemployment rate climbed over 25 percent nationwide and was more than 50 percent in many major cities.

The problem is that the economics profession never considered this type of recession until a few years ago because it never allowed for the possibility of a private sector that sought to minimize debt. The entire theoretical toolkit of economics, built over many decades, was predicated on the assumption that the private sector is always trying to maximize profits.

Because recessions driven by private-sector attempts to minimize debt had never been discussed by economists, the public was totally unprepared for the balance sheet recessions that hit them in 1929 and again in 2008. Even Keynes, who argued for an increase in government spending in 1936, seven years after the Great Depression began, failed to free himself from the notion that the private sector is always maximizing profits.

With no economists talking about balance sheet recessions in 1929, it did not occur to political leaders of the time that the government should mobilize fiscal policy and act as borrower of last resort. On the contrary, most economists and policymakers argued strongly in favor of a balanced budget.

When the recession started in 1929, both President Herbert Hoover in the U.S. and Chancellor Heinrich Brüning in Germany insisted the government should balance the budget as quickly as possible. The Allied Command, the victors of World War I, also insisted that the German government balance its budget and continue to make reparation payments. That was the worst possible policy one could have implemented in this type of recession because if the government stopped serving as "borrower of last resort," the $100 leakage from the income stream would be left unaddressed and the economy would fall into a deflationary spiral. Soon enough, the German economy fell into deflationary spiral that caused unemployment rates to soar to 28 percent.

Although the Americans had only themselves to blame for getting caught up in a bubble, Germany was still recovering from the traumatic hyperinflation that followed its defeat in World War I and was very much dependent on U.S. capital when the New York stock market crashed. The extent of its reliance on American capital can be inferred from the saying in Germany in the 1920s that train passengers in the first-class cabin do not speak German at all, those in second class speak a little German, and those in the ordinary cars speak good German. With American capital rushing back to the U.S. after the crash and the Allied powers demanding both a balanced budget and reparation payments, the German economy had no place to go but down.

The extreme hardship and poverty this mistaken policy imposed on the German people forced them to find a way out. With only limited social safety net and established center-right and center-left political parties largely beholden to orthodox economics and insisting on a balanced budget, the only choice left for the German people after four years of terrible suffering was to vote for the National Socialists, who argued against both austerity and reparation payments.

Thus the Nazis, considered by most Germans just a few years earlier to be a gang of hoodlums, ended up winning 43.9 percent of the vote and securing the chancellorship in 1933. It was not as if nearly half the German population woke up one morning and suddenly began hating immigrants and Jews. What happened was that they finally lost faith in established parties that remained beholden to fiscal orthodoxy. People voted for the Nazis because the established parties, the Allied governments, and the economists had proved totally incapable of rescuing them from the four years of horrendous poverty that followed the crash of 1929. The Nazis were swept to power because policymakers of that period failed to understand the balance sheet recession mechanics (the deflationary spiral described above) that led to so much suffering for the German people.

For better or for worse, Adolf Hitler quickly implemented the kind of fiscal stimulus needed to overcome a balance sheet recession—the construction of the autobahn expressway system was among the many public works projects undertaken by the Nazi party. By 1938, just five years later, Germany's unemployment rate had fallen to 2 percent.

This was viewed as a great success by people both inside and outside Germany—in contrast, the democracies of the United States, France, and the UK continued to suffer from high unemployment as policymakers were unable to think outside the box of orthodox fiscal consolidation. The stark contrast between the two made Hitler seem like an attractive alternative, and even those who used to look down their noses at the ranting lance corporal from Austria began to worship him.

Germany's spectacular economic success also led Hitler to think that this time the nation could win a war—its economy, after all, was in a virtuous cycle and generating plenty of taxes to support rearmament efforts, while the U.S., UK and French economies were in a vicious cycle of unattended balance sheet recessions with ever-dwindling tax receipts and military budgets.

That is what led to the tragedy of the Second World War. Nothing is worse than a dictator with the wrong agenda having the right economic policy. And the problem was made far worse in the 1930s by the inability of democracies to switch to the right economic policy until hostilities began.

Once war broke out, however, the democracies were able to introduce the same sorts of policies Hitler had implemented six years earlier. In other words, Allied governments started acting as borrower and spender of last resort to procure tanks and fighter planes, and the U.S. and UK economies jumped back to life, just as the German economy had done six years earlier. The combined productive capacity of the Allies soon overwhelmed that of the Third Reich, but not before millions had perished.

Every country has its share of extreme nationalists who blame immigrants and foreigners for society's problems. But their ability to garner enough votes and actually emerge victorious in Germany despite the region's democratic traditions and high levels of education suggests that ordinary people who traditionally voted for parties espousing democratic values switched allegiance in desperation. It has been observed time and again that when survival is at stake, respect for individuals and human rights is often thrown out the window. And that is when things can go wrong in a big way.

The Nazis' initial successes and the tragedies that followed were attributable largely to a lack of understanding of balance sheet recessions among the period's economists and policymakers. If Allied governments and the Brüning administration had understood the mechanics and dangers of balance sheet recessions and administered sufficient fiscal stimulus to fight deflationary pressures in Germany, most Germans would never have voted for a ranting extremist like Hitler.

If Allied governments had also administered sufficient fiscal stimulus to prevent deflationary spirals in their own economies, Hitler's success would not have appeared so spectacular by contrast. And if strong Allied economies had been able to present a credible military deterrent, Hitler might have thought twice about starting a war. The failure of economists in the democracies to understand balance sheet recessions in the 1930s therefore contributed significantly to the Nazis' initial success and all the human suffering that followed.

## History Repeating Itself Since Global Financial Crisis (GFC) in 2008

With 50 million lives lost in World War II, readers may think this mistake could never be repeated. Unfortunately, that is not the case, especially in Europe.

When housing bubbles burst on both sides of the Atlantic in 2008, the Western economies fell into a severe balance sheet recession, with the private sectors in these countries increasing savings or paying down debt in spite of zero or negative interest rates.

Figure 7.1 illustrates the financial position of the private sector in Eurozone countries that experienced housing bubbles. The figure shows that the private sectors in these countries were borrowing huge sums of money to invest in houses during the bubble (i.e., in financial deficit), but after the bubble burst they all began saving, some to a huge extent, in spite of zero interest rates (i.e., in financial surplus). That puts these economies fully in Cases 3 and 4 of Figure 1.3.

Since the bubble was in housing, a closer look at the household sectors of these countries reveals an even more dramatic change before and after bubble burst in 2007. For Spain and Ireland, where the bubbles were huge,

FIGURE 7.1  Private Sectors[1,2,3] in Eurozone Are Saving Massively, but Member Governments Are Only Focused on Reducing Deficits

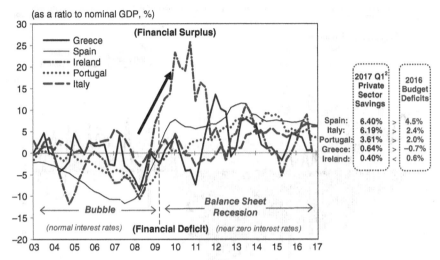

*Notes:* 1. Private Sector = Household Sector + Non-Financial Corporate Sector + Financial Sector. 2. All entries are four-quarter moving averages. For the latest figures, four-quarter averages ending in 2017 Q1 (only for Greece and Ireland, 2016 Q4) are used. Budget deficits in Euro area in 2016 are from May 2017 release by European Commission. 3. Except Greece.

*Sources:* Based on the flow-of-funds data from Bank of Greece, Banco de España, National Statistics Institute, Spain, The Central Bank of Ireland, Central Statistics Office Ireland, Banco de Portugal, Banco d'Italia and Italian National Institute of Statistics, and IMF

flow-of-funds data for the non-financial corporate sector are also included. As noted in Chapter 2, a white bar above zero in these charts (starting with Figure 7.2) means the household sector is increasing its financial assets, i.e., increasing savings. A white bar below zero means the household sector is reducing its financial assets, i.e., drawing down savings. Similarly, a shaded bar below zero means the sector is increasing its financial liabilities, i.e., increasing borrowings. And a shaded bar above zero means the sector is reducing its financial liabilities, i.e., paying down debt. The net number is shown as the broken line. This is not exactly the same as the household lines shown in Figures 2.6, 2.7, and 2.8 because it is seasonally adjusted while the latter are four-quarter moving averages.

FIGURE 7.2 Spanish Households Increased Borrowings After Dotcom Bubble, But Are Now Deleveraging

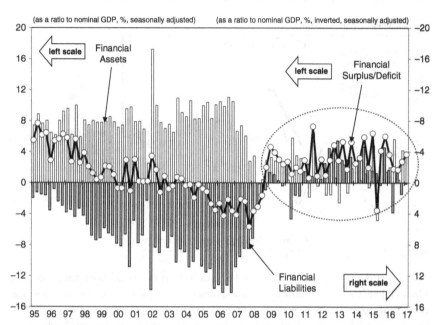

*Notes:* Seasonal adjustments by Nomura Research Institute. Latest figures are for 2017 Q1.

*Source:* Nomura Research Institute, based on the flow-of-funds data from Banco de España, National Statistics Institute, Spain

The Spanish household sector, shown in Figure 7.2, behaved very conservatively until the bubble hit and then began borrowing massively. When the bubble burst in 2007, not only did borrowing stop altogether in spite of zero and now negative interest rates, but the whole sector began paying down debt (shaded bars above zero) in a trend that continues to this day.

Although the Spanish economy has been doing better since the second half of 2016, it seems unlikely that domestic demand has grown substantially as long as the household sector continues to minimize debt and the Spanish non-financial corporate sector is not borrowing either (Figure 7.3). This suggests that the recent recovery may be due to increased competitiveness made possible by years of (painful) internal deflation, something that is discussed later in regard to the path of unit labor cost in Figure 7.10.

It is also worth noting that the white bars for the non-financial corporate sector in Figure 7.3 went below zero for seven consecutive quarters

**FIGURE 7.3** Spanish Non-Financial Corporations Have been in Financial Surplus since GFC

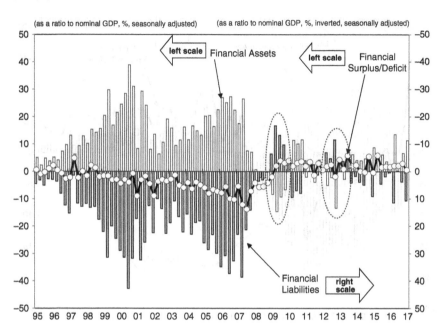

*Notes:* Seasonal adjustments by Nomura Research Institute. Latest figures are for 2017 Q1.

*Source:* Nomura Research Institute, based on the flow-of-funds data from Banco de España, National Statistics Institute, Spain

starting in 2008. White bars below zero are a bad sign in that they usually indicate a credit crunch (or a drop in income) that is forcing the sector to draw down past savings just to make ends meet. A corporate treasurer who has lived through a credit crunch usually becomes extremely averse to borrowing from banks, and this aversion can last for years. This aversion may explain at least some of Spanish corporations' reluctance to borrow since then.

The Irish household sector, shown in Figure 7.4, went through even more dramatic changes. Starting from a very conservative position around 2000, it went deeply into debt during the bubble. But after the bubble burst, borrowing stopped completely and debt repayment (shaded bars above zero) continued almost every quarter until today. This indicates that the supposedly strong performance of the Irish economy observed recently has little to do with the household sector. Since Irish non-financial corporations

FIGURE 7.4  Irish Households Increased Borrowings After Dotcom Bubble, But Are Now Deleveraging

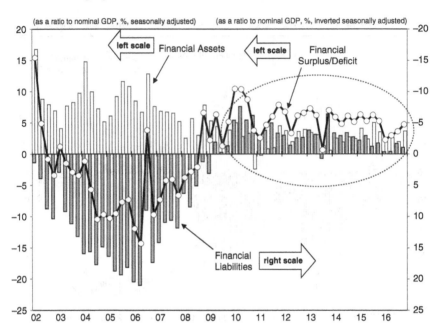

*Notes:* Seasonal adjustments by Nomura Research Institute. Latest figures are for 2016 Q4.

*Source:* Nomura Research Institute, based on the flow-of-funds data from Central Bank of Ireland and Central Statistics Office, Ireland

have been mostly net savers (Figure 7.5) except for the latest quarter, the recent growth is likely to be coming mainly from lower wages due to internal deflation (see Figure 7.10) and of the country's position as a tax haven.

Greek households (Figure 7.6) were not as highly leveraged as their Spanish or Irish counterparts even though Greek house prices also soared (Figure 2.4). Nevertheless, the sector has been paying down debt since 2010. This is a natural reaction for any sector caught in a bubble.

What is disturbing about Greece's household sector is that it has been drawing down financial assets since the end of 2009, as indicated by the white bars below zero. As noted earlier, white bars below zero are very bad signs in that they represent the withdrawal of past savings to make ends meet. Such withdrawals are typically triggered by a credit crunch involving troubled financial institutions or in response to a fall in income. With Greek GDP nearly 30 percent below where it was in 2008 (Figure 7.7), it is understandable that many Greek households are being forced to dis-save just to

FIGURE 7.5 Irish Non-Financial Corporations Have been Mostly in Financial Surplus since GFC

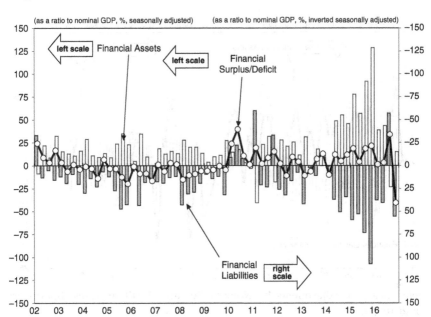

*Notes:* Seasonal adjustments by Nomura Research Institute. Latest figures are for 2016 Q4.

*Source:* Nomura Research Institute, based on the flow-of-funds data from Central Bank of Ireland and Central Statistics Office, Ireland

pay for daily necessities. Some Greek households might have indeed withdrawn euro notes from the banks in anticipation of the country's possible departure from the euro, but such moves should not affect the flow-of-funds data because both bank deposits and cash are financial assets. The point is that the low savings figure for Greece in Figure 7.1 is not because of strong investment but because of weak income.

In contrast to the peripheral countries mentioned above, Germany, the largest of the Eurozone countries, experienced no housing bubble (Figure 2.4). But that was because it entered a balance sheet recession in 2000 when the dotcom bubble burst. This can be seen from Figure 7.8, which shows that German households not only stopped borrowing money after 2000 but also started paying down debt even though the ECB took interest rates down to their lowest level in the postwar period. This change happened because German households and businesses, who are usually very conservative, apparently lost their heads over the Neuer Markt, the German equivalent of Nasdaq, which went up tenfold from 1998 to 2000

FIGURE 7.6 Greek Households Deleveraging But Also Drawing Down Savings to Survive

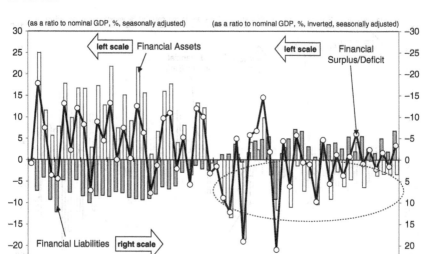

*Notes:* Seasonal adjustments by Nomura Research Institute. Latest figures are for 2016 Q4.

*Source:* Nomura Research Institute, based on the flow-of-funds data from Bank of Greece and Hellenic Statistical Authority, Greece

FIGURE 7.7  Greece's Nominal GDP Falls Far Below IMF "Forecasts"

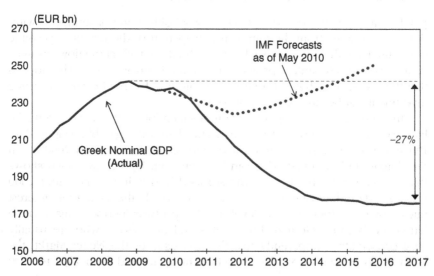

*Sources:* Nomura Research Institute, based on Hellenic Statistical Authority, Greece; IMF, "IMF Executive Board Approves €30 Billion Stand-By Arrangement for Greece" on May 9, 2010

**FIGURE 7.8** German Households Stopped Borrowing Altogether After Dotcom Bubble

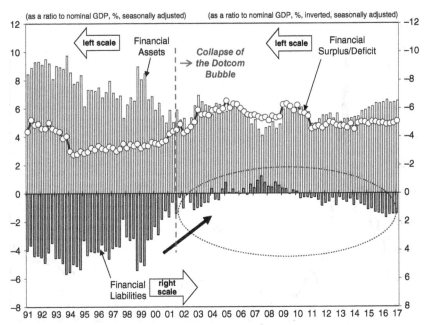

*Notes:* Seasonal adjustments by Nomura Research Institute. Latest figures are for 2017 Q1.

*Source:* Nomura Research Institute, based on flow-of-funds data from Bundesbank and Eurostat

(Figure 7.9)[1]. When the bubble burst and the market lost 97 percent of its value, the financial health of the German private sector was devastated.

The German private sector then went on to save as much as 10 percent of GDP and pushed the economy into a serious balance sheet recession. Not realizing that the German economy was in balance sheet recession and monetary policy does not work well in such recessions, the ECB promptly brought interest rates down to a postwar low of two percent to save the largest economy in the Eurozone, but to no avail. This inability to revive Germany's economy with record low interest rates led to the notion that the country was "the sick man of Europe."

The Germans, in turn, began to push for structural reforms known as Agenda 2010 when in fact their problems were rooted in the balance sheet. After all, it is difficult to explain the sudden shift in German private-sector savings behavior starting in 2000 (Figure 7.8) with structural issues that

---

[1] Neuer Markt changed its name to Tec DAX on March 24, 2003.

FIGURE 7.9 Collapse of Neuer Markt in 2001 Pushed German Economy into Balance Sheet Recession

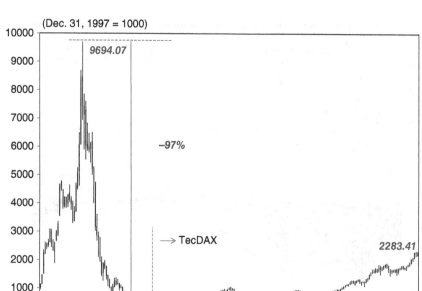

were in place decades before then. This fundamental misdiagnosis created distortions in Eurozone economies after 2000 and continued to do so after 2008, when Germans began demanding that other Eurozone economies implement the same structural reforms they had gone through even though the problems were due largely to balance sheet—not structural—problems.

While Germany was struggling with both balance sheet recessions and painful structural reforms, the Eurozone countries that had stayed away from the dotcom bubble and had clean balance sheets responded enthusiastically to the ECB's monetary easing. In no time, these countries were engulfed in huge housing bubbles. That allowed the Germans to export their way out of the balance sheet recession.

The fact that Germany was in a balance sheet recession and the rest were in housing bubbles opened up a large competitive gap between the two. Slow money supply growth in Germany with its balance sheet recession led to stagnant wages and prices, while rapid money supply growth in the rest of the bubble-ridden Eurozone resulted in rapidly rising wages and prices. Readers interested in seeing how the competitiveness issue evolved in the Eurozone are referred to Chapter 5 of the author's previous book, *The Escape from Balance Sheet Recession and the QE Trap*, for a more detailed discussion.

If the private sector as a whole is saving, someone outside the private sector must borrow and spend those savings to keep the economy out of a deflationary spiral. Unfortunately, in spite of dramatic increases in post-2008 private-sector savings, the concept of balance sheet recessions was still absent from economic textbooks, and powerful figures on both sides of the Atlantic started pushing for fiscal consolidation in a repeat of the 1930s.

In the U.S. this move was spearheaded by the Tea Party faction of the Republican Party, and in the Eurozone it was the Germans, led by Chancellor Angela Merkel and Finance Minister Wolfgang Schäuble, who took the initiative. In the UK, Prime Minister Gordon Brown understood balance sheet recessions and initially administered the required fiscal stimulus, but he was soon voted out of office in favor of David Cameron, who also opted for deficit-reduction efforts.

Fortunately for the U.S., policymakers from Ben Bernanke to Larry Summers recognized soon after the GFC that they were facing a balance sheet recession, the same economic sickness that had afflicted Japan. As mentioned in Chapter 2, they realized that with the entire U.S. private sector engaging in massive deleveraging in spite of zero interest rates, the government must administer sufficient and sustained fiscal stimulus to keep the economy from entering a deflationary spiral. They then used the expression "fiscal cliff" in their efforts to stop premature fiscal consolidation.

Even though the U.S. came close to falling off the fiscal cliff on several occasions with its government shutdowns, debt-ceiling debates and sequesters, it ultimately managed to avoid that predicament and is now doing much better. It is doing better because private-sector balance sheets are becoming healthier after eight years of fiscal support. Some businesses and households are actually starting to borrow again, as shown in Figure 2.16.

## Defective Maastricht Treaty an Invitation for National Socialists to Return

In the Eurozone, where policymakers did not understand balance sheet recessions or the need for government to act as borrower of last resort in such situations, one country after another fell off the fiscal cliff, with devastating consequences. The Maastricht Treaty that created the euro made no provision whatsoever for this type of recession and actually prohibited governments from borrowing more than three percent of GDP *regardless* of the size of private-sector savings. In other words, Eurozone governments are prevented from acting as borrower of last resort beyond three percent of GDP.

This is not surprising given that the Treaty was ratified in 1998, when no one outside Japan knew anything about balance sheet recessions. But when the housing bubbles burst in 2008, triggering Europe's balance sheet recessions, policymakers were left with no tools to stop the deflationary spiral, resulting in deep recessions and tremendous human suffering not unlike what the Germans went through in the early 1930s.

For example, the Spanish private sector saved an average of 7.15 percent of GDP in the eight years starting in Q3 2008 (Figure 1.1). But since the government was allowed to borrow only three percent of GDP, savings equal to more than four percent of GDP leaked out of the nation's income stream. Shockingly, the Treaty offers no advice on how a government should address this kind of deflationary gap because it was created based on the assumption that situations like Cases 3 and 4 in Figure 1.3 could never happen. It is this fundamental defect in the Treaty that is killing the Eurozone economies in balance sheet recessions.

In reality, weakened economies saw tax receipts fall and budget deficits rise to more than three percent of GDP. An increase in the deficit due to economic weakness is referred to in economics as an automatic stabilizer because the increase in government borrowing and spending forced by lower tax revenues helps stabilize the economy.

But instead of strengthening this function by increasing government borrowing to match the increase in private-sector savings, Eurozone governments were forced to reduce their borrowing to three percent of GDP. Instead of ending the recession, these government actions actually made it worse. The Spanish unemployment rate shot up to 25 percent, and many other countries suffered a similar fate. With center-left and center-right political parties alike insisting on the fiscal consolidation mandated by the Maastricht Treaty, average citizens, not unlike the Germans in the early 1930s, grew increasingly destitute and desperate.

This disastrous outcome was perfectly predictable given the Treaty's limitations. The author tried to warn Europeans in his 2003 book, *Balance Sheet Recession*: "Since fiscal stimulus is the most effective—if not the only—remedy for a balance sheet recession, as soon as the symptoms of balance sheet recessions are observed in Europe, the EC Commission is strongly advised to take action to free the Eurozone economies from the restrictions of the Maastricht Treaty. Failure to do so may result in Europe falling into a vicious cycle with an ever-larger deflationary gap. Indeed, of the three regions—Japan, the U.S. and Europe—Europe is by far the most vulnerable when it comes to balance sheet recessions because of the restrictions placed on it by the Maastricht Treaty."[2] Unfortunately, this warning went unheeded, and one Eurozone economy after another fell into a prolonged balance sheet recession.

The author then warned about the political consequences of this problem in his 2008 book *The Holy Grail of Macroeconomics*, arguing that ". . . forcing a country or region in a balance sheet recession to balance the budget out of misguided pride or stubbornness will not benefit anyone. Indeed, forcing an inappropriate policy on a nation already suffering from a debilitating recession can actually put its *democratic* structures at risk by aggravating the downturn."[3] This warning, too, went unheeded, and extremist parties have gained ground in all of these countries, as predicted.

Although none of the extremist parties has actually gained power as of this writing, the fact that a large portion of the population now supports them is a dangerous sign because it indicates that people are losing confidence in established center-right and center-left political parties. By May 2014, people had become so desperate that nationalist anti-EU parties shocked the political establishment by emerging victorious in European Parliament elections in the UK, France and Greece. The UK actually voted itself out of the EU in 2016, with some arguing that "the only continent that had lower growth rates than Europe was Antarctica!" These election results underscore just how many people are unhappy and distrustful of the European political and economic establishment.

The gains made by the Eurosceptics prompted both the establishment and the media to warn about a loss of momentum in the fiscal consolidation and structural reform efforts they consider essential to the region's economic revival. The powers-that-be have labeled the triumphant Eurosceptics "populists" and are desperately trying to paint them as irresponsible extremists.

All of the anti-EU parties that performed well in recent elections have elements of irresponsible populism in the sense that they blame immigrants for many of their countries' domestic problems. There is no reason why stricter controls on immigration would meaningfully improve the lives of people suffering from unattended balance sheet recessions (or other factors mentioned later in Chapter 9). In other words, these parties all have some elements of National Socialism in them.

---

[2] Koo, Richard (2003) *Balance Sheet Recession: Japan's Struggle with Uncharted Economics and its Global Implications*, Singapore: John Wiley & Sons (Asia), p. 234.

[3] Koo, Richard (2008) *The Holy Grail of Macroeconomics: Lessons from Japan's Great Recession*, Singapore: John Wiley & Sons (Asia), p. 250.

## Policymakers Need to Ask Why Eurosceptics Made Such Gains

On the other hand, the establishment's argument that it has pursued responsible policies deserves to be critically reexamined. Most countries in Europe fell into severe balance sheet recessions after the housing bubble collapsed, yet not a single government has recognized that and responded with the correct policies. To make matters worse, establishment policies have centered on fiscal consolidation, which is the one policy a government must *not* implement during a balance sheet recession. That policy mistake has had painful consequences for the people of Europe.

Moreover, the establishment has made the situation worse by mistaking balance sheet problems for structural problems. While every Eurozone country, as a post-LTP pursued economy, need to address a variety of structural problems to stay ahead of pursing economies, the recessions currently unfolding in Europe are due mostly—perhaps about 80 percent—to balance sheet problems, with structural issues responsible only for the remaining 20 percent or so. After all, it is difficult to attribute the sudden collapse of these economies in 2008 and their subsequent stagnation to structural factors that existed for decades prior to that. Furthermore, these economies were all responding correctly to conventional macroeconomic policies until 2008 (until 2000 in Germany).

As mentioned in Chapter 5, all advanced countries are facing two challenges: the fact that they are being pursued and the fact that they are in balance sheet recessions. Structural reforms are necessary to address the former, but fiscal stimulus needed to deal with the latter is more urgent when the deflationary gap brought about by private-sector deleveraging is so large. In some sense, the present situation is more serious than in the 1930s when policymakers only had to deal with balance sheet recessions.

Moreover, as mentioned in Chapter 5, structural reforms which often take a decade or more to produce macroeconomic results are no substitute for fiscal stimulus when the economy is in balance sheet recession. The political leaders, therefore, must make it clear to the voters that structural policies are needed to stay ahead of the pursuing countries, but fiscal stimulus is urgently needed to offset the deflationary pressures coming from private-sector deleveraging.

The situation also varies from one country to the next. In Spain and Ireland, which experienced particularly large bubbles, balance sheet problems are responsible for a greater percentage of the ongoing recession, while in Italy, which did not see a major bubble, problems are probably more structural in nature.

Regardless of national differences, that the Eurozone as a whole is in a balance sheet recession should be clear from the fact that net private-sector savings for the whole region amounted to 4.62 percent of GDP in 2017 Q1 (Figure 2.8) in spite of negative interest rates. This means that private-sector borrowers have not only disappeared from the scene, but are actually paying down debt or increasing savings. At such times the economy will not improve unless the government does the opposite of what the private sector is doing—i.e., unless it borrows and spends the unborrowed private-sector savings amounting to 4.62 percent of GDP.

Unfortunately, neither the European Commission nor European Central Bank (ECB) President Mario Draghi seem cognizant of the scale of private-sector savings. As a result, they continue to argue in favor of fiscal consolidation and structural reform while ignoring the need to put unborrowed private-sector savings back into the economy's income stream. This means that they are still operating on the textbook assumption that the Eurozone economy is in Case 2, where there are willing borrowers but a shortage of lenders. That assumption led the ECB to introduce LTROs, TLTROs (Targeted Longer-Term Refinancing Operation), quantitative easing, and a negative-interest-rate policy—all of which are designed to increase *lending* on the assumption that there are plenty of willing borrowers. Although some of these ECB policies did help the Eurozone economy move somewhat closer to Case 3 from Case 4 (but not completely, as explained later in Chapter 8), the actual growth in credit extended to Euro-area residents over the last nine years was only 1 percent, as shown in Figure 2.10.

The Eurosceptics have been successful in recent elections not because they are populists. They were successful *in spite of* their populist leanings because the established center-left and center-right parties were unable to break out of their policy orthodoxy. It was the establishment's bad policy choices that dragged the economy down and left residents no choice but to vote for the Eurosceptics. For people whose lives have been devastated by their governments' inaction (or worse) on the deflationary gap, the first step toward a solution is to free their countries from the fiscal straitjacket imposed by the defective Treaty—hence the surge in support for anti-EU parties.

If it was the populist aspect of these parties that had attracted voters in the recent election, their historical election performance would have been much better than it actually was. Their much-improved showing in recent polls can be attributed instead to the fact that, after waiting for eight fruitless years, voters realized the situation was not going to improve as long as the established parties remained in power. And those are exactly the circumstances under which Adolf Hitler and the National Socialists came to power in Germany in 1933.

It is truly ironic that it is the Germans who are imposing this fiscal straitjacket on every country in the Eurozone even though they were the first victims of a similar fiscal orthodoxy in 1929, when Allied governments imposed austerity on the Brüning administration. Those demands devastated the German economy and pushed its unemployment rate up to 28 percent, as noted earlier. But with established center-right and center-left political parties largely beholden to orthodox economics and insisting on a balanced budget, the only choice left for the German people after four years of suffering was to vote for the National Socialists, who argued against both austerity and reparation payments.

Perhaps Germans today are so appalled by the utter brutality of the Nazi regime that everything Hitler did is now automatically rejected. This kind of total repudiation of a person or an era can be dangerous because people will be naïve and unprepared when the next Hitler comes, since they were never taught all the *right* things he did to win the hearts of the German people.

With so many Nazi-like political parties gaining ground in countries suffering from balance sheet recessions but unable to do anything about them because of the ill-designed Maastricht Treaty, it is urgent that the people of Europe be made aware of this economic disease as quickly as possible. Without correct understanding of the disease, some member countries may find their economic crisis accompanied by a crisis in democracy.

Social safety nets today are far more extensive than in the 1930s, making modern democracies more resistant to such recessions and policy mistakes. Indeed social safety net themselves are a form of fiscal stimulus which did not exist in the 1930s. Nevertheless, people's mistrust and unhappiness could eventually explode if complacent politicians, economists, and bureaucrats continue to implement misguided policies.

## European Recovery Led by Internal Deflation

Economies do adjust given sufficient time. In spite of the misguided policies described above, some European economies have been doing better since the second half of 2016 as a result of painful internal deflation brought about by double-digit unemployment rates that lasted for so long. Figure 7.10 shows that unit labor costs of high-unemployment countries such as in Spain, Ireland, Portugal, and Greece have all fallen quite substantially from their peaks. According to the OECD, unit labor costs fell 14.3 percent from their previous peak in Greece, 6.52 percent in Spain, and 5.14 percent in Portugal. In Ireland, they plunged 33.6 percent from the peak, although this decline may have been exaggerated by discontinuities in Irish GDP data. With German unit labor costs rising 22.2 percent from their low in Q3 2007, the decline in unit labor costs in the peripheral countries made them quite competitive vis-à-vis Germany and the rest of the world.

Consumer prices in the Eurozone have increased by 10.2 percent since 2008. To the extent that declines in unit labor costs represent a fall in real

FIGURE 7.10 Euro Crisis Depressed Unit Labor Costs in Peripheral Countries

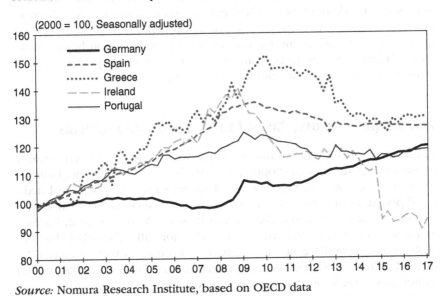

*Source:* Nomura Research Institute, based on OECD data

income for workers, it should come as no surprise that those at the receiving end of internal deflation are casting their votes for the Eurosceptics, the only parties to come out against austerity.

In this sense, some of the self-congratulatory remarks coming from (northern) European policymakers since the second half of 2016 give cause for concern. They are now saying that most countries in the Eurozone—with the possible exception of Greece—are well on their way to recovery, with both Spain and Ireland recording high growth rates. But the flow-of-funds data for those countries have yet to show significant improvements, suggesting the growth is not necessarily domestically generated.

Economists also have a bad habit of using the term "recovery" to mean a return of the growth rate to positive territory. For the public, however, "recovery" often means returning to where they were before. In other words, economists are talking about the rate of change while the average public is talking about the level.

When one looks at the level, especially in terms of real per capita GDP or industrial production, most countries have yet to recover to where they stood in 2008. Many people might have already exhausted their savings or unemployment benefits trying to make ends meet during the last eight years. Some in Portugal told the author they had exhausted their savings during the crisis and actually had to rely on friends and relatives to make ends meet. That means they could still vote for extremist parties if things go wrong or the established political elite appear complacent or irresponsive to their needs. Although none of the extreme-right parties has actually won power as of this writing, the fact that some of them received 30 percent or more of the vote means any mistake on the part of the establishment could tip the balance in their favor, with most unpleasant consequences. In that sense, this is no time to be complacent in Europe.

## Two Simple Measures Needed to Fix Eurozone Problems

Unlike many famous American economists who argue that the Euro was a disastrous experiment that should never have been tried, the author believes the Euro is one of humanity's greatest achievements, with bright and dedicated people from across the region striving for years to make it work. And it worked quite well before 2008, when most economies were in Cases 1 and 2. When they fell into balance sheet recessions after the bubble burst in 2008, however, the Euro ran into massive problems that were predicted by the author in his 2003 book because its architects (or its antagonists, for that matter) never made provisions for economies in Cases 3 and 4.

Since Cases 3 and 4 were never anticipated, monetary policy was the only tool policy makers had to address recessions. It was what Mario Draghi called "the only game in town." As a result, when Germany fell into a balance sheet recession in 2000, the ECB had to create bubbles elsewhere to save it. When those bubbles burst and other countries fell into balance sheet recessions in 2008, the ECB had to encourage bubbles in German real estate and other places with quantitative easing (QE) and negative interest rates in a feeble attempt to help the rest. But fighting balance sheet recessions in one part of the Eurozone by creating bubbles in other parts is no way to run a currency union.

The author also does not agree with those who argue that extensive fiscal union, together with structural reform and greater fiscal stimulus in surplus countries like Germany, is needed to make the single currency work. This is because the fundamental cause of the crisis is the Eurozone's inability to handle economies in Cases 3 and 4, not the absence of a fiscal union or lack of progress in structural reforms.

With regard to solutions, two modifications should be made to the Stability and Growth Pact. First, the Pact should enable governments to borrow more than three percent of GDP to stabilize the economy when the private sector is saving more than three percent of GDP at near-zero interest rates. This would allow the Pact to deal with both ordinary downturns and balance sheet recessions. It would also maintain the spirit of the original treaty by allowing member governments to borrow more than three percent of GDP *only* if the private sector is saving more than three percent of GDP at near-zero interest rates.

Second, Eurozone governments should introduce differentiated risk weightings or similar measures to encourage the excess private-sector savings of countries in balance sheet recessions to flow into those countries' government bond markets. This is needed because the self-corrective mechanism of economies in balance sheet recessions (see Chapter 2) does not function well in the European Monetary Union (EMU).

Elsewhere in the world, government bond yields typically fall to unusually low levels during this type of recession because fund managers who must invest funds in local-currency-denominated, fixed-income assets have no choice but to buy bonds issued by the one remaining domestic borrower: their own government. This rush to buy government bonds brings yields down to levels that would have been unthinkable when the economies were in Cases 1 and 2. Extremely low yields, in turn, not only encourage the government to administer necessary fiscal stimulus but also make many infrastructure projects self-financing.

However, the EMU contains nineteen government bond markets, all of which are denominated in the same currency. This means there is no assurance that Spanish savings will be invested in Spanish government bonds or that Portuguese savings will be used to buy Portuguese government bonds. Indeed, a huge amount of private-sector savings from the peripheral countries went into German government bonds (Bunds), pushing their yields to unthinkably low levels while raising the yields on their own governments' bonds. The foreign exchange risk that ring-fenced government bond markets and channeled domestic savings to their own government bond markets during balance sheet recessions in non-Eurozone countries could not do the same in the Eurozone.

This intra-Eurozone capital flight at the onset of the EMU turbulence in 2010 robbed many peripheral countries of their "fiscal space." Even though the private sectors in peripheral countries (except Greece) were all generating massive savings, their governments could not tap those savings to stabilize their economies. If peripheral countries in balance sheet recessions had had their own currencies, those private-sector savings would have lowered bond yields and allowed governments to finance the fiscal stimulus needed to keep them away from the fiscal cliff.

This problem of capital flight among the nineteen different Eurozone bond markets is unique to the Eurozone but was never addressed by the Maastricht Treaty that created the euro. Some unscrupulous speculators also made the situation worse by shorting peripheral government bonds while flooding the media with talk of so-called redenomination risk, i.e., the imminent disintegration of EMU.

This crisis was contained only because ECB President Mario Draghi came out and said he will do "whatever it takes" to defend the EMU. Although that helped protect one of mankind's greatest achievements from unscrupulous speculators, a formal mechanism is needed to address the instability caused by intra-Eurozone capital flight problems so that a similar crisis will not happen again.

This could be achieved by implementing measures to (1) keep savings from leaving the country of origin or (2) bring back savings that have already left the country of origin. One way to achieve (1) and keep savings from leaving is to assign lower risk weights to institutional investors' holdings of domestic government bonds relative to foreign government debt. In other words, institutional investors would be required to hold more capital against foreign government bonds than against domestic government bonds. This could be justified on the grounds that investors should know the risk characteristics of their home market best.

This way, Spain's excess savings would be encouraged to flow into Spanish government bonds and Portugal's savings into Portuguese government bonds. The resulting purchases of domestic government bonds would lower yields and provide peripheral countries with the fiscal space they need to engage in necessary fiscal stimulus.

The point is that any country in a balance sheet recession, by definition, should be able to self-finance the necessary fiscal stimulus if the excess private-sector savings that is causing the recession is channeled into its own government bond market. The low government bond yields that result should also make many public works projects self-financing or nearly so. If differentiated risk weights enabled this self-corrective mechanism to work in the Eurozone, then the member economies would be doing no worse than the U.S., which utilized this mechanism to the fullest.

## Misplaced Fear of Negative Feedback Loop

Unfortunately, the widespread but misplaced fear of a negative feedback loop between sovereign and banking risk has prompted Eurozone officials to make it more difficult for countries to use their own excess private-sector savings to fight balance sheet recessions. Indeed, the current push is to make it difficult for financial institutions to hold their own government's bonds. But such a fear is misplaced because the very origin of the negative feedback loop is Eurozone governments' inability to use fiscal stimulus to fight balance sheet recessions.

Because of this inability to use fiscal stimulus, when a debt-financed bubble bursts, Eurozone economies in balance sheet recessions are *forced* to implode, greatly exacerbating their banking sector problems. The banking problems arise not only because banks have lent money to participants in the bubble, but also because the imploding economy and falling incomes make it difficult for borrowers to service their debts.

When people realize that the government is unable to stop the implosion of the economy or the explosion of NPLs in the banking system, they become rightfully scared and move their money abroad, leading to capital flight and higher government bond yields at home. The higher yields then force greater austerity on the government, which makes the problems in the economy and the banking sector that much worse in a vicious cycle.

That increases the pressure on Germany, the recipient of savings from other countries (which are responsible for its rock-bottom bond yields), to engage in more fiscal stimulus. Yet instead of forcing a reluctant Germany, already at full employment, to do more, Europe should be allowing peripheral countries to use their own excess savings to restart their economies.

The correct way to address this negative feedback loop is to allow governments to fight balance sheet recessions with fiscal stimulus from the outset, so that there will be no vicious cycle. This can be achieved by allowing the government to borrow more than 3 percent of GDP when the private sector is saving more than 3 percent of GDP at near-zero interest rates. With no implosion of domestic economy, excess savings in the country will head toward its own government bonds with the help of favorable risk weights instead of toward higher-priced/lower-yield foreign government bonds. Once the peripheral economies begin to move forward, the funds that fled these countries for German or Dutch government bonds are likely to return, and that will mark the start of a *positive* feedback loop for these economies.

The option (2)—of recycling peripheral savings back to peripheral countries—is possible in theory but is likely to be difficult in practice. For recycling to work smoothly, capital inflows to countries like Germany would have to be borrowed by the receiving countries first and then re-lent back to countries like Spain in some sort of automatic arrangement. It has to be automatic so bond market participants would not have to worry about bond yields being pushed higher by uncertainties surrounding delays or insufficient recycling.

Net-inflow countries such as Germany would also have to quickly determine how much they need to borrow and recycle to Spain, Portugal, etc. But the politics of such a mechanism—including the question of how much to borrow and who will assume the risk—are likely to be difficult to resolve. If recycling is politically difficult, differentiated risk weights or similar measures to keep excess savings from leaving countries in balance sheet recessions should be introduced.

As of this writing, EMU unemployment is still 2.7 million higher than it was before the financial crisis. Coupled with the turmoil surrounding refugees, this is straining Europe to its political and economic limits. Amending the European treaties in the manner recommended here would not be easy, but the EU has already made numerous supposedly difficult procedural changes in response to EMU challenges, such as inaugurating the banking union or addressing the crisis in Cyprus.

The two straightforward but essential measures proposed here will put European economies back on track for a full recovery by allowing the countries to tap their own excess private-sector savings. That will allow the ECB to retract its ill-conceived policies of negative interest rates and quantitative easing, both of which have little impact when there are no borrowers but will cause huge problems when borrowers return. This should be good news for the Germans and many others who are concerned about the end game of the ECB's "crazy" monetary easing policies. The proposed measures will also free Germany from the pressure to implement more fiscal stimulus.

Simply put, the recovery of Eurozone economies does not require more fiscal union, more structural reforms, more quantitative easing, more negative interest rates, or more fiscal stimulus from Germany. All that is needed is to ensure that excess private-sector savings generated in countries suffering from balance sheet recessions are channeled to their own government bond markets and that governments can borrow and spend those domestically generated savings to fight recessions.

The refugee crisis would be far easier to address both politically and economically if the policies noted above had been implemented, providing jobs for the 2.7 million who have become unemployed. It is hoped that the EU, the ECB, and the German government will open their eyes to the reality of balance sheet recessions and implement these two simple measures before it is too late. If they do, Europeans will resume voting in a direction more conducive to the proper functioning of democracy. The UK may also change course if it sees the Eurozone regaining its economic health and demonstrating robust growth.

In the never-ending Greek crisis, Greece's GDP fell so sharply partly because the IMF, which was called in to help Greece following the deficit-fudging scandal in 2010, had no understanding of balance sheet recessions at the time (it does now). The Fund then forced the country to engage in draconian fiscal consolidation in the hope that that would win back the trust of its creditors. Although that would be the right course of action for a country in an ordinary fiscal crisis, Greece was also in a balance sheet recession, and the austerity triggered the $1,000–$900–$810–$730 deflationary spiral, causing nominal GDP to contract by nearly 30 percent (Figure 7.7).

As a result, Greece is the only country where the private sector as a whole has continued to run a financial deficit (Figure 7.1). This deficit is a sign of depressed income, not strong investment demand. This can be seen from the fact that the white bars in Figure 7.6 have been mostly below zero since 2010, indicating that the country is so poor that its private sector has to live off its past savings. There is no way such a country can pay its foreign creditors back.

The Greek government lost the market's trust when its newly elected administration revealed in October 2009 that the previous government had been fudging the budget deficit numbers and the actual deficit was much larger than reported. However, the IMF and the EU also lost their credibility in the eyes of the Greek people when the economic package they imposed on Greece not only failed to meet its own targets, but also ended up devastating the nation's economy. Now that both sides have made one massive mistake each, it is time for them to call it even and move forward.

## Three Problems with Milton Friedman's Call for Free Markets

When Milton Friedman, Nobel Laureate and champion of free markets, monetary policy, and small government, visited Japan in the 1950s and spoke to Kazushi Nagasu, an economist, he said: "I am a Jew . . . I do not think I need to tell you what kind of horrible deaths Jewish people had to face. The real drive behind my argument for free markets is the bloodied cries of Jewish people who perished under Hitler's and Stalin's regimes, and their message is that the best way to happiness is to have a mechanism that brings people together where states, races and political systems have no influence."[4]

Although many sympathize with Friedman and agree that a free market is ideal, he is wrong on at least three counts. The first is his assumption that markets driven by a profit-maximizing private sector can never go wrong. Every several decades the private sector loses its head in a bubble, something observed most recently in the pre-2000 dotcom bubble and the pre-2008 housing bubble. During a bubble, the private sector in a frenzy of speculation ends up misallocating trillions of dollars of resources which no government could ever hope to match. In other words, markets work well when businesses and households have cool heads, but not when a bubble has formed.

When the bubble bursts, the private sector comes to its senses and realizes it must restore its financial health by shifting priority from maximizing profits to minimizing debt. But the economy will fall into the fallacy-of-composition problem called a balance sheet recession if everyone does that at the same time.

---

[4] Uchihashi, Katsuto (2009), Shinpan Akumu-no Saikuru: Neo-riberarizumu Junkan ("The cycle of nightmares: the recurrence of neoliberalism"), updated version, in Japanese, Japan: Bunshun Bunko, pp. 88–89.

This is where Friedman made his second mistake. He argued that monetary policy—whereby the central bank supplies liquidity and lowers interest rates—should be mobilized to counter recessions. But once the private sector is minimizing debt to repair its balance sheet, the economy is in Case 3 or 4 and monetary policy is no longer effective. It stops working because the absence of borrowers means funds supplied by the central bank to the financial sector have no way to enter the real economy even at zero interest rates.

His third mistake was that he vehemently opposed the use of fiscal stimulus, which is basically government borrowing and spending, to fight recessions. But in a balance sheet recession, the government *must* act as borrower of last resort. There is no other way to keep the economy out of a deflationary spiral and give the private sector the income it needs to pay down debt and rebuild its balance sheet.

Friedman's overriding emphasis on small government and the supremacy of markets and monetary policy allows no room for government to act as borrower of last resort. But it was the failure of the Brüning government to do just that that paved the way for Adolf Hitler's rise to power in Germany in 1933. The failure of the French, UK, and U.S. governments to act as borrowers of last resort not only enhanced Hitler's reputation, but also prevented those governments from presenting a credible deterrent to his rapidly expanding military. To prevent the tragedy of another Holocaust, it is essential that the public be taught what a balance sheet recession is and how to fight it with fiscal stimulus.

# CHAPTER 8

# Banking Problems in the Other Half of Macroeconomics

When a bubble bursts, the economy typically faces an absence of both lenders and borrowers (Case 4). Lenders disappear from the scene because they lent money to participants in the bubble, many of whom became insolvent when the bubble burst. The resultant increase in non-performing loans (NPLs) erodes banks' capital, leaving them unable to lend. In fact, many lenders may find themselves effectively bankrupt.

## Two Externalities of Banking System

When impaired balance sheets leave banks unable to function fully, the broader society suffers in two ways. First, banks are at the core of the settlement system. Because everything from utility bills to college tuition is paid via the banking system, a breakdown here can have a devastating impact on the economy. Banks' second function is to ensure that saved funds are borrowed and spent, thereby keeping the economy functioning. A failure of this function will lead to the sort of $1,000–$900–$810–$730 deflationary spiral discussed earlier.

On the first point, banks have to make hundreds of thousands of payments on behalf of depositors for a wide variety of purposes every day. In making those payments, banks are merely *passive* executors of requested transactions. They have no prior knowledge of when a depositor will purchase something or what the price will be.

A bank also receives a large number of payments on behalf of depositors from depositors at other banks. But there is no guarantee that the payments it receives one day will match the payments it has to make to other banks that day. To deal with this daily but significant uncertainty, interbank markets and central banks were created to ensure that banks always have enough reserves to meet payment requirements.

The interbank market was created to allow banks with net inflows to lend their surplus reserves to banks experiencing net outflows. Since the aggregate inflows and outflows for the banking system should sum to zero, a fully functioning interbank market should keep the payment system from running into difficulties.

When a bubble bursts and many borrowers go bankrupt, however, banks begin to distrust each other because they are all saddled with large and growing portfolios of non-performing loans. Banks with net inflows then refuse to loan out excess funds on the interbank market because they worry the borrowing bank may go under without repaying the loan. Dysfunctional interbank market, in turn, threatens the continued functioning of the settlement system, which is crucial to the economy.

Central banks were created as lenders of last resort to address this vulnerability of the interbank market. If the interbank market becomes dysfunctional or when a bank faces an excessively large outflow, it goes to the central bank to borrow the reserves needed to make the payment. Since the advent of central banks, virtually all payments in the economy have been settled through accounts that banks have with the central bank. In the U.S. these are known as "Fed funds."

On the second function of banks, when a bubble bursts and banks incur losses from non-performing loans, sending their capital-adequacy ratios below the required minimum, they have to abstain from lending because their capital is not considered sufficient to absorb the risks associated with lending. They must also abstain from lending if their access to reserves via the interbank market is constrained or uncertain. This inability to lend is also known as a "credit crunch."

When banks are unable to lend the savings entrusted to them, the entire economy suffers because saved funds cannot re-enter the economy's income stream. Indeed, this lender-side problem can also trigger the $1,000–$900–$810–$730 deflationary spiral. These two lender-side difficulties, coupled with borrowers' debt overhang, throw the economy into Case 4.

These two externalities of the banking sector mean that the government cannot treat banks as just another private-sector business. That is why they are closely supervised by the government in any country. When banking problems arise, the government and the central bank implement the sorts of policies described under Case 2 in Chapter 1. For example, if the interbank market has become dysfunctional, the central bank is expected to act as lender of last resort to help banks experiencing net outflows.

If the NPL-induced credit crunch is so bad that it triggers a deflationary spiral, the government must inject capital into the banks to enable them to lend again. Japan recapitalized the banking sector in 1998–99 and the U.S. did the same in 2008, although these actions were extremely unpopular in

FIGURE 8.1 What to Expect When a Bubble Bursts

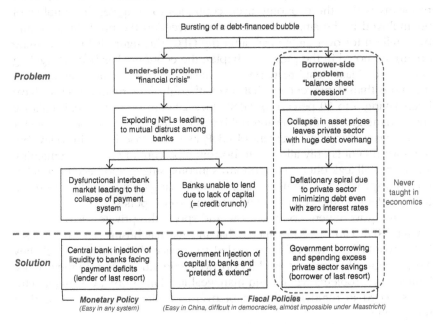

both countries. The point is that the necessary remedies are well known and, once implemented, will usually resolve lenders' problems within one to two years.

While central bank monetary policy is largely useless in helping borrowers, it is absolutely essential in helping lenders emerge from a financial crisis. Lenders' and borrowers' problems are summarized in Figure 8.1. Once the banking system resumes functioning, the economy moves from Case 4 to Case 3.

## Eurozone Banking Problems Still Unresolved?

When Lehman Brothers' failure triggered the global financial crisis in 2008, both the West and Japan faced massive banking-sector problems. While the U.S., the UK, and Japan implemented the kinds of measures noted above to address the banking crisis in the first two years, the Eurozone continues to struggle with these problems fully eight years after the GFC. The situation has improved significantly since the crisis peaked five years ago as a result of efforts by the ECB. However, Deutsche Bank, Germany's largest lender, came under the spotlight in early 2016, and Italian banks, among others, are reported to be still carrying large amounts of NPLs.

Needless to say, the primary cause of the Eurozone's banking-sector problems is that the economy itself continues to struggle: the number of unemployed in the single-currency zone exceeded the pre-Lehman figure by 4 million for over eight years after the GFC (this figure is finally coming down). As noted in the previous chapter, the economy has been struggling because the Maastricht Treaty prevents member governments from borrowing more than 3 percent of GDP even though their private sectors have been saving 5 to 10 percent of GDP since 2008 in order to repair balance sheets damaged by the housing bubble's collapse. But if the private sector in aggregate is saving 7 percent of GDP, as is the case in Spain today, but the government is only allowed to borrow 3 percent of GDP, the remaining 4 percent will leak out of the economy's income stream and become a deflationary gap. With governments unable to fill that gap, it is hardly surprising that problems in the economy and banking sector persist.

If the government could borrow and spend the private sector's excess savings GDP can be maintained. That means that businesses and households would have the income needed to service their debts even if they were technically insolvent. And if borrowers continue to service their debts, banks' NPL problems will remain manageable. Many borrowers might actually succeed in removing their debt overhang altogether with their debt repayments.

Japanese banks went through a similar experience to that of post-2008 European banks in 1997 as a result of premature fiscal consolidation. The Hashimoto administration opted for austerity at a time when the private sector was still saving more than 5 percent of GDP to repair balance sheets damaged when the bubble burst in 1990. Japan's economy promptly fell into a classic deflationary spiral starting in April of 1997 and contracted for five straight quarters. That proved to be the final blow for both borrowers and lenders in Japan, and a nationwide banking crisis erupted in October 1997. That forced the Japanese government to mobilize all the policy tools at its disposal, including a recapitalization of the banking sector, to overcome the crisis. Even with all the efforts, it still took until 1999, nearly two years later, for things to return to normal (this point is discussed further below with regard to Figure 8.4).

## Two Misunderstandings Regarding Banking-Sector Problems

Banking crises are frequent occurrences in post-bubble economies, but the Eurozone authorities also made a number of mistakes in handling the crisis that delayed the recovery in both the banking sector and the real economy.

In particular, they seem to have misunderstood the lessons of Japan and the U.S. and, even worse, have implemented policies based on those misunderstandings. On Japan, they appear to believe that the country's long economic slump occurred because banks and the government were unwilling to address NPL problems until the Koizumi administration came along in 2001, more than ten years after the bubble burst in 1990.

On the post-2008 U.S., they seem to think the economy recovered quickly because monetary authorities there required the banks to dispose of their bad loans quickly in accordance with market principles. As a result, they have concluded that banks must dispose of their NPLs quickly in order for the Eurozone economy to recover.

## Japanese Banks Began Writing off Bad Loans Early On

Many Western pundits over the last two decades have indeed attributed Japan's economic stagnation to banks' tardiness in writing off bad loans. But this view is completely mistaken, as I noted at the time. How this myth was created by certain self-serving groups is discussed later in the chapter.

The first political leader in Japan to raise the issue of NPLs was none other than Prime Minister Kiichi Miyazawa, who argued in 1993 that a quick resolution of this problem would reduce the future cost to taxpayers. Unfortunately, ignorant media pundits and politicians rejected Miyazawa's plan not only because bank rescues are politically unpopular, but also because they had no understanding of how to handle a banking crisis, since Japan had not experienced such a crisis since the war.

This rejection postponed the clean-up process by about two years, but that was the extent of the delay. Japanese banks began setting aside huge provisions against NPLs starting in 1995 (Figure 8.2). Consequently, some 80 percent of the losses from NPLs had already been provisioned against before Junichiro Koizumi became prime minister in 2001. It is simply not true that Japanese banks were slow to deal with their NPLs.

## Why NPLs Did Not Decline Even as Provisions Rose

In spite of the above, most overseas analysts continue to believe that Japan was slow to address its bad loan problems based on official data that show NPLs increasing until 2001 (Figure 8.3). The value of outstanding NPLs continued to rise on paper because the tax authorities, out of a desire to bolster revenues, refused to accept those loans as NPLs long after they had been designated as such by both the banks and the Ministry of Finance's Banking Bureau. Banks were therefore forced to keep the loans on their books and make provisions using after-tax earnings. This ridiculous state of affairs

FIGURE 8.2 Japanese Banks' Losses on Bad Loan Disposals

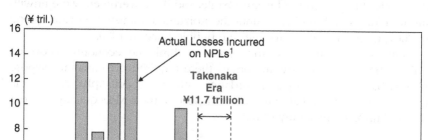

*Notes:* Includes commercial banks only; investment banks, insurance companies, and other financial institutions are NOT included.

*Source:* Financial Services Agency, Japan, "FSA publishes the status of loans held by all banks as of the end of March 2016, based on the Financial Reconstruction Act"

FIGURE 8.3 Japanese Banks' NPLs

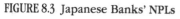
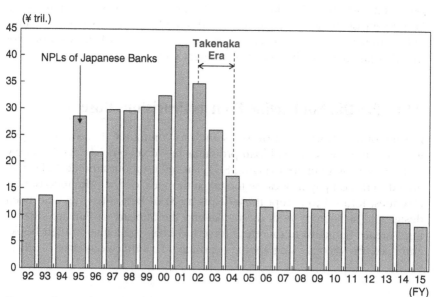

*Source:* Financial Services Agency, Japan

continued until the tax authorities finally recognized each individual NPL as a complete loss, a process that took years. The point is that Japan's NPL statistics did not reflect the loan-loss provisions already made by the banks.

Faced with such an unfavorable tax regime, the MOF came up with a "grand bargain" in 1998 to provide an incentive for banks to proceed quickly with NPL disposals. This agreement allowed Japanese lenders to count as capital (deferred tax assets) the taxes they had paid and would eventually recoup—and which would not have been due if the loans had been properly classified as NPLs.

This led to an unusual situation in which deferred tax assets increased massively after 1998 (Figure 8.4) and accounted for a substantial portion of Japanese banks' capital (Figure 8.5). The Koizumi administration's financial services minister Heizo Takenaka, who did not understand the tax issue behind this grand bargain, sparked turmoil in Japan's financial sector by demanding that banks reduce their deferred tax assets to levels in line with those in the U.S., in what became known as the "Takenaka Shock." He was apparently totally unaware of the differences in tax treatment of NPLs in Japan and the U.S. The point here is that Japanese banks did not delay their

FIGURE 8.4 Deferred Tax Assets of Japanese Banks Jumped After 1998 "Grand Bargain"

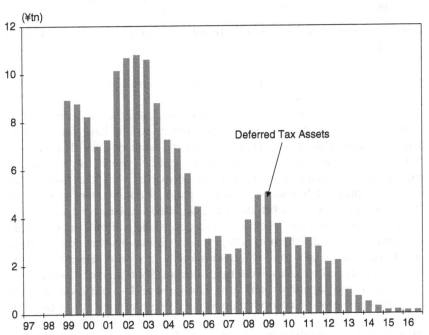

*Source:* Nomura Research Institute, based on data from Japanese Bankers Association

FIGURE 8.5 Deferred Tax Assets' Share of Japanese Bank Capital Skyrocketed After 1998

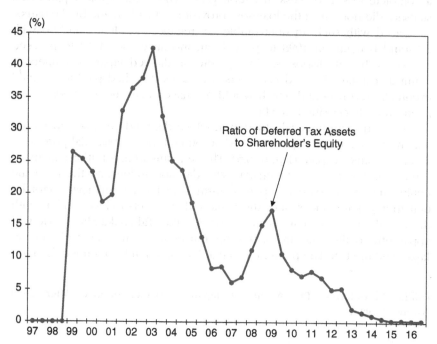

*Source:* Nomura Research Institute, based on data from Japanese Bankers Association

bad loan disposals to the extent suggested by some official statistics or by overseas commentators.

Takenaka and other "reformists" who dominated the media in the late 1990s also pushed strongly for bail-ins which would have forced large depositors and creditors to accept losses during bank closures. They argued that pressure from depositors and other creditors would force banks to improve their management. They even concocted the fake notion that Japan's adoption of bail-ins was an international commitment in order to ensure the country's blanket deposit guarantee implemented in 1995 is removed. Although some discipline from depositors is useful under certain circumstances, forcing them to accept losses via bail-ins was nothing short of national suicide at a time when so many banks were experiencing the same problem and were also suffering from rock-bottom credit ratings.

By then, no Japanese bank was rated above D-, and most were at the lowest rating of E in Moody's financial strength ratings[1] when ordinary

---

[1] Moody's stopped publishing these ratings in 2015.

FIGURE 8.6 Credit Ratings of Japanese Banks in 2002 Were Too Low to Implement Bail-ins (= Removal of Blanket Deposit Guarantee)

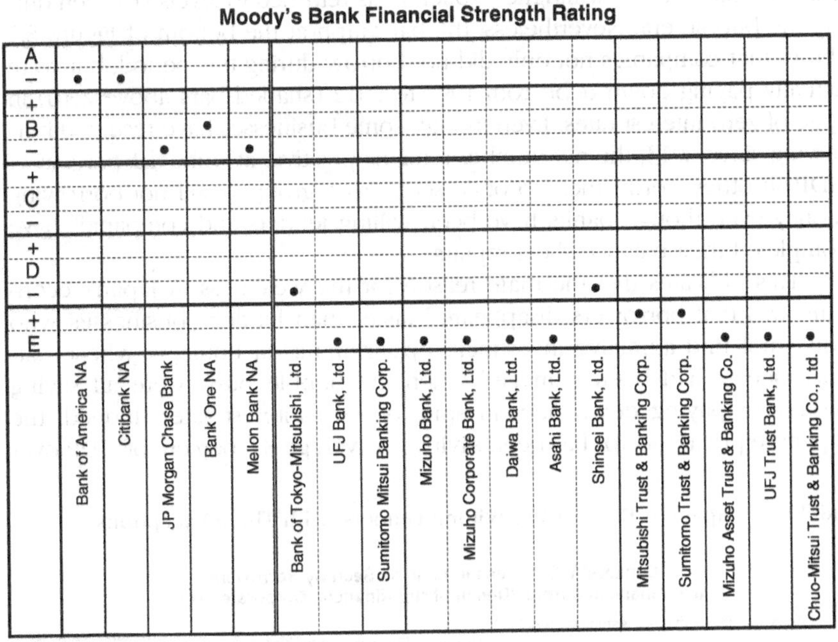

**Moody's Bank Financial Strength Rating**

| Bank | Rating |
|---|---|
| Bank of America NA | A− |
| Citibank NA | A− |
| JP Morgan Chase Bank | B+ |
| Bank One NA | B− |
| Mellon Bank NA | B− |
| Bank of Tokyo-Mitsubishi, Ltd. | D− |
| UFJ Bank, Ltd. | E |
| Sumitomo Mitsui Banking Corp. | E |
| Mizuho Bank, Ltd. | E |
| Mizuho Corporate Bank, Ltd. | E |
| Daiwa Bank, Ltd. | E |
| Asahi Bank, Ltd. | E |
| Shinsei Bank, Ltd. | D− |
| Mitsubishi Trust & Banking Corp. | E+ |
| Sumitomo Trust & Banking Corp. | E+ |
| Mizuho Asset Trust & Banking Co. | E |
| UFJ Trust Bank, Ltd. | E |
| Chuo-Mitsui Trust & Banking Co., Ltd. | E |

*Note:* As of November 1, 2002

*Source:* Moody's

banks are expected to be rated around B or higher (Figure 8.6). With all of Japan's banks carrying rock-bottom ratings, any closure accompanied by a bail-in would have created a massive panic among large depositors at all banks. This sort of madness was only narrowly avoided when the author convinced Shizuka Kamei, then chairman of the LDP's Policy Planning Committee, to postpone the introduction of bail-ins in December 1999. Interestingly, when Takenaka himself served as Financial Services Minister from 2002 to 2005, he did not implement a single bail-in.

## Real Cause of Japan's Slump Can Be Traced to Borrowers, Not Lenders

As for the impact of Japan's banking crisis on the real economy, the Bank of Japan has for decades been asking 10,000 large and small businesses for their views on the "lending attitude of financial institutions" in its quarterly Tankan survey (upper portion of Figure 8.7). According to this survey of corporate borrowers, Japanese banks have been willing lenders for most of the last 27 years except for three cases of credit crunches. Indeed, recent data indicate that bankers' willingness to lend has returned to levels last seen during the bubble era. Nevertheless, the bar graph at the bottom of Figure 8.7 shows that companies not only did not borrow during this period, but were actually paying down debt from 1997 to 2012 (shaded bars above zero) in spite of zero interest rates. Even though some businesses have resumed borrowing since 2013, the net number remains positive, at some 4.1 percent of GDP. In other words, the corporate sector as a group is still not borrowing money even though banks have been willing lenders and companies have completed their balance sheet repairs.

This indicates that the main reason for the weakness in Japan's economy was that borrowers disappeared faster than lenders: businesses who could not find attractive investment opportunities at home or whose balance sheets had been damaged when the bubble burst were all saving money or paying down debt in spite of zero interest rates. Indeed, the Japanese private sector has been saving on average 8.6 percent of GDP over

FIGURE 8.7 Japanese Banks Were Willing Lenders, with Three Exceptions

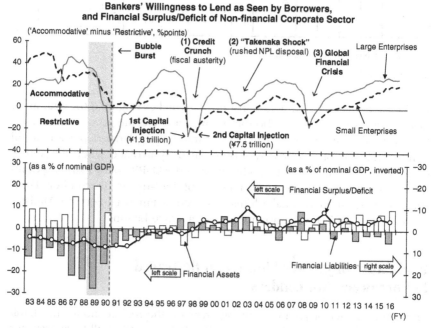

*Note:* Shaded areas indicate periods of BOJ monetary *tightening.*

*Sources:* Bank of Japan, *Tankan, Flow of Funds Accounts,* Cabinet Office, Japan, *National Accounts*

the last 20 years at a time of zero interest rates. Japan's economy has been stuck in Case 3 except for three brief periods in 1997, 2002 and 2008, when it found itself in Case 4.

When the private sector as a whole is saving money at zero interest rates, the economy will fall into a deflationary spiral unless the government steps up to serve as borrower (and spender) of last resort. It is precisely because the Japanese government has largely fulfilled that role for the past 25 years (the one exception being 1997–98) that the nation's GDP has never fallen below bubble-peak levels.

The IMF, which was surprised to learn the truth about Japan's banking problems after the author pointed it out, flew him to participate in a seminar titled "How Japan Recovered from Its Banking Crisis: Possible Lessons for Today" at the annual meeting of the IMF and the World Bank in Istanbul on October 6, 2009. The goal was to try to foster a proper understanding of what actually happened in Japan. Unfortunately, people will believe anything if it is repeated often enough, and in spite of the IMF's efforts in Istanbul, most people in Europe continue to argue that Japan offers a cautionary tale for Europe in terms of its reluctance to deal with bad loans.

## U.S. Rescue of Commercial Real Estate Went Against Market Principles but Led to Recovery

Turning to the post-2008 U.S., many European banking officials continue to believe that the U.S. authorities forced banks to dispose of NPLs quickly, when in fact they did just the opposite. In particular, European officials appear to be completely unaware of the "Policy Statement on Prudent Commercial Real Estate Loan Workouts"—commonly known as "pretend and extend"—that was implemented jointly by the Federal Reserve, the Federal Deposit Insurance Corporation (FDIC), and the Office of the Comptroller of the Currency (OCC) on October 30, 2009[2] in an attempt to rescue both the banks and the commercial real estate market.

Under this program, U.S. authorities took the highly unusual step of asking banks to roll over existing commercial real estate loans even when the loan's outstanding balance far exceeded the value of the underlying collateral. This request was crucial because by October 2009, commercial real estate prices had already plunged 40 percent from their peak (Figure 6.3), and the refinancing crisis for commercial real estate loans was so bad that many thought commercial real estate would be the next pillar to collapse after the residential housing market. A collapse of commercial real estate market at that juncture would have completely devastated the U.S.

---

[2] https://www.federalreserve.gov/boarddocs/srletters/2009/SR0907.htm

economy and its banks and made the recovery many times more difficult and expensive.

The "pretend and extend" policy for the banks, combined with President Obama's $787 billion fiscal stimulus package for the real economy, solved this problem and laid a foundation for the subsequent economic recovery. Figure 6.3 indicates very clearly that the "pretend and extend" policy sparked a recovery in the commercial real estate market. U.S. commercial real estate prices today are substantially higher than at their 2008 peak.

## Volcker's "Pretend and Extend" Was Effective During Latin American Debt Crisis

October 2009 was by no means the only time U.S. banking authorities had implemented a "pretend and extend" policy. A similar policy was adopted during the Latin American debt crisis which erupted in 1982, which left seven out of the eight largest U.S. banks technically insolvent and hundreds of others in very bad shape. Indeed, it was then the country's worst-ever postwar financial crisis. The author was personally involved in resolving this crisis as the Federal Reserve Bank of New York economist in charge of syndicated Eurodollar loans, the instrument U.S. banks used to lend money to Latin American borrowers. He can attest that the U.S. survived the crisis only because then-Chairman Paul Volcker announced a "pretend and extend" policy on the day the crisis erupted and kept it in place for a full *seven* years thereafter.

Specifically, Volcker instructed all U.S. banks with more than $1 million in exposure to Mexico to continue rolling over loans that came due even though the country was effectively bankrupt in August 1982. He also assured banks that the authorities would not treat those loans as bad loans (even though they were). This assurance was necessary to free the banks from the pressure to write off NPLs, which would have caused massive fallacy-of-composition problems and made the crisis far worse. This is because, with so many banks facing the same problem at the same time, there would have been no buyers for the NPLs dumped onto the market. The resultant free-fall of asset prices would have made the banking crisis even worse. This policy, which was also enacted jointly by the Fed, the FDIC, and the OCC, remained in place for seven years, giving U.S. banks all the time they needed to rebuild their balance sheets.

In 1989, after lenders had finally regained their financial health, the authorities brought the saddest chapter in postwar U.S. banking history to an end with the introduction of Brady bonds. While many have heard of the bonds, few are aware of the measures taken by U.S. authorities in the preceding seven years.

These two examples from 1982 and 2009 show that while the U.S. banking authorities seek market-based solutions when banking problems are limited in scale, that approach goes out the window during a systemic financial crisis, when a large number of banks are confronting the same problem at the same time. U.S. policymakers then opt for pragmatism above all else.

European officials seem curiously unaware that the U.S. adopted a policy of "pretend and extend" in both 1982 and 2009 to address systemic banking crises. This misreading of events in the U.S., coupled with a mistaken belief that Japan's prolonged slump was caused by an unwillingness to write off bad loans, has pushed European policy in an increasingly counterproductive, market-fundamentalist direction.

## Eurozone Suffers from Systemic Banking Crisis

For the Eurozone, which is facing the same systemic crisis that Japan confronted in 1997 and the U.S. did in 1982 and 2009, demands for higher capital and the rushed disposal of NPLs will only exacerbate the paralysis in the banking sector, with corresponding negative implications for the economy. Forced bail-ins in Europe are also scaring away potential providers of capital to European banks.

There are far fewer providers of capital when so many financial institutions are facing similar problems at the same time. That increases the cost of capital if it is available at all. But expensive capital may actually increase the pressure on banks. Faced with prohibitively expensive capital, banks will cut lending in order to economize on capital and achieve required capital-to-asset ratios, but that only exacerbates the credit crunch that is already choking the economy. The resultant weakness in the economy then aggravates banks' NPL problems.

The extent to which European banks are economizing on capital, and the resultant credit crunch, can be observed in Figure 8.8, which illustrates flow-of-funds data for Eurozone financial institutions. It shows that while the initial shock triggered by the Lehman bankruptcy was not that severe, the situation grew much worse in 2012 when the shaded bars went above zero and the white bars went below zero (the circled area). In effect, banks were reducing both assets and liabilities in order to economize on capital and enhance their capital ratios. But reducing assets was tantamount to a reduction in lending, otherwise known as a credit crunch.

FIGURE 8.8  Credit Crunch in Eurozone Financial Sector

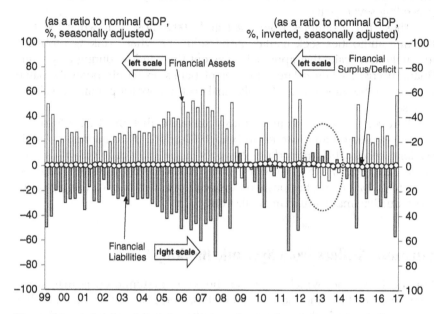

*Notes:* Seasonal adjustments by Nomura Research Institute. Latest figures are for 2017 Q1.

*Source:* Nomura Research Institute, based on the data from ECB and Eurostat

For some countries, this was indeed a devastating period for banks and their borrowers. Figure 8.9 illustrates the flow-of-funds for the Spanish financial sector. It shows that there was a massive contraction at Spanish banks from mid-2012 onward as they reduced financial assets and liabilities alike in order to economize on capital.

Irish banks were hit particularly hard when the nation's housing bubble burst. This can be seen from the flow-of-funds data in Figure 8.10, which shows white bars below zero and shaded bars above zero from mid-2010 through the end of 2013.

In Portugal, which did not experience a large housing bubble, banks were relatively calm until the Eurozone crisis hit in 2012 (Figure 8.11). The white bars then moved deep into negative territory and the shaded bars deep into positive territory until the end of 2015, indicating a huge contraction in Portuguese banking activity during this period.

Even in Germany, which had no housing bubble, banks have been shrinking their balance sheets since 2008 because many of them were caught holding U.S. Collateralized Debt Obligation (CDOs) containing subprime loans. German banks bought CDOs in response to the disappearance of domestic

FIGURE 8.9  Credit Crunch in Spanish Financial Sector

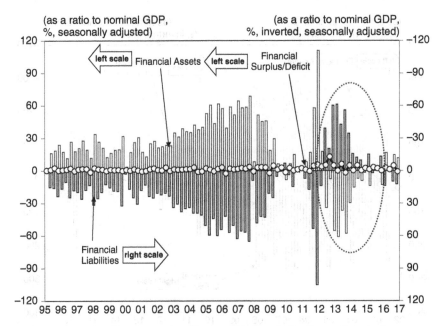

*Notes:* Seasonal adjustments by Nomura Research Institute. Latest figures are for 2017 Q1.

*Source:* Nomura Research Institute, based on flow-of-funds data from Banco de España, National Statistics Institute, Spain

private-sector borrowers after the dotcom bubble burst in 2000, as noted in the previous chapter. Indeed, the post-2008 reaction of German banks was far more violent than when they faced the collapse of the dotcom bubble in the Neuer Markt back in 2000. In most quarters from 2008 to 2013, the white bars were below zero and the shaded bars were above zero (Figure 8.12), a very distressing state of affairs that was seldom observed in the past.

All of the above is to demonstrate that the Eurozone was indeed suffering from a systemic banking crisis. The correct way to address such a contraction and the resulting credit crunch is for the government to relax capital requirements by postponing their imposition date and/or inject capital directly into the banks, as Japanese and U.S. authorities did in 1998–99 and 2008, respectively. The imposition of bail-ins was also totally counterproductive under the circumstances.

The Japanese and U.S. decisions indicate that if the policy choice is between ending the credit crunch and fixing the banks, the authorities must

FIGURE 8.10 Credit Crunch in Irish Financial Sector

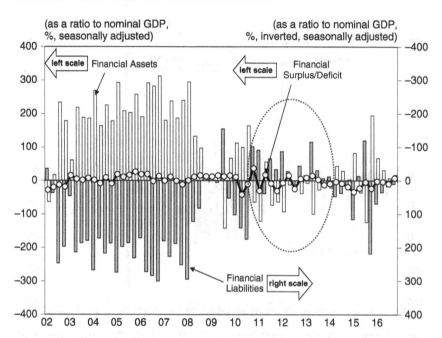

*Notes:* Seasonal adjustments by Nomura Research Institute. Latest figures are for 2016 Q4.

*Source:* Nomura Research Institute, based on flow-of-funds data from Central Bank of Ireland and Central Statistics Office, Ireland

end the credit crunch first. Allowing it to continue means that saved funds are not borrowed and spent, resulting in an ever-weaker economy. A weaker economy, in turn, makes it difficult for borrowers to service their debts, thus increasing banks' NPLs and undermining the effort to fix the banks.

Unfortunately, European banking authorities continued with this market-fundamentalist orthodoxy, simultaneously demanding higher capital ratios, bail-ins and quick disposals of NPLs. This resulted in a sustained credit crunch and a weaker economy, which eventually prompted desperate voters to opt for extreme-right political parties.

## The Right Way to Inject Capital

If capital is to be injected, it must be injected to a large number of banks at the same time in order to avoid the issue of stigma. The government must also ensure that the injected capital is used to support lending and not to

FIGURE 8.11 Credit Crunch in Portuguese Financial Sector

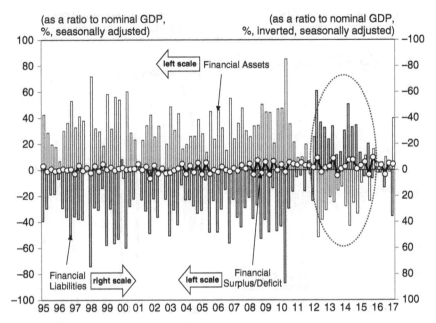

*Notes:* Seasonal adjustments by Nomura Research Institute. Latest figures are for 2017 Q1.

*Source:* Nomura Research Institute, based on flow-of-funds data from Banco de Portugal

write off NPLs. This is important because cleaning up NPLs and ending the credit crunch are two *contradictory* goals: the faster banks dispose of their bad loans, the more their capital will shrink, impeding their efforts to lend. While both are ultimately desirable goals, the authorities—given the choice—should strive to end the credit crunch first and allow banks to use their earnings to write off NPLs over the medium term. Moreover, a collective attempt by banks to sell off their bad loans when there are so few buyers will accelerate the decline in the value of those assets, creating a fallacy-of-composition problem as mentioned earlier in which bank balance sheets, instead of improving, only get worse.

When the author spearheaded the effort to recapitalize the Japanese banks starting in late 1997 via numerous TV and parliamentary appearances, he had to make sure the fresh capital was used to support lending and not to dispose of bad loans.

The author also recommended that NPL disposals proceed *slowly* in Japan to avoid the fallacy-of-composition problems mentioned above based on his involvement in the rescue of American banks in the 1982 Latin

FIGURE 8.12 Credit Crunch in German Financial Sector

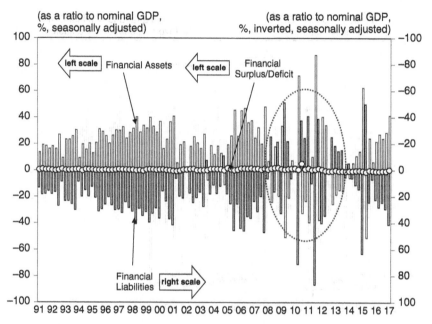

*Notes:* The assumption of Treuhand agency's debt by the Redemption Fund for Inherited Liabilities in 1995 is adjusted. Seasonal adjustments by Nomura Research Institute. Latest figures are for 2017 Q1.

*Source:* Nomura Research Institute, based on flow of funds data from Bundesbank and Eurostat

American debt crisis. This public stance made the author very unpopular with U.S. investment houses and their asset-stripper friends who sought to buy Japanese assets on the cheap. On the other hand, he received the support of Paul Volcker, who published a piece in leading Japanese economic journal *Toyo Keizai*[3] arguing that the government should establish a *speed limit* on the pace of bad loan write-offs to prevent fallacy-of-composition problems. His recommendation (and mine) is, of course, the exact opposite of what Eurozone officials are demanding of banks today.

As the examples above indicate, banking authorities face a minefield of contradictions and fallacy-of-composition problems when addressing a systemic banking crisis. But few people in the Eurozone today seem capable

---

[3] Volcker, Paul A. (2001) Jinssoku na Furyo-saiken Shori ga Hitsuyo daga Shori no Seigensokudo wa Daiji ("Prompt disposal of NPLs is needed, but so is setting a speed limit"), *Shukan Toyo Keizai*, June 23, 2001, p. 58.

of drawing a distinction between an ordinary banking crisis involving only a few banks and a systemic crisis involving a large number of lenders. In the former case, a market-based solution may be appropriate if the rest of the economy is large and strong enough to absorb the shock, but in the latter case, such a solution could easily result in massive contradictions and self-defeating fallacy-of-composition problems.

Unless these distinctions are drawn and the contradictions addressed, the Eurozone is likely to continue its current market-fundamentalist approach of more bail-ins, higher demands for capital, and faster bad loan disposals. Such measures are likely to result in a sustained credit crunch and sub-par economic performance until policymakers realize that a more pragmatic approach is needed to address systemic banking challenges.

## Ghosts of U.S. Asset Strippers Killing European Banks

The irony here is that it was mostly American asset strippers and their investment banking friends in the 1990s who championed the view that the Japanese economy was stagnating because its banks were not writing off their NPLs fast enough. They spread these rumors because they had come to Japan to buy distressed assets on the cheap but were unable to purchase them at attractive prices. Disappointed, they started telling the Western media and policymakers that the Japanese economy was not recovering because banks were not writing off their NPLs fast enough.

Western journalists in Japan not only had no knowledge of how the U.S. handled the Latin American debt crisis, they did not even speak Japanese. They therefore had to rely on Western financial institutions for their stories, since they never knew whether the person who picked up the phone at a Japanese bank would speak English. Not only did Western journalists fail to get the Japanese side of the story, but they were bombarded with stories from Western asset stripers and investment bankers, who insisted the Japanese economy was doomed until its banks cleaned up their NPLs. Those stories ultimately reached Washington, where equally uninformed officials began repeating the story invented by the self-serving asset strippers.

It was also quite astonishing to see so many high-ranking U.S. officials making the same argument without realizing that the U.S. also had to use the same "pretend and extend" policy when it faced problems of similar scale in the 1982 Latin American debt crisis. Indeed, the ignorance of U.S. officials, academics, and investment bankers (but not commercial bankers) regarding the "pretend and extend" policies of 1982 and 2009 is appalling. The only banking crisis with which they seem to be familiar is the 1989 savings and loan crisis, which was tiny compared with the 1982 Latin American debt crisis. Those same ignorant officials and economists then went on to lecture the Japanese (and other Asians after the 1997 Asian currency crisis) what to do in a banking crisis without knowing anything about their *own* nation's crises.

Today, Japanese banks are considered some of the healthiest in the world, but the Japanese economy remains slow. This indicates that those who blamed the banks for the nation's economic stagnation 20 years ago largely misunderstood the situation. The Japanese economy has been sluggish not because of a lack of lenders but because of a lack of *borrowers*.

The irony in all of this is that the self-serving pronouncements by U.S. asset strippers talking their book on Japanese banks twenty years ago has convinced unsuspecting Europeans that they must rush ahead with NPL disposals, further compromising their response to the systemic banking crisis. True to form, asset strippers and investment bankers are also telling European officials that they should push ahead with NPL disposals so that they can buy distressed European assets on the cheap. Since that is basically the job description of asset strippers, one cannot expect them to recommend a gradualist approach to bad loan disposals. But just as Paul Volcker warned the Japanese in 2001, European officials charged with looking after the broader economy should have the courage to consider the gradualist option during a systemic banking crisis.

## Too-Big-To-Fail Has Little to Do with Global Financial Crisis (GFC)

It should be noted that not all of the U.S. authorities' post-2008 policy responses were on the mark. In particular, the emphasis on "too-big-to-fail" and the orderly dissolution of such institutions missed the key lessons of the systemic banking crisis. An absence of provisions for an orderly dissolution of non-banks such as Lehman and AIG was not responsible for the severity of the GFC. The crisis would have unfolded even if there had been a textbook-perfect resolution of Lehman.

The crisis in September 2008 was not a result of Lehman being too big to fail. The problem was that so many other financial institutions faced the same problems as Lehman. When all institutions face the same problem at the same time, everyone distrusts everyone else because they know that others are in the same boat. And the problem was that nobody knew the value of their huge CDO holdings because the market for those securities had completely collapsed. This means that no one knew how big their losses were or whether they were still solvent. It was this uncertainty and mutual distrust that triggered the GFC.

Problems of this magnitude do not happen often, but when they do, the authorities must have the power to implement "pretend and extend" policies the way Paul Volcker did with the Latin American debt crisis in 1982. As noted above, the 1982 crisis engulfed a huge number of financial institutions around the world via their participation in syndicated loans. With hundreds of banks around the world holding claims on Latin American borrowers that were collapsing in value, the situation resembled the Lehman crisis.

To contain the crisis on the day it erupted, Volcker made a superhuman effort of calling the heads of central banks around the world and telling them to instruct their banks to stay with Latin American borrowers while maintaining their credit lines with American banks, knowing fully well that both were insolvent.

When the crisis erupted on a Friday morning (New York time) in August 1982, the 13-hour time difference meant that most people in Japan had already left the office. When Paul Volcker, after many emergency meetings and conversations with other central bankers, called BOJ Governor Haruo Maekawa, it was close to midnight in Tokyo, and only a handful of people remained at the Bank.

It fell to Mr. Shuzo Aoki, who happened to be still working, to respond to the call from the chairman of the Federal Reserve. To the harried and agitated Fed chairman, Aoki could only say that the governor had left for his country home in Karuizawa which was a four-hour drive from Tokyo in those days. And there were no mobile phones.

A flabbergasted Volcker yelled at the BoJ official, "If you cannot get Governor Maekawa on the phone in the next few hours, there will be no U.S. banks left on Monday!" Shocked, Aoki and his staffers worked desperately to find a way to contact Maekawa so he could call the Fed chairman. When he finally succeeded, Volcker basically told Maekawa that Mexico and American banks needed all the help Japanese banks could offer.

While Volcker in Washington was frantically calling foreign central bankers and asking them to instruct their banks to keep on lending to insolvent Mexico and U.S. institutions, the author and other Federal Reserve staff were calling hundreds of U.S. banks, urging them to continue lending to the bankrupt state of Mexico. The author recalls that the instruction from Washington at that time was: "Do not let a single U.S. bank with an exposure of more than one million dollars to Mexico leave Mexico." Although these efforts succeeded in avoiding a GFC-like outcome with tens of millions of jobs lost, the legality of the actions taken by U.S. authorities was perhaps questionable. After all, asking a bank to lend to a bankrupt borrower goes beyond the typical mandate of a bank supervisor.

Volcker had the courage to save the world first and only then worry about the legality of his actions. A lesser central banker might worry about overstepping his authority and desist from taking the necessary actions until it was too late. This problem seems to be particularly acute in the Eurozone, where national banking authorities must consult so many different institutions before taking action (witness the situation in Italy in the spring of 2017). Such powers should be explicitly given to the authorities so that they can act at the first indication of a systemic banking crisis, where many banks face the same problem at the same time.

Talking about too-big-to-fail is politically popular because no one likes big banks or fat bankers. But if Lehman were an isolated case, it would never have morphed into a global crisis that eventually claimed 8 million jobs on each side of the Atlantic. No "orderly resolution" of a bankrupt Lehman or AIG would have prevented that outcome, either.

What is needed is an explicit granting of emergency powers in a systemic crisis so that banking authorities can move to save *all* banks quickly. Lesser minds may object to such policies, citing moral hazard and the cost to taxpayers. But the extraordinary actions taken by Paul Volcker not only did not lead to a debilitating credit crunch or economic slowdown, but actually cost the U.S. taxpayer almost nothing, even though most of the largest U.S. banks were insolvent for nearly seven years.

Volcker's actions in 1982 also proved that bail-ins championed by Jeroen Dijsselbloem, the chairman of the Eurogroup of finance ministers, are by no means the only way to save taxpayers' money. Indeed, "pretend and extend" policies in 1982 and 2009 not only cost taxpayers nothing, but were crucial in keeping the economy functioning despite massive problems in the banking sector. And in both cases, the relatively strong economy made possible by these policies gave the banks the income they needed to repair their balance sheets over time.

What Europeans need above all else, therefore, is pragmatism. They could also use someone like Paul Volcker who is willing to take unpopular actions in order to save the economy, jobs, and taxpayers.

## Are Reserve Requirements and Money Multipliers Obsolete?

Putting aside the topic of NPLs for the moment, some economists have objected to the author's use of concepts such as reserve requirements and money multipliers, arguing that they are no longer useful in understanding monetary policy. Some even say they were *never* applicable. In particular, economists who believe bankers actually create money out of nothing tend to argue that reserve requirements and the money multiplier are outdated, irrelevant concepts.

This point is made by M. McLeay, A. Radia, and P. Thomas at the Bank of England (2014)[4] as well as by Z. Jakab and M. Kumhof (2015)[5] and R. Werner (2016),[6] among others. The latter two actually examined how banks account for money-lending transactions. Kumhof worked for Barclays Bank and Werner worked with Raiffeisenbank to conclude that when a banker grants a loan, he simply credits the bank account of the borrower with the amount of the loan without any corresponding debits. They then concluded that the bankers create money out of thin air (or with a stroke of a pen), that this action has nothing to do with the availability of reserves in the banking system.

But these economists failed to ask what happens when the borrower actually uses the loaned funds. When the loan is used to purchase a car, for instance, the car dealer must be paid. If the seller insists on cash payment, the borrower must withdraw the required amount from the bank that granted him the loan (Bank A) in bills and coins. This means Bank A must either have that cash on hand or get it from the nearest central bank office.

In the first case, Bank A will have to debit its cash holdings. In the second case, it will have to debit its account at the central bank. Since Bank A's account at the central bank is where its reserves are kept, this transaction effectively reduces its reserves with the central bank.

If the car is purchased with a check drawn on Bank A, the seller will deposit the check with his bank (Bank B). Bank B will then present the check to Bank A for payment, and Bank A will debit its account at the central bank by the amount of the purchase and credit the same amount to Bank B's account at the central bank. It is only after Bank B acknowledges that its account at the central bank has received the funds from Bank A that the transaction is considered complete.

What this means is that a bank *must* have sufficient cash or reserves at the central bank to make the loan. Otherwise, it cannot make any payments or grant any loans. The notion that a bank can create money out of nothing is therefore complete nonsense. Only banks that have plenty of cash or reserves can grant loans.

In response to this, the authors above would probably argue that reserves do not represent a constraint on bank lending because they are available from the central bank "on demand." Although it is true that banks

---

[4] Bank of England, Quarterly Bulletin 2014 Q1, pp. 14–27.

[5] Jakab, Zoltan and Kumhof, Michael (2015) "Banks Are Not Intermediaries of Loanable Funds—and Why This Matters," *Bank of England Working Paper*, No. 529. www.bankofengland.co.uk/research/Documents/workingpapers/2015/wp529.pdf.

[6] Werner, Richard A. (2016) "A Lost Century in Economics: Three Theories of Banking and the Conclusive Evidence," *International Review of Financial Analysis*, 46, pp. 361–379.

can borrow reserves from the central bank by posting high-quality collateral, both the availability of such collateral and the stigma attached to such borrowing (see below) discourage banks from relying on the central bank as a source of reserves except in emergencies.

In the U.S., reserves borrowed from the Fed by commercial banks are called "borrowed reserves," and this data series was used earlier in Figure 2.12. If the authors above are correct, borrowed reserves should have grown more or less in line with the growth in bank lending. Figure 8.13, which tracks borrowed reserves since 1959, indicates that not only was there no growth, but that borrowed reserves represented just 0.86 percent of total reserves held by the banks even before quantitative easing (QE). This means 99.14 percent of the reserves held by banks are obtained from private-sector sources who are willing to entrust their money with the bank, such as depositors, bond holders and shareholders.

The notion that a bank can create money out of thin air because the central bank is always ready to provide reserves "on demand" is therefore complete nonsense. Banks do whatever they can to avoid borrowing from the central bank. Consequently, only banks with plenty of reserves grant loans.

At the moment the loan is granted, there is no corresponding debit at the bank because the money has not moved. But as soon as that loan is used to

**FIGURE 8.13** Banks Use Borrowed Reserves only in Emergencies

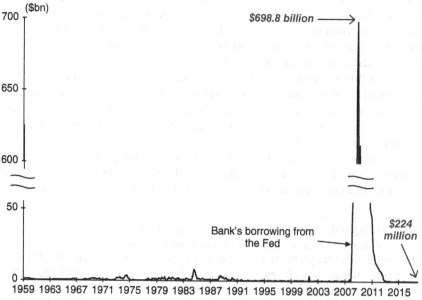

*Source:* Board of Governors of the Federal Reserve System

make a payment, the debit appears, either in the form of reduced reserves at the central bank or reduced cash holdings at the bank office that granted the loan. Since most if not all loans are used to make payments, the bank granting the loan must have sufficient cash or reserves to fund the loan.

For individual loan officers, however, the availability of reserves is not a major concern unless the bank is in serious difficulty or the requested loan amount is exceptionally large. This is because the reserve requirement applies to the *entire* bank, not to individual branches. As such, only those in the treasury department of the head office are closely monitoring the bank's reserve requirement. Others have no idea where the bank stands relative to its requirement. However, if the requested loan was large enough, even loan officers who would not normally check with headquarters would probably call the treasury department to make sure the loan could be funded.

Perhaps this rather silly confusion among academic economists could have been avoided if government regulators had required banks to have two reserve accounts at the central bank, one to handle general payments and the other for loan withdrawals. As soon as a loan is granted (but not paid out), the bank would move the amount of the loan from the general reserve account K to the loan reserve account L, and when the loan is paid out, it would be paid out from the reserves in account L. That way, there will be a visible debit to correspond with the granting of the loan for academic economists to see. In real life, banks make no distinction within the reserve account because debits from loan withdrawals are no different from hundreds of other withdrawals the bank has to process every day on behalf of depositors.

The vast majority of these payments are settled through the accounts that banks maintain with the central bank. When outflows exceed inflows, the bank's reserves with the central bank are drained, while reserves increase if the reverse is the case. Whether the bank has sufficient reserves or not is therefore a hugely important issue in running a bank.

Because banks earn next to nothing for processing a massive number of payments every day, they are allowed to earn interest by lending the deposits entrusted to them. While they have an incentive to lend as much as possible to maximize interest income, they may run into ugly payment problems if they lend too much. To ensure banks that do not lend excessively and jeopardize their role as payment processors, government regulators have imposed reserve requirements. This requirement is generally set at a low level because inflows and outflows tend to even themselves out over a period of time, especially at the larger banks.

Within this framework, large banks, which are expected to have full access to the interbank market, are expected to turn to the central bank for reserves far less often than smaller regional banks, which may have only limited access to the interbank market. When the author was at the Federal

Reserve Bank of New York and was involved in a project to familiarize the U.S. offices of foreign banks with access to the Fed discount window, money center banks (the category which included the domestic offices of foreign banks) were allowed to access the discount window up to three times per month, while small regional banks could do so up to six times each month.

If a bank exceeded that maximum, the Fed would send a team of supervisors to audit it and determine the cause of its reserve management problems. Since a Fed audit, like a tax audit, is not a pleasant affair, banks did their best to meet their reserve requirements. There was also a strong stigma attached to borrowing from the Fed because frequent borrowing implied the institution was poorly managed.

These maximums were considered guidelines, inasmuch as banks were granted almost unlimited access to the discount window in the case of a systemic crisis. As the upper part of Figure 8.13 indicates, the borrowed reserves increased to $700 billion during the GFC from about $200 million just prior to it. This 3500 times increase indicates just how dysfunctional interbank market had become following the Lehman Shock.

To borrow from the Fed, banks also had to post collateral to ensure that taxpayers' funds were not placed at risk. Although many economists with no experience in bank supervision, including those on the payrolls of central banks, the IMF, and the BIS, often talk as though reserves are freely available from the central bank at the going interest rate, any bank that borrows from the central bank faces a myriad of costs, and those who borrow too often will face highly unpleasant audits. This explains why borrowed reserves constituted only 0.86 percent of bank reserves even before QE.

More recently, the guidelines mentioned above have been relaxed for banks in "good standing" with the Fed. The Fed is also trying to remove some of the stigma attached to the use of its discount window for banks in good standing. But the "good standing" designation presumably means the bank is meeting its reserve requirements and other regulations most of the time.

In Japan, an officer at the Bank of Japan who is responsible for overseeing a particular bank will monitor the institution's progress in meeting its reserve requirements. When the bank looks likely to miss the target, she will make a phone call a few days before the end of the reserve maintenance period to ensure the bank makes the necessary adjustments.

It was mentioned earlier that only banks with sufficient reserves grant loans. Although most well-managed banks can extend loans most of the time, they will stop lending altogether when they feel their supply of reserves is exhausted or uncertain. At such times, banks put aside their profit-maximizing motive and stop granting loans so that they can earmark remaining reserves for the more urgent need of making payments.

Banks also refrain from lending when they feel that their capital is insufficient to absorb the risk associated with lending. Credit crunches were observed in the U.S. in the early 1990s following the savings and loan debacle, in Japan during its banking crisis from 1997 to 1999, and in Western economies after the GFC in 2008. Some of the post-2008 credit crunch continues today in many parts of the Eurozone. At times like these where many banks are involved at the same time, monetary authorities must act quickly to recapitalize the banks or, if there are borrowers, provide "fat spread" (= unusually wide spread between deposit and lending rates) to help the banks recapitalize themselves. They should also provide sufficient reserves as lender of last resort to make sure that the settlement system does not run into problems. The authorities should push the banks to dispose of NPLs only after the debilitating credit crunch has subsided.

In the post-2008 world, where central banks have flooded the system with excess reserves via QE, most banks have no problem meeting their reserve requirements. Indeed, the UK suspended its reserve requirement when the Bank of England embarked on its massive QE program in 2009.

But reserve requirements will become relevant again when the private sector finishes repairing its balance sheets and resumes borrowing. Indeed, some in the U.S. are already arguing that a higher reserve requirement might be needed—together with higher interest rates—if the unwinding of QE described in Chapter 6 turns out to be too slow to contain inflationary pressures as the economy recovers.

Indeed, if the economy's recovery turns out to be stronger than expected, the central bank is likely to mobilize every means at its disposal to remove or sterilize excess reserves. Such measures may include raising interest rates or raising reserve, capital and liquidity requirements. The central bank may also try to borrow those funds from the banks to keep the banks from lending them to the private sector. There may also be some arm-twisting via window guidance when push comes to shove. None of these measures is likely to be pleasant or pretty. But with massive excess reserves sloshing around the system, central banks will have no choice but to mop them up or sterilize them if they hope to maintain price stability as the economy recovers.

# Individually banks are financial intermediaries, but collectively they are money creators

So how does money get created in this system? It starts when the central bank buys government bonds or other assets from a private-sector entity such as an insurance company. When the transaction is consummated, the central bank (1) credits the account of the insurance company's bank (Bank E) with the amount of the purchase, and Bank E (2) credits the insurance company's account with the same amount. Since the money supply represents the aggregation of all bank accounts plus notes and coins in circulation, transaction (2) increases the money supply.

Because transaction (1) boosts the reserves of Bank E, the bank can grant loans to earn interest income if there are any willing borrowers. If a borrower with a high enough credit score appears, the bank will grant her the loan by (3) crediting her bank account with the amount of the loan. Since the money supply includes all bank accounts, transaction (3) will also expand the money supply. The amount of the loan is capped by the amount of the increase in reserves minus the larger of either (a) required reserves or (b) whatever sum bankers consider it appropriate to keep within the bank.

When the borrower then uses the borrowed money to buy an automobile from a car dealer, the dealer's bank (Bank F) will (4) credit the dealer's account by the amount of the purchase, which increases the money supply. Bank E, however, will (5) debit the account of the borrower by the same amount, which reduces the money supply. Transactions (3) and (5) therefore cancel each other out in terms of their impact on the size of the money supply. That leaves only the increase in the money supply due to transactions (2) and (4).

The transaction between Banks E and F is settled through their accounts with the central bank. Bank E's reserves with the central bank are therefore reduced, while Bank F's reserves with the central bank increase.

Bank F, which now has more reserves, will try to lend the money to earn interest income *if there are any willing borrowers*. If a qualified borrower shows up and borrows the money to buy furniture, the initial increase and subsequent decrease in the borrower's bank account will offset each other, but (6) the increase in the furniture store's bank account will remain, thereby increasing the money supply. This also means the furniture store's bank (Bank G) will try to lend the inflow of reserves *if there are any willing borrowers*.

This process will not continue forever because banks cannot lend out all incoming reserves—after all, the insurance company, car dealer or furniture store may want to withdraw money for their own purposes. The reserve requirement prescribes the minimum amount banks must set aside to prepare for the possibility of withdrawals. When the full amount of reserves supplied by transaction (1) is set aside for this purpose after all the lending, the process of money supply creation has reached its apogee.

The process will come to a halt much sooner if demand for loans from borrowers is insufficient or non-existent. For economies in Cases 3 and 4, where the private sector as a whole is either paying down debt or saving money, this money creation process will not only fail to engage but may actually go into reverse with people paying down debt, triggering the kind of money supply shrinkage observed during the Great Depression.

The ratio of total bank deposits created (i.e., the sum of transactions (2), (4), (6), . . . .) to the initial injection of reserves (1) is called the money multiplier, a term first used in this book in Chapter 2. This number will reach its maximum value if there is strong demand for funds (as is the case during the golden era) and all reserves are fully set aside for meeting reserve requirements.

But during the pursued phase, when demand for loans becomes very weak, the multiplier is likely to be a fraction of its maximum potential value. It may actually turn negative at the margin if the private sector as a whole is paying down debt. As long as the money multiplier is not at its maximum, loan officers should be able to grant loans without worrying about whether there are sufficient reserves.

If the multiplier is at its maximum but there is still unmet demand for funds, perhaps because regulated interest rates are too low, banks begin competing for deposits. This phenomenon has been observed in many countries during their golden eras before interest rates were fully deregulated.

This discussion should make it clear that while individually banks are financial intermediaries, collectively they are creating tremendous amounts of bank deposits because of their ability to lend money under the fractional reserve banking system. It also means the fractional reserve system is helpful—if not essential—in ensuring that saved funds are borrowed and spent, thereby keeping the economy going.

Finally, it should be noted that this process of money creation does not make society any richer. The increase in the money supply is matched by the increase in debt held by those who borrowed to purchase the car and the furniture. So the net increase in wealth is zero. If the borrowed money is used to fund viable investment projects that generate value, society will be richer at the end, but that is the result of the wise use of funds and not of money creation itself.

# CHAPTER 9

# The Trump Phenomenon and the Conflict Between Free Capital Flows and Free Trade

The disappointment and despair felt by many in the Eurozone is due largely to glitches in the Maastricht Treaty that have prevented member governments from responding correctly to balance sheet recessions. However, there is also a widespread sense of frustration among those in advanced countries over income inequality and stagnant wages, along with a general feeling of helplessness. At the same time, the establishment figures and "experts" responsible for the Great Recession are losing credibility everywhere. Even in the U.S., where the economy is doing better than most of its counterparts, Donald Trump, a complete outsider, was elected president at least partly because of his opposition to free trade and other establishment policies.

## Backlash Against Globalism in Pursued Countries

One reason for the frustration and social backlash witnessed in the advanced countries is that these countries are experiencing the post-Lewis Turning Point (LTP) pursued phase for the first time in history. As noted in Chapter 5, many were caught off guard, having assumed the golden era that they enjoyed into the 1970s would last forever. It comes as no surprise that those who have seen no improvement in their living standards for many years but still remember the golden age, when everyone was hopeful and living standards were steadily improving, would long for the "good old days."

The June 2016 Brexit vote, where older people tended to vote for an exit from the Eurozone while younger people voted to stay, suggests that the older generation is still hoping for a return of "great" Britain, when the country was second to none. In the U.S., too, the Trump phenomenon, which has depended largely on the support of blue-collar white males, suggests that people are longing for the life they enjoyed during the golden era, when U.S. manufacturing was the undisputed leader of the world.

Participants in this social backlash in many of the pursued economies view globalization as the source of all evil and are trying to slow down the free movement of both goods and people. Donald Trump and others like him are openly hostile toward immigration while arguing in favor of protectionism and the scuttling of agreements such as the TPP that seek even freer trade.

The real target of this backlash, however, seems to be the market fundamentalism—also known as neoliberalism—espoused by individuals like Milton Friedman. It is the belief that individuals and companies should be allowed to do anything—so long as it does not violate the law—in the pursuit of profit. This view also holds that whatever increases the freedom of the private sector will result in a better allocation of resources. According to this view, companies should invest in countries like China and Mexico as long as it is more profitable than investing in the U.S., and that they should strive to reduce the number of high-cost employees in their home countries as long as that enhances the bottom line.

President Trump, on the other hand, has openly opposed U.S. businesses' decision to fire workers at home and replace them with less expensive labor abroad. He has gone so far as to describe executives who take such actions as "getting away with murder." The fact that some major corporations in the U.S. responded almost immediately to Mr. Trump's request not to move factories abroad is a sign that they realize this is a social issue, not a legal issue. If it were a legal issue, they could simply hire an army of lawyers to fight the pressure from Washington. But such a response would backfire if this is viewed as a social issue. It is indeed unprecedented for major U.S. corporations to alter their business plans solely on the basis of tweets by a man who, at the time, had not even become president.

This unusual turn of events may be a result of corporate executives waking up to the deepening social backlash against their past behavior, something that was underscored by Trump's ascendancy. Some of them may feel guilty about having closed so many domestic factories and moved production to China and Mexico solely in order to boost shareholder returns. No matter how loud the calls for enhancing shareholder returns, executives are bound to feel pangs of conscience for firing people they worked together with for years or even decades simply to enrich faceless shareholders who may unload their shares in the company tomorrow.

The cost of neoliberal policies is that society as a whole must look after the "victims" of such policies. This is not a major problem as long as there are relatively few "losers." Indeed, economists have traditionally argued that while free trade creates both winners and losers within the same country, it offers significant overall welfare gains for both trading partners because the gains of the winners are greater than the losses of the losers. In other words, there should be more winners than losers from free trade. The task for policymakers, according to this view, is to ensure that the losers are looked after so that free trade can continue to benefit the entire society.

This conclusion, however, is based on one key assumption: that imports and exports will be largely balanced as free trade expands. When—as in the U.S. during the past 30 years—that assumption does not hold and a nation continues to run massive trade deficits, free trade may produce far more losers than theory would suggest. With the U.S. running a trade deficit of almost $740bn a year, or about four percent of GDP, there were apparently enough losers from free trade to put the protectionist Donald Trump into the White House. The fact that Hillary Clinton was also nominated to be the Democratic Party's candidate for president in the arena full of banners saying "No to TPP" indicates that the social backlash has grown very large indeed.

Trade and current account deficits are important because they represent a transfer of income from one country to another. Exports are added and imports subtracted when calculating a country's gross national product or GDP. The U.S. current account deficit amounted to some 2.6 percent of GDP in 2016, and the UK ran a deficit totaling more than 4.3 percent of GDP. This means that a great deal of income (and employment) was transferred from these countries to their trading partners.

Deficit countries receive goods made by the surplus countries, so it is not a total loss. But with the IMF and others warning countries for decades that an external deficit of more than 3 percent of GDP is unhealthy, it is easy to see why Donald Trump and other policymakers in deficit countries are concerned about external imbalances. Indeed, the size of the social backlash in some pursued countries is now so large that it is beginning to threaten not only free trade but also the very foundations of democracy.

On the other hand, outright protectionism is likely to benefit the working class in the short term only. In the long run, history has repeatedly shown that protected industries always fall behind on competitiveness and technological advances, which means the economy will stagnate and be overtaken by more dynamic competitors. A nation that relies on protectionism to save jobs may therefore drop off the list of "advanced" countries.

This does not mean that free trade as practiced since 1945 and globalism in general have no problems. They both have major issues, but these can be addressed if properly understood. A correct understanding is important here because even though increasing imports is the most visible feature of an economy in a pursued phase, trade deficits and the plight of workers displaced by imports have been made far worse by the free movement of capital since 1980, a point that will be revisited after the inadequacies of the current WTO-based system of free trade are discussed.

## GATT and WTO Rules Ended up Favoring Latecomers

The problem with the General Agreement on Tariffs and Trade (GATT) and the current World Trade Organization (WTO) is that they do not provide sufficient safeguards for existing members when a country in a different stage of economic development joins the system at a later date. Both GATT and WTO, which are at the heart of the postwar free-trade regime, are based on two fundamental principles: most-favored-nation treatment, under which treatment granted to one trading partner must be granted to all, and national treatment, under which imported products must be treated the same as domestically produced goods.

This is a very generous system in the sense that it allows a country to set tariff rates according to its national priorities as long as those rates apply to all member countries. For example, a country may set high tariffs on automobile imports as long as those tariffs apply to automobile imports from all member countries.

It could also be argued that this system is unfair to automakers and their employees in countries that happen to levy low or no import duties on motor vehicles. For example, if country A, which is running a large trade surplus with country B, has higher tariff rates on imports from country B than country B has on imports from country A, people in country B will naturally get upset. It is this point that Trump made with respect to China and others that are running large and persistent trade surpluses with the U.S. while imposing much higher tariffs on U.S.-made goods than the U.S. charges on their exports.

How did this (in a sense) unfair trade framework come to be? When the GATT was created in 1947 after World War II, its members were all developed countries of the West with similar levels of economic development. In other words, countries with similar wages and productivity levels were lowering tariffs among themselves to facilitate trade. At the same time, the U.S. was dominant in all sectors and was running massive trade surpluses with the rest of the war-torn world. And rebuilding the devastated economies of Japan and Western Europe was a key priority for the U.S. as it faced the Soviet threat.

Along with the GATT, the U.S. also created a number of international "public goods" around this time in an attempt to prevent another world war. These included the Bretton Woods currency regime, the United Nations, the IMF, and the World Bank. Of these, the one that made the greatest long-term contribution to postwar peace and prosperity was the free-trade framework made possible by the GATT, as noted in Chapter 3.

## Adoption of Free Trade Marked End of Imperialism. . . But Also Led to Stagnant Incomes for U.S. Workers

Before the GATT, import duties were decided in bilateral trade negotiations. This prompted countries to erect numerous barriers to trade, and some even used multiple exchange rates for different product lines in an attempt to gain the upper hand in trade negotiations. In this world, the dominant principle was the imperialist view that maximizing the geographic scope of national power was essential for economic development. This principle was also the cause of countless wars throughout human history.

Once the U.S. opened up its massive markets to the world after 1945 and the GATT-based system of free trade was adopted, nations belonging to this system found that it was possible to achieve economic growth without territorial expansion as long as they could produce competitive products. The first countries to recognize this were the vanquished nations of Japan and West Germany, which then decided to devote their best people to developing globally competitive products. The two countries soon overtook the victorious UK and France to become the world's second- and third-largest economies as a result. They were subsequently followed by Taiwan, South Korea, and ultimately China, as noted in Chapter 4.

By the end of the 1970s, however, the West began losing its ability to compete with Japanese firms as the latter overtook their U.S. and European rivals in many sectors, including home appliances, shipbuilding, steel, and automobiles. This led to stagnant income growth and disappearing job opportunities for Western workers.

When Japan joined the GATT in 1963, it still had many tariff and non-tariff trade barriers. In other words, while Western nations had been steadily reducing their own trade barriers, they were suddenly confronted with an upstart from Asia that still had many barriers in place. But as long as Japan's maximum tariff rates were falling as negotiated and the remaining barriers applied to all GATT members equally, GATT members who had opened their markets earlier could do little under the agreement's framework to force Japan to open its market (the same problem resurfaced when China joined the WTO 38 years later). That led to much frustration among Japan's trading partners and sparked ugly trade frictions between the West and Japan.

When U.S.–Japan trade frictions began to flare up in the 1970s, however, exchange rates still responded correctly to trade imbalances. In other words, when Japanese exports to the U.S. outstripped U.S. exports to Japan, there were more Japanese exporters selling dollars and buying yen to pay employees and suppliers in Japan than there were U.S. exporters selling yen and buying dollars to pay employees and suppliers in the U.S.

Since foreign exchange market participants in those days consisted mostly of exporters and importers, excess demand for yen versus the dollar caused the yen to strengthen against the dollar. That, in turn, made Japanese products less competitive in the U.S. As a result, trade frictions between the U.S. and Japan were prevented from growing any worse than they did because the dollar fell from ¥360 in mid-1971 to less than ¥200 in 1978 in response to widening Japanese trade surpluses with the U.S.

But this arrangement, in which the foreign exchange market acted as a trade equalizer, broke down with financial liberalization, which began in the U.S. with the Monetary Control Act of 1980. Japan's efforts to liberalize capital flows based on the misguided U.S. pressure explained below started the same year. European countries also began allowing the free movement of capital around this time.

These changes prompted huge capital outflows from Japan as local investors sought higher-yielding U.S. Treasury securities. Since Japanese investors needed dollars to buy Treasuries, their demand for dollars in the currency market outstripped the supply of dollars from Japanese exporters and pushed the yen back to ¥280 against the dollar. This rekindled the two countries' trade problems, because few U.S. manufacturers were competitive vis-à-vis the Japanese at that exchange rate.

When calls for protectionism engulfed Washington, President Ronald Reagan, a strong supporter of free trade, responded with the September 1985 Plaza Accord, which took the dollar from ¥240 in 1985 down to ¥120 just two years later. The dollar then rose to ¥160 in 1990 but subsequently fell as low as ¥79.75 in April 1995, largely ending the trade-related hostilities that had plagued the two nations' relationship for nearly two decades.

The news for U.S. workers was not all good, unfortunately, because Japan was soon replaced by Taiwan, South Korea, and finally China. Meanwhile, the North American Free Trade Agreement (NAFTA) led to the emergence of Mexico as a leading destination for U.S. manufacturers seeking to relocate their factories.

Capital transactions made possible by the liberalization of cross-border capital flows also began to dominate the currency market. Consequently, capital inflows to the U.S. have led to continued strength of the dollar—and stagnant or declining incomes for U.S. workers—even as U.S. trade deficits continue to mount. In other words, the foreign exchange market lost its traditional function as an automatic stabilizer for trade balances, and the resulting demands for protectionism in deficit countries are now at least as great as they were before the Plaza Accord in 1985.

## Trump Administration Views Two WTO Principles as Being Unsuited to Current Conditions

Donald Trump won the election in November 2016 by giving a voice to these unhappy workers. He argued that while the WTO framework may have been acceptable when the U.S. was economically dominant, it needed to be reconsidered now that the U.S. has lost that position. He effectively exposed a key contradiction in the WTO framework: the fact that China levies high tariffs on imports from all WTO nations is no reason why the U.S.—which runs a huge trade deficit with China—should have to settle for lower tariffs on imports from China.

This problem arose because the developed-world members of the WTO had already lowered tariffs among themselves before developing countries such as China, with their significantly lower wages and higher tariffs, were allowed to join. When they joined, developing countries could argue that they were still underdeveloped and needed higher tariffs to allow infant domestic industries to grow and to keep their trade deficits under control. Although that was a valid argument for developing countries at the time and their maximum tariff rates have come down as negotiated, the effective rates remained higher than those of advanced countries long after those countries became competitive enough to run trade surpluses with the developed world.

The negotiations required to join the WTO are not easy for developing countries, but they are often influenced by industry representatives from the developed countries. For example, aspiring members may have to commit to opening their insurance or banking sectors to foreign firms by a certain date. Since many businesses in the developed world are eager to enter emerging markets, these negotiations can become quite tense. However, there are apparently few negotiations at the macroeconomic level that might, for example, link the country's trade performance to its overall tariff rates.

Because the WTO system is based on the principle of multilateralism, with rules applied equally to all member nations, this framework provides no way of addressing bilateral imbalances between the U.S. and China. It is therefore not surprising that the Trump administration has decided to pursue bilateral, not multilateral, trade negotiations.

In retrospect, what the WTO should have done is to impose a macroeconomic condition stating that new members must lower their tariff and non-tariff barriers to advanced-country norms after they start to run significant trade surpluses with the latter. Here the term "significant" might be defined to mean running a trade surplus averaging more than, say, two percent of GDP for three years. If a country fails to reduce its tariffs to the advanced-nation norm within say five years after reaching that threshold, the rest of the WTO community should then be allowed to raise tariffs on products from that country to the same level that country charges on its imports. The point is that if the country is competitive enough to run trade surpluses vis-à-vis advanced countries, then it should be treated as one.

If this requirement had existed when Japan joined the GATT in 1963 or when China joined the WTO in 2001, subsequent trade frictions would have been far more manageable. Under the above rules, Japan would have had to lower its tariffs starting in 1976, and China would have had to lower its tariffs from the day it joined the WTO in 2000! Such a requirement would also have enhanced the WTO's reputation as an organization that supports not only free trade but also fair trade.

## U.S. May Seek Tariff Equality from Trade Partners Running a Surplus

The Trump administration has already indicated that its goal in bilateral negotiations is to lower the tariffs U.S. exporters face abroad, especially in countries that are running large trade surpluses with the U.S. This means it is effectively trying to achieve the above-noted requirement that the WTO failed to impose on developing countries when they joined the organization. In all likelihood, the Trump administration will threaten to raise U.S. tariffs to the same level as the tariffs imposed by those countries in order to force them to lower their import duties on U.S. goods.

Naturally, the U.S. also has the option of unilaterally raising its own tariff rates, but that would lead to a contractionary equilibrium for the global economy. A reduction of import duties in surplus countries, on the other hand, would lead to an expansionary equilibrium that would benefit the global economy.

President Trump may also apply a similar approach to non-tariff barriers. When a country has erected non-tariff barriers to keep out U.S. products, the U.S. may adopt similar barriers targeting imports from that country.

Ideally, however, the WTO should (belatedly) impose the rule mentioned above on all members. In other words, it should require all post-1947 "newcomers" to lower their tariffs to the advanced country average within, say, five years if they are running significant trade surpluses with those countries. That will not only keep the multilateral spirit of the WTO alive but will also address the fairness issue raised by President Trump while nudging the global economy toward an expansionary equilibrium.

At the time of this writing, it is not clear how China will respond to the challenges posed by President Trump, but if Chinese President Xi Jinping understood the gravity of the situation, lowered Chinese tariffs on all imports to U.S. levels, and applied those tariffs to imports from *all* WTO member countries effective immediately, the result would be a new Chinese-led WTO regime that is both free and fair. That could transform China into the new leader of free trade, possibly replacing the protectionist and anti-WTO U.S.

Unfortunately, China has a bad habit of using trade as a policy instrument in diplomatic disputes. For example, it stopped exports of rare earth to Japan in response to a dispute over the Senkaku Islands and boycotted South Korean businesses when Seoul had to deploy Terminal High Altitude Area Defense (THAAD) missiles to defend itself from the ever-expanding North Korean missile threat. These actions and many others are all contrary to the spirit of the WTO and are likely to prevent China from claiming the moral high ground on free trade vis-à-vis the U.S.

## Fixing WTO Without Fixing Capital Flows Problem Leads Nowhere

Attaining a level playing field on tariffs and non-tariff barriers, however, is no guarantee that the trade accounts of countries will come closer to balance. This is because the foreign exchange market is now dominated by capital flows, which means that exchange rates no longer help to reduce trade imbalances. This free movement of capital that began in the 1980s was justified by the neoliberal notion that anything that increases the freedom of the private sector will increase its welfare. It was also implemented without careful thought on the part of economists. And it is those carelessly implemented aspects that are causing problems. This also means the term "globalization" as used today actually has two components: free trade and the free movement of capital.

Of the two, it was argued in previous chapters that the system of free trade introduced by the U.S. after 1947 led to unprecedented global peace and prosperity. Although free trade produces winners and losers and providing a helping hand to the losers is a major issue in the pursued economies, the degree of improvement in real living standards since 1945 has been nothing short of spectacular in both pursued and pursuing countries. It is said, for example, that an average U.S. resident today is better off than the Queen of England in 1900 thanks to massive advances in technology and free-trade-driven competition, which made air conditioners, automobiles, and smartphones affordable for ordinary people.

The same cannot be said for the free movement of capital, the second component of globalization. Manufacturing workers and executives in the pursued economies feel so insecure not only because imports are surging but also because exchange rates driven by portfolio capital flows of questionable value (explained later) are no longer acting to equilibrate trade.

To better understand this problem, let us take a step back and consider a world in which only two countries—the U.S. and Japan—are engaged in trade, and each country buys $100 in goods from the other. The next year, both countries will have the $100 earned from exporting to its trading partner, enabling it to buy another $100 in goods from that country. The two nations' trade accounts are in balance, and the trade relationship is sustainable.

But if the U.S. buys $100 from Japan and Japan only buys $50 from the U.S., Japan will have $100 to use the next year, but the U.S. will have only $50, and Japanese exports to the U.S. will fall to $50 as a result. Earning only $50 from the U.S., the Japanese may have to reduce their purchases from the U.S. the following year. This sort of negative feedback loop may push trade into a "contractionary equilibrium."

When exchange rates are added to the equation, the Japanese manufacturer that exported $100 in goods to the U.S. must sell those dollars on the currency market to buy the yen it needs to pay domestic suppliers and employees. However, the only entity that will sell it those yen is the U.S. manufacturer that exported $50 in goods to Japan.

With $100 of dollar selling and only $50 worth of yen selling, the dollar's value versus the yen will be cut in half. This is how a surplus country's exchange rate is pushed higher to equilibrate trade.

Continuing with this example, if Japanese life insurers, pension funds, or other investors who need dollars to invest in U.S. Treasury bonds sold yen and bought the remaining $50 the Japanese exporters wanted to sell, there would then be a total of $100 in dollar-buying demand for the $100 the Japanese exporter seeks to sell, and exchange rates would not change. If Japanese investors continued buying $50-worth of dollar investments each year, exchange rates would not change, in spite of the sustained $50 trade imbalances.

Although the above arrangement may continue for a long time, the Japanese investors would effectively be lending money to the U.S. This means that at some point the money would have to be paid back.

Unless the U.S. sells goods to Japan, there will be no U.S. exporters to provide the Japanese investors with the yen they need when they eventually sell their U.S. Treasury bonds to pay yen obligations to Japanese pensioners and life insurance policyholders. Unless Japan is willing to continue lending to the U.S. in perpetuity, therefore, the underlying 100:50 trade imbalance will manifest itself when the lending stops.

At that point, the value of the yen will increase, resulting in large foreign exchange losses for Japanese pensioners and life insurance policyholders. Hence this scenario is also unsustainable in the long run. The U.S., too, would prefer a healthy relationship in which it sells goods to Japan and uses the proceeds to purchase goods from Japan to an unhealthy one in which it funds its purchases via constant borrowings.

In the real world, there are over 200 countries trading with each other, not just two. Moreover, cross-border capital flows from investors around the world easily dwarf foreign exchange transactions driven by exporters and importers. Exporters of oil and other natural resources also complicate the situation. In this complex multilateral environment, it is neither possible nor desirable to balance each and every bilateral trade.

The complexity of the actual world, however, does not change the fundamental fact that a deficit country must borrow from abroad to maintain its exchange rate and imports. The IMF and other organizations have also been warning countries for decades that external deficits of more than three percent of GDP are potentially unsustainable and should therefore be corrected. President Trump's pledge to improve his country's trade imbalances also signals a political desire to put an end to this sort of unhealthy trade relationship. This means there has to be a balance between the complex realities of the multilateral trading (and investing) world and the income and job losses that deficit countries can tolerate.

## Open Capital Markets a Relatively New Phenomenon

The major economies opened their markets to cross-border capital flows only three decades ago. As noted earlier, U.S. financial markets were not liberalized until the Monetary Control Act of 1980, which started the deregulation of interest rates. The Monetary Control Act itself was a response to the double-digit inflation which the U.S. economy experienced in the late 1970s, which made it difficult to maintain administered interest rates.

Before this act, there had been a raft of controls and regulations that insulated U.S. financial markets from the rest of the world. These included Regulation Q, which controlled domestic interest rates, Eurodollar reserve requirements, which discouraged arbitrage between domestic and offshore markets, and the Fed's "Bank of America letter," which discouraged domestic financial institutions from offering foreign-currency-denominated instruments to U.S. retail customers.

The deregulation of Japan's capital markets also started in 1980, when the Foreign Exchange Law was amended to allow, in principle, investments in foreign assets for the first time. Washington pushed hard for Japan to open its capital markets via the so-called Yen Dollar Committee, based on the mistaken notion that it would attract more foreign capital to Japan and strengthen the yen. But as soon as the floodgates were opened in the early 1980s, a huge amount of capital flowed *out* of Japan in search of higher yields elsewhere. Those outflows completely overwhelmed foreign capital inflows to Japan and prompted a significant decline in the value of the yen.

Many European countries also started removing controls on cross-border portfolio flows during the 1980s. These liberalization efforts accelerated in the mid-1990s as part of the preparations for the single currency. The point is that, even in advanced countries, it was only in the last thirty years that cross-border capital flows really got off the ground.

## Capital Flows Distorting Trade Flows

When financial markets are liberalized, capital moves to equalize the expected return in all markets. To the extent that countries with strong domestic demand tend to have higher interest rates than those with weak demand, money will flow from the latter to the former. Such flows will strengthen the currency of the former and weaken the currency of the latter. They may also add to already strong investment activity in the former by keeping interest rates lower than they would be otherwise, while depressing already weak investment activity in the latter by pushing interest rates higher than they would be otherwise.

To the extent that countries with strong domestic demand tend to run trade deficits and those with weak domestic demand run trade surpluses, these capital flows will exacerbate trade imbalances between the two by pushing the deficit country's currency higher and pushing the surplus country's currency lower. In other words, these flows are not only not in the best interests of individual countries, but are also detrimental to the attainment of balanced trade between countries. The widening imbalances then increase calls for protectionism in deficit countries.

Furthermore, the equalized rate of return on capital obtained in this way might not be in the best interest of any individual country. For example, if market forces are trying to equalize global interest rates at, say, three percent, countries requiring rates either above or below three percent will suffer. Indeed, the market-driven three percent interest rate may not be in the interest of any individual economy.

In the world that existed before efforts to liberalize capital flows commenced in the early 1980s, trade was free, but capital flows were regulated, so the foreign exchange market was driven largely by trade-related transactions. The currencies of trade surplus nations therefore tended to strengthen, and those of trade deficit nations to weaken. That encouraged surplus countries to import more and deficit countries to export more. In other words, the currency market acted as a natural stabilizer of trade between nations.

Today, it is said that only about five percent of foreign exchange transactions involve trade, while the remaining 95 percent are attributable to capital flows. And those capital flows are seeking to equilibrate investment returns across countries. With no mechanism to balance trade, global imbalances have expanded to an unprecedented level. The U.S. current account and trade account deficits reached as much as six percent of GDP in 2006, when three percent is already considered far too high. New Zealand's deficit was 7.8 percent of GDP in 2006 Q1. Today it is the UK that has the largest trade deficit, at 6.9 percent of GDP.

If imbalances and job losses prove too much for the deficit country to tolerate, the market or politicians will act, usually with unpleasant consequences. The market's reaction may include a collapse of the deficit country's currency (the dollar fell from ¥360 in 1971 to ¥75 in 2011). The foreign exchange losses incurred by surplus-country investors could wipe out earlier gains and put a temporary stop to the sorts of capital flows illustrated in Figure 9.1.

But once investors in the surplus countries get over their losses in a couple of years, they will see that the U.S. trade deficit is declining with a weaker dollar. They will then conclude that "the dollar has fallen enough." This will prompt a resumption of the capital flows indicated in Figure 9.1, and they will not stop until another crash forces another temporary suspension. Indeed, the world may repeat this silly cycle of destabilizing capital flows and financial crashes for decades without any benefits or efficiency gains accruing to participants.

FIGURE 9.1  Ultimate Outcome of Free Capital Movement?

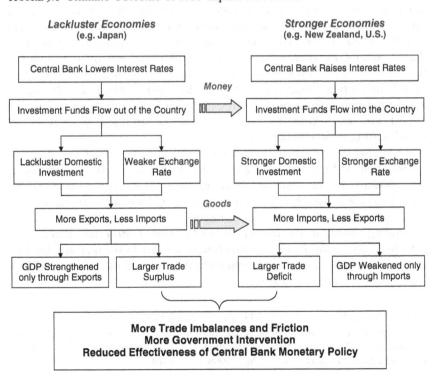

If the politicians are forced to act, it could mean protectionism and a collapse of global trade, as exemplified by the Smoot–Hawley Tariff, which triggered the global depression in the 1930s. More recently, with no mechanism left to balance trade, a massive expansion of trade deficits has ignited protectionist sentiment in the U.S. and elsewhere. As mentioned in Chapter 6, since the Fed announced its intention to normalize monetary policy in September 2014, the dollar has appreciated over 20 percent on a trade-weighted basis and more than 60 percent against the Mexican peso at one point (Figure 6.5) as portfolio investors sought potentially higher interest rates in the U.S. Such a large and abrupt appreciation made life difficult for U.S. manufacturers and their employees and contributed in no small way to the election victory of Donald Trump, who openly argued in favor of protectionism.

## Efficiency Gains from Capital Flows?

Some may argue that there must be efficiency gains for the global economy as a whole if capital is earning a higher return abroad. Although that may be true for intra-country investments, the final outcome is not so clear when different countries and currencies are involved. Japanese investors ended up incurring huge foreign exchange losses when the dollar fell from ¥240 in 1985 to ¥80 in 1995. The Chinese also sustained massive losses on their dollar investments when the RMB appreciated 40 percent against the dollar from 2005 to 2015. Large investments in the U.S. from 2001 to 2003 also ended up costing Europeans dearly as the euro climbed sharply higher against the dollar. Similarly, U.S. investors with foreign-currency assets suffered heavy losses when the dollar became the strongest currency in the world starting in September 2014.

It is also difficult to argue that the massive purchases of U.S. Treasuries that helped fund the U.S. budget deficit—by the Japanese starting in the 1980s and by the Chinese starting in the 1990s—were the best use for those funds. When the average American is living far better than the average Japanese or Chinese, it makes no fundamental sense for the latter two to be lending money to the former. Richard Cooper (1997)[1] has also argued that there are many cases of cross-border capital flows that are hard to justify on efficiency grounds, among them flows driven by differences in tax laws and accounting treatment.

---

[1] Cooper, Richard N. (1997) "Should Capital-Account Convertibility Be a World Objective?" in Peter B. Karen et al. (eds), "Should the IMF Pursue Capital-Account Convertibility?" *Essays in International Finance 207*, Princeton: Princeton University International Finance Section, May 1998, pp. 11–19.

The point is that the massive capital flows that are influencing exchange rates are of dubious value because it has *never* been proven that such flows actually improve the welfare of all concerned. Economists and financial market participants who pushed for ever-freer capital flows simply *assumed* that whatever increases the freedom of the private sector will result in a better allocation of resources along the neoliberal tradition. Although that is largely true in a closed economy, a positive result is not at all assured in an open international context with multiple currencies.

## Capital Flows Undermining Effectiveness of Monetary Policy

The rapid expansion of cross-border flows is also making it difficult for central banks to implement monetary policy. Today, it is just as easy for Japanese households to invest their savings in U.S. dollars as it is for Croatian households to arrange home mortgages in Japanese yen. The ease with which these transactions can be undertaken would have been unthinkable just twenty years ago.

Indeed, the pre-2008 housing bubbles in Europe were made possible to some extent by people taking out home mortgages in Japanese yen or Swiss francs in what was known as the "carry trade." This trade refers to investments financed with borrowings in currencies offering lower rates of interest. Even if the ECB tried to rein in housing bubbles in Spain and other Eurozone countries by raising interest rates, those borrowing in yen to buy houses would not be affected, because the interest rates they pay are determined by the Bank of Japan.

Higher euro interest rates as a result of ECB tightening, however, will widen the yield spread between the euro and the yen. That, in turn, lifts the euro against the yen by enticing capital away from the yen and into the euro. The weaker yen reduces the liabilities of those borrowing in yen, emboldening even more people to fund their investments with borrowed yen. In other words, the growth of the Swiss franc and yen carry trades undermined the effectiveness of ECB policy in its own market.

When the Fed announced its intention to normalize monetary policy in September 2014, the U.S. was already nearing full employment, and some asset prices were displaying bubble-like tendencies. In particular, commercial real estate prices had already returned to their pre-crisis peak and were still moving higher, as shown in Figure 6.3. Any central banker in these circumstances would want to begin tightening to forestall inflation and an asset bubble.

What followed, however, was very different from what the Fed expected. When the Fed announced in September 2014 that it would normalize interest rates, Japan and Europe were still in the process of expanding quantitative easing (QE) and lowering interest rates. As a result, massive amounts of funds left those two regions for the U.S. in search of higher yields. U.S. funds that had left the country following the GFC in 2008 in search of higher emerging market yields also began to return.

Those capital inflows pushed the dollar sharply higher while putting downward pressure on long-term U.S. bond yields. Instead of higher bond yields putting the brakes on a commercial real estate bubble, therefore, domestic and foreign appetite for U.S. debt kept Treasury yields low and actually helped expand the bubble in commercial real estate. Commercial real estate prices are now 26 percent higher than at the 2008 bubble peak.

The same capital inflows also transformed the dollar into the world's strongest currency. The strong dollar then made life difficult for U.S. exporters and firms competing with imports, thereby enlarging the already alarming size of U.S. current account deficit and adding to protectionist pressures from both workers and businesses.

The U.S., which wants and needs stronger exports and a cooler commercial real estate market, is getting the opposite results because of cross-border capital inflows, while the Japanese and Europeans have the same problem in reverse. Both are running large external surpluses while suffering from weaker domestic demand, which is why they eased monetary policy in the first place. But monetary easing prompted investment funds to leave in favor of the U.S., weakening their currencies and encouraging their exporters to export more.

## National Policy Objectives Inconsistent with Free Capital Flows

No economics textbook offers any guidance as to what the Fed or the Bank of Japan should do under these circumstances. This is because most of the research done by academic economists on so-called "open economies" dealt with open trade in goods only and seldom included open trade in capital. In other words, the economics profession has never envisioned a world with a globalized financial market, in which anyone, anywhere can borrow and invest in any currency at any time. But that world is here today, and for the first time. The world economy is truly entering uncharted waters.

In this world, central banks that set low interest rates end up stimulating investment outside their borders via the carry trade, while those setting higher rates end up attracting a disproportionate share of global savings. At the moment, the Bank of Japan and the ECB find themselves in the former position with negative interest rates, while the Fed is in the latter position with a strong dollar, but this is not a problem specific to any individual country. It is a problem for *all* central banks in a globalized financial market.

No economist would argue that such a world is desirable on the grounds of either efficiency or equity. Moreover, the adverse exchange rate movements created by these capital flows have caused global imbalances to reach alarming levels and pushed desperate working families in deficit countries into the protectionist camp. If no one wanted this outcome, how did it come about?

It came about because the opening of capital markets in these countries brought financial sectors together into a single global market, while governments and labor markets remained strictly local. The conflict stems from market forces trying to integrate the world's economies into a single market but the people and governments of individual countries have no intention of becoming a single country.

To see this, assume that Japan and the U.S. were planning to become one country. Their relationship would then be similar to that of the states of California and New York, and no one would give a second thought to trade imbalances between the two, no matter how large they might become. The balance of trade between states like California and New York is not an issue because people, capital, and goods are free to flow between the two. If New York has a booming economy but California is in the midst of recession, people will move from California to New York in search of better job opportunities. Similarly, if investment opportunities are more attractive in California than in New York, capital will flow from New York to California in search of higher returns.

Even if people are not so free to move, the federal government in Washington can use its powers to redistribute income from the area experiencing an inflow of income (i.e., a trade surplus) to the area experiencing an outflow of income (i.e., a trade deficit). This is possible because both California and New York are part of the U.S.

With all factors of production free to move between New York and California, it also makes no sense for the two states to have separate monetary policies. Given the ease with which money can move between them, any difference in interest rates between the two would immediately result in massive arbitrage that would equalize rates.

Today, capital is moving between countries *as though* they were going to become a single nation. This is why investors pay so little attention to the huge current account deficits of the U.S. or the current account surpluses of China. This also explains why monetary policy is losing its effectiveness at the national level, in the same way that New York and California cannot have separate monetary policies.

The problem, however, is that neither Japan nor the U.S. plans to merge into a single nation. Both set limits on immigration that restrict the free movement of labor between the two countries. They also have different value systems, different languages, and different traditions. In other words, they are and will remain separate nations.

The fundamental conflict stems from the fact that countries are trying to remain independent while their financial markets are behaving as though they were about to merge into one nation. Trump and others blame free trade for today's problems, but it is actually the free movement of capital that is causing these huge global imbalances. The calls for protectionism and the rhetoric against free trade in the U.S. would have been much more manageable if dollar exchange rates had not gone up as much as they did after September 2014. To the extent that capital flows are allowed to enlarge the external imbalances of individual countries, trade frictions and imbalances are likely to remain important political issues for years to come.

## Financial Types Have No Choice Either

The financial market participants behind these capital flows are unable to act any differently since their job is to place funds where expected returns are highest, even though such actions may worsen global imbalances and add to protectionist pressures. Their actions can also undermine the effectiveness of central banks in their own economies, as higher interest rates designed to cool domestic investment end up attracting more investment funds from abroad, while low interest rates designed to stimulate domestic investment end up pushing domestic investment funds overseas.

Global investors have also paid virtually no attention to trade or current account imbalances during the last twenty years. As the chief economist of a research institute associated with the largest investment bank in Japan, the author's main job is to brief the bank's global investor clients all over the world. When the author mentions trade imbalances as a potentially important determinant of exchange rates (based on his own involvement with the pre-1995 U.S.-Japan trade frictions, as noted in Chapter 5), most young investors stare back in disbelief. They cannot imagine that trade-related transactions, which account for only about five percent of total foreign exchange transactions, could have such an impact.

Instead, they are interested mainly in the direction of monetary policy in various countries and the resultant interest rate differentials. This is in spite of the fact that monetary policy has lost much of its effectiveness in advanced countries (Figures 2.9 to 2.14 and Figure 4.1), all of which are in a pursued phase and are suffering from balance sheet recessions.

It is indeed fascinating to note that, regardless of where they reside, these investors are all looking at basically the same economic, market, and policy indicators when making investment decisions. Thus the questions the author gets from investors in New York are no different from those he hears in Singapore, Frankfurt, Tokyo, or London. They really are part of one huge global market working to equalize returns on capital.

Foreign exchange market participants have ignored massive U.S. trade deficits for the last twenty years and supported the dollar based on a belief that continued deficits on this scale do not matter. However, Mr. Trump's election victory and the social backlash he represents are an indication that trade deficits *do* matter, and that there is something fundamentally wrong with the views of currency traders.

The fact that the dollar has been flat or even weaker since Trump's inauguration in spite of the Fed's push to normalize monetary policy may reflect a new realization among foreign exchange market participants that trade imbalances *do* matter. After all, they do not want to be caught long dollars when the President of the United States starts talking (tweeting?) down the dollar to reduce the U.S. trade deficit.

## Converse of Optimal Currency Theory Needed

In economics, there is a rich literature on the concept of optimal currency areas. It argues that if two regions have free movement of capital, labor, and goods, they should adopt a common currency. It also states that, if there is to be a common currency, there should also be free movement of people, goods, and capital. In areas such as the Eurozone, where governments have invested a great deal of time and effort to enable the free flow of people, capital, and goods, a single currency will provide major benefits for all concerned. Globally, however, governments making such efforts are the exception rather than the rule.

Theory and reality are at greatest odds when it comes to the flow of people, because immigration remains a thorny issue in most countries. Even if immigration were fully liberalized, differences in language, race, religion, and culture would continue to hamper the free movement of people. The world consists of 200 independent nations mostly because there are 200 different value systems and national identities. The barriers created by the differences in these values cannot be overcome by economic exchanges alone.

Nor is it realistic to expect the advent of a world government capable of redistributing income across national borders. As long as nations have no intention of becoming a single country or giving up an important part of their sovereignty to a "world government" anytime soon, trade imbalances—which signify the transfer of income from deficit to surplus nations—will remain a major political issue.

Although individual governments and the IMF seek to reduce trade imbalances, their efforts often run contrary to financial markets' trend toward globalization. Indeed, the IMF itself seems to be schizophrenic, with one part of the organization pushing for freer movement of capital while the other is fighting trade imbalances brought about by the same. This contradiction between free capital flows and the trade tensions resulting from a lack of political integration will be with us for decades.

The key question facing the world economy today, therefore, is really the *converse* of the optimal currency area concept. In other words, if the free movement of one or more factors of production is not achievable, should the remaining factors be allowed to move freely? More specifically, if labor is not allowed to move freely across national borders, should capital be allowed to do so?

Providing a full answer to this question would probably require volumes of research. And that research should commence immediately given the growing threat of protectionism in so many pursued countries. Policymakers and scholars must re-examine the benefits and costs of the unrestricted opening of capital markets instead of blindly assuming that anything that increases the freedom of the private sector is good for the economy. Although the economics profession has proved that open trade in goods improves the welfare of the concerned economies, it has *not* demonstrated that open trade in capital will produce the same result when there are multiple currencies involved and other factors of production are not free to move. The profession should also look into the welfare implications of prolonged unbalanced trade.

## The Case for Government Intervention in the Foreign Exchange Market

For policymakers facing protectionist threats today, however, waiting for the results of such research may not be an option: they may have to take action now to protect free trade (and world peace). To the extent that the explosion of cross-border capital flows during the past three decades contributed to larger global imbalances and more calls for protectionism, they may want to consider placing some restrictions on those flows.

Alternatively, they may wish to consider more direct government involvement in the foreign exchange market if capital flows themselves are to be left to the private sector. For example, they may consider implementing something similar to the Plaza Accord of 1985 to realign exchange rates in order to forestall protectionism and prevent destructive cycles of capital flows and financial crashes.

As noted earlier, a strong dollar left the U.S. facing widespread calls for protectionism in the summer of 1985. Only a handful of U.S. companies were still competitive against the Japanese with the dollar hovering around ¥250. Indeed, it was said at the time that there were only two U.S. companies that were still in favor of free trade: Boeing and Coca-Cola. Everyone else was opposed. President Ronald Reagan, a strong believer in free trade, then had to convene a meeting of the G5 countries on September 22, 1985 to create the Plaza Accord, which was designed to save free trade by weakening the dollar.

Although markets were initially highly skeptical, the G5 (later G7) countries succeeded in halving the value of the dollar to ¥120. By 1988 the agreement had completely neutralized the protectionist threat in the U.S. Although the dollar did return briefly to ¥160 in 1990, it never touched ¥200 again, indicating that forceful government action can have a lasting impact.

Plaza Accord-like government interventions are considered "politically incorrect" in a neoliberal academic climate, which views with suspicion any market restrictions or interventions undertaken by the government. But if capital flows are to remain free, policymakers must also have the ability to ensure that trade balances do not go out of whack. Oddly enough, protectionist measures are the only tool policymakers have to keep trade imbalances within politically or socially acceptable bounds under the current regime of liberalized capital flows and a hands-off policy toward foreign exchange rates.

Deciding what constitutes the correct exchange rate is no easy task, of course. After all, this is largely a zero-sum game, and no country wants to be stuck with an uncompetitive rate. The current "hands-off," market-determined exchange rate regime adopted by the developed countries is in some sense a cop-out by policymakers who find it impossible to agree on an exchange rate. But given the groundswell of protectionism, policymakers simply cannot leave the exchange rate to the whims of international investors and speculators who care little about trade imbalances or job losses.

## Central Bank Intervention Can Be Effective If It Sides with Trade Flows

Some argue that even if central banks decide to intervene in the foreign exchange market on behalf of governments, their actions are bound to be ineffective because private capital flows are now so much larger than the amounts that central banks can mobilize. But the impact of such interventions can far exceed the actual amounts of money being mobilized if central banks side with trade flows and coordinate their actions. Siding with trade flows means buying the currencies of surplus countries and selling the currencies of deficit countries.

Central banks are the only participants in the foreign exchange market who do not have to worry about profits and losses. When they side with trade flows and start pushing exchange rates in such a direction as to reduce trade imbalances, private-sector participants, who *do* have to worry about losing money, get scared. After all, they are in the market not to prove how strong they are, but to make money. When they see central banks charging their way, many would prefer to avoid confrontation, because central banks pushing in the same direction as trade flows have potentially unlimited resources. This is because the central bank of a deficit country wishing to weaken its currency can print potentially unlimited amounts of its own currency and sell it on the foreign exchange market to depress the currency's value.

To avoid such confrontations, investors who have been betting on an appreciation of deficit-country currencies will square their positions by selling the currencies of deficit countries and buying the currencies of surplus countries. Their selling of the deficit country's currency multiplies the impact of the central bank's initial sale of the deficit-country currency and pushes exchange rates in the desired direction.

The best example of this was in the two years after the Plaza Accord of September 1985, when G5 central banks successfully pushed the overvalued U.S. dollar down from ¥240 to ¥120. However, central bank interventions tend to be ineffective or easily overpowered by the market when they go against trade flows.

## Risk of Capital Flight in Adjusting Exchange Rates

Although a central bank can influence the exchange rate if it is acting on the side of trade flows, its influence may come at a high cost if it triggers capital flight. To understand this risk, imagine a world where the U.S. government started to openly push for a weaker dollar. In face of such overt government action, anyone holding dollar assets, including U.S. investors, would probably consider dumping those assets in exchange for foreign-currency-denominated assets and buying back the dollar assets later, once they have become cheaper in foreign-currency terms.

If these investors sold their holdings of U.S. bonds, bond prices would be pushed lower, sending yields higher and putting highly unpleasant pressure on U.S. financial markets and the economy. Indeed, this sort of capital flight could lead to sharply higher bond yields and the dreaded "big mess" scenario mentioned in Chapter 6, something the Fed has been trying to avoid at any cost.

Although largely forgotten by both market participants and academics, such a capital flight actually occurred 30 years ago in March 1987, roughly a year and a half after the start of the Plaza Accord. By then the dollar had fallen to just above ¥150 from ¥240 in September 1985, and U.S. authorities were satisfied with the extent of the adjustment in exchange rates. To indicate their satisfaction, the G7 countries in February 1987 concluded the Louvre Accord, which basically stated that the dollar had fallen enough. The Japanese government was also busy assuring investors, who had suffered huge foreign exchange losses on their U.S. bond holdings, that ¥150 marked the bottom for the dollar.

But a few days before the all-critical end of the Japanese fiscal year on March 31, the dollar suddenly slipped below ¥150, shocking Japanese investors who had refrained from selling the dollar and dollar assets on the understanding that ¥150 marked the bottom. Feeling betrayed, they dumped U.S. bonds and bought Japanese government bonds (JGBs), sharply widening the interest rate differential between the two bond markets, starting on the day the dollar fell below ¥150 (Figure 9.2).

U.S. policymakers and market participants, who seldom look to Asia for answers, initially had no idea what was happening and blamed the sudden increase in U.S. bond yields on domestic inflationary fears. From his vantage point in Japan, the author could see what was happening and quickly telephoned former colleagues at the Federal Reserve Bank of New York to inform them that the long-feared capital flight was now unfolding, knowing that Paul Volcker, the Fed chairman, had been worried about this risk from the outset of the Plaza Accord. The author told U.S. authorities to look at what was happening to (1) the yen/dollar exchange rate, (2) U.S. Treasury bond yields, and (3) JGB yields after the dollar slipped below ¥150.

Once U.S. authorities realized that the dollar had triggered this move in bond prices, the Fed chairman announced that the Fed was ready to raise interest rates to defend the dollar. This announcement had an impact since it was the first indication since the Plaza Accord that the U.S. was willing to defend the dollar, and the dollar returned to ¥150 by early July. The divergence in U.S. and Japanese government bond yields that had begun in March was also reversed.

But when the dollar again fell below ¥150 just a few days after Alan Greenspan became the Fed chairman in August, policymakers' credibility was lost, and U.S. bond yields renewed their upswing, eventually triggering the Black Monday stock market crash in October 1987. On Black Monday, U.S. bond yields were fully 270 basis points higher than when the dollar had fallen below ¥150 for the first time six months earlier.

This incident indicates that U.S. policymakers must be careful with exchange rate adjustments if U.S. financial markets are vulnerable to capital flight out of the dollar. If U.S. bond yields rose 270 basis points from where they are now, not only the U.S. housing market but also the commercial real estate market (with its extremely low capitalization rates) and the stock market (with its extremely high valuations) would likely suffer mightily.

FIGURE 9.2 Risk of Capital Flight in Adjusting Exchange Rates

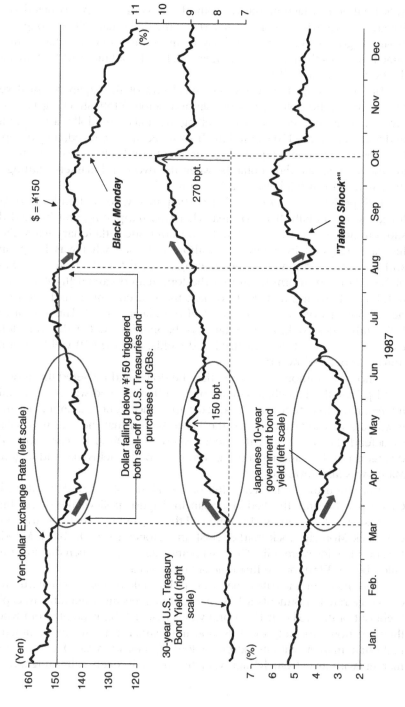

*Note:* *Japanese chemical company Tateho loses massively in JGB futures trading, triggering panic in the JGB market.
*Sources:* Federal Reserve Bank of New York, Board of Governors of the Federal Reserve, Japan Bond Trading Company

## "Paying Back Our Fathers' Debt"

The above incident also begs the question as to why Japanese investors in the late 1980s did not dump the dollar earlier while it was falling from ¥240 to ¥150 and whether similar patience could be expected from Japanese and other investors today. The Japanese investors refrained from selling the dollar until March 1987 for two reasons. First, they had large unrealized capital gains in their domestic stock portfolio that could be used to absorb losses elsewhere. Those gains had accumulated on their cross-holdings of Japanese equities, an arrangement that started in the 1950s. Because the Japanese economy had grown rapidly in the 30 years to 1987 and share prices had also surged, investors had accumulated large unrealized capital gains by the time the Plaza Accord was implemented.

But having unrealized capital gains is no reason for Japanese investors to hold on to dollar assets when the U.S. government is openly pushing for a weaker dollar. Here, a very different mindset was at work in the late 1980s—in effect, many Japanese investors told themselves that, by not selling dollar assets, they were paying back their fathers' debt to the U.S.

Their fathers' debt refers to the help the U.S. extended after the war to rebuild Japan, a former enemy. The author actually heard this phrase many times from Japanese institutional investors during those years. By not selling their dollar assets and absorbing the losses, they were helping the U.S. bring its exchange rate down nearly 40 percent without a major disruption to its economy and its markets. What should not have been possible became possible because of the peculiar way Japanese investors viewed the war debt of their fathers.

When the dollar fell below ¥150 in late March 1987, however, even these investors found themselves unable to hold on to their sentimental positions any longer. But it was still extremely fortunate for the U.S. that this happened at ¥150 to the dollar and not at ¥180 or ¥200.

The stock market crash in Tokyo starting in 1990 wiped out Japanese investors' unrealized gains. Besides, mark-to-market accounting is now the norm and cross-holdings of shares have been reduced drastically, both under pressure from the U.S. While Japanese investors had a major presence in the U.S. bond market during the 1980s, today Chinese and other investors also play important roles, and they are likely to think and act very differently than the Japanese did 30 years ago.

It should also be noted that not all of the capital flight observed in the late 1980s and into the 1990s was due to Japanese investors. In March 1988, about a year after the events described above, it was reported again that selling by the Japanese had triggered another plunge in the U.S. Treasury market, sending the dollar lower. Japanese investors—who were *not* selling this time—actually made an official statement to that effect through the Life

Insurance Association of Japan.[2] Eventually it was discovered that it was U.S. investors, worried that their Japanese counterparts were about to start selling, who had moved preemptively to unload their U.S. bond holdings.

Today, the potential for investors to move preemptively, correctly or otherwise, is far greater than it was 30 years ago given the prevalence of quick-acting hedge funds and computer-driven program trading. This means that if the Trump administration wants to adopt a weak-dollar policy, it needs to assume that there will be a certain amount of capital flight. In other words, the Trump administration should be able to weaken the dollar because the U.S. is a deficit country, but it has to be careful when doing so to ensure that capital flight out of the dollar—and the higher domestic interest rates that would result—do not get totally out of control.

## Not Perfect, but Better Than Today

Even if exchange rates are moving to equilibrate trade, there will still be some grievances from workers in pursued countries. This is because exports from pursued countries are likely to be more capital- and technology-intensive, while those from pursuing countries will tend to be more labor-intensive. Consequently, even if trade is balanced, the pursued countries end up "importing labor" because of the higher labor content of their imports. However, that is still far better than the situation today, where deficit countries could continue losing income and jobs to surplus countries for decades because no mechanism exists to equilibrate trade.

To their credit, economists did point out that even though free trade will improve the welfare of the countries involved, there are winners and losers within each country. They also noted that since the winners' gains are larger than losers' losses, the entire society should benefit from trade as long as the winners share some of their gains with the losers.

While that is true in theory, actually structuring a loss-sharing arrangement between free-trade winners and losers is not easy, since even the losers enjoy some benefits as consumers. This practical difficulty may be the reason why political leaders have never implemented loss-sharing arrangements. Given the strong anti-free-trade sentiment in so many pursued countries today, however, policymakers should consider measures, including currency realignments, to ensure that free trade "losers" are not left behind.

It was argued in Chapter 5 that the easy days are over for those in post-LTP pursued countries who do not put in the effort to improve their human

---

[2] *Asahi Shimbun* (1988), Endaka 'Seiho-Hannin-Setsu' ni Kyoukai ga Kirei no Hanron ("Accusation that life insurers are responsible for strong yen is absurd"), in Japanese, March 30, p. 9.

capital. At the same time, the explosion of social backlash against trade deficits and job losses in pursued countries means that the easy days are over for emerging countries whose economies are open only on the export side. Those days when they could export all they want without opening domestic market for imports are rapidly coming to an end. They must open their markets faster or accept higher exchange rates if they want to continue enjoying access to the markets of pursued countries.

## Two Types of "Equalizing" Capital Flows and the Quality of Investors

Much will also depend on the quality of the investors involved, as well as whether capital flows are driven by direct investment or portfolio investment. If investors paid more attention to trade imbalances and refrained from investing excessively in trade deficit countries, some of the adverse currency movements noted above would also be contained.

The distinction between direct and portfolio investment is important because even though both are in some sense "equalizing" returns on capital across national borders, their impact on exchange rates can be very different. Most investors who are sending money abroad as direct investment are likely to be non-financial operating companies who have done careful studies of the host country, including its trade balance, because once they build a factory or set up operations there, they cannot leave easily.

These businesses are investing abroad because of higher returns on capital, as discussed in earlier chapters. But returns are higher because of real competitive reasons and not because of higher interest rates. This means that direct investment flows will tend to push up the exchange rates of increasingly competitive recipient countries while depressing the exchange rate of the increasingly uncompetitive home countries. Hence these investment flows tend to move exchange rates in a direction that equilibrates trade flows.

Portfolio investors, on the other hand, will often buy the financial assets of deficit countries as long as they offer higher interest rates. Such flows tend to move exchange rates in a way that will enlarge existing trade imbalances, as noted earlier.

Another problem facing portfolio investors is that they often have only limited time to study the countries they are investing in, especially when they are competing against global stock market indexes such as the MSCI. If a sudden boom in a certain country's stock market pushes the MSCI index higher, for example, fund managers who are competing with that index but do not own any of that country's stocks will come under tremendous pressure to include those stocks in their portfolios. Too often they end up rushing to buy those stocks without fully understanding all the issues surrounding the country.

When something unexpected happens, these uninformed portfolio investors tend to rush to the exit simultaneously in a massive panic that hurts both the market and the country's economy. Although academic economists tend to assume that investors are always rational and know what they are doing, the actual market is littered with examples of ignorance or worse. The all-too-frequent formation of asset price bubbles proves just how irrational investors can be.

Both the Latin American debt crisis of 1982 and the Asian currency crisis of 1997 were preceded by supposedly sophisticated Western financial institutions lending billions of dollars to poorly managed public-sector borrowers in Latin America and to investment projects with huge financial mismatch (short-term foreign-currency financing for long-term domestic projects) in Asia. Although the Latin American crisis was stopped from getting worse by Paul Volcker as mentioned in Chapter 8, no-one stopped the outside investors from rushing to the exit at the same time in the Asian crisis, resulting in massive panic and confusion. These two crises demonstrated that nothing is worse for emerging economies than an influx of cash-rich but ignorant investors from the developed world investing huge amounts in projects they do not fully understand.

In the wake of the 1997 Asian crisis, for example, many Western investors complained bitterly about a wide range of structural problems in Asia, including crony capitalism and the inadequacy of Thai bankruptcy laws. But their very complaints proved that they had done no homework on the countries they were investing in. In other words, they showed themselves to be totally unqualified to invest in Thailand: it was their duty to investigate those laws *before* investing in the country.

In view of the quality of investors in the real world, the authorities might want to consider implementing higher risk weights for institutional investors' holdings of assets located in current account deficit countries or denominated in the currencies of such countries. The purpose of such a measure would be to remind investors that their decision to invest in such assets may contribute to the widening of global imbalances that could cost them dearly in the end.

Risk weights can also be used to rein in the carry trade, which has undermined monetary policy in many parts of the world. The Russian central bank, for example, has successfully reined in the market for foreign-currency-denominated home mortgages by imposing higher risk weights on banks' holdings of such mortgages.

The point is that, even though both direct and portfolio investment flows move to equilibrate the return on capital across national borders, the former is based on real competitive reasons which tend to move exchange rates in the direction needed to equilibrate trade balances, while the latter is often based on interest rate differentials, which tend to move exchange rates in the opposite direction. It is this latter type of capital flow that is problematic.

## Chilean Solution to Deter Uninformed Investors

The authorities of emerging countries receiving portfolio inflows may also want to consider the Chilean solution. Chile was a victim of the Latin American debt crisis in 1982, when U.S. banks that understood little about Latin America lent billions of (petro) dollars to public-sector borrowers there in the belief that governments do not go bankrupt. When Mexico duly went belly up in August 1982, all other borrowers south of the U.S.–Mexico border were caught up in the contagion and suddenly lost access to the market, resulting in devastating recessions that lasted for over a decade.

From this bitter experience, the Chileans correctly concluded that it is dangerous to accept money from foreign investors who have not done their homework. They realized that investors with insufficient knowledge of the country will quickly panic when things go wrong and collectively rush to the exit, causing devastating turmoil in the market and the economy.

To ensure that those who bring money to the country have done their homework, Chile imposed a high tax rate on portfolio inflows that stayed in the country only briefly. The tax rate gradually declined with the length of the capital's stay. Although this tax helped enhance the stability of the Chilean economy by forcing outside investors to do homework on Chile, it was later removed, apparently under pressure from U.S. authorities.

The value of Chilean approach was proved again fifteen years later when Malaysia imposed a similar tax in the midst of the Asian currency crisis. The tax succeeded in quickly stabilizing the economy and markets but was harshly condemned by the U.S. Treasury Department. One of Treasury's top officials declared that the Malaysian economy would not recover for the next ten years given such bad policy choices. In reality, the country was the *first* to recover, emerging from the currency crisis in just 18 months and proving that free portfolio capital flows provided few benefits to Malaysia at that stage of economic development.

The Malaysian experience also means the IMF and the U.S. government should be more careful when asking countries to allow free portfolio capital flows. For Wall Street types, more-open foreign capital markets mean more playgrounds to play in. But there is no proof that the benefits of foreign capital flows to the host country outweigh the negatives of heavy fluctuations in asset prices and exchange rates.

As noted above, financial liberalization in the U.S. started in the early 1980s in response to the high inflation rates of the late 1970s. Double-digit inflation rates, for example, made a mockery of Regulation Q's administered (low) interest rates and led to a wholesale shift of funds from banks with regulated interest rates to unregulated money market mutual funds. That, in turn, forced the Fed to abandon Regulation Q with the Monetary Control Act of 1980.

Today, however, virtually all advanced economies are in the pursued phase and face private-sector balance sheet problems. That puts them in Case 3 or 4, where inflation is not likely to be a problem. This means that some of the rationale for financial deregulation that was valid when the economy was in a golden era and inflationary pressures were rampant is no longer relevant today. In other words, it may be possible to roll back some of the financial liberalization that took place 30 years ago without adverse consequences now that inflation is no longer a major issue.

## Time to Rethink Capital-Market Liberalization

Financial globalization makes sense if the world is eventually going to become a single nation. The current turmoil, including the social backlash, stems from financial globalization proceeding at a time when *no* country seeks global political integration. Nor has there been any move to create a global government with the authority to redistribute income.

The free-trade component of globalization has not only improved the lives of billions of people on this planet, but has also contributed tremendously to human peace and happiness since 1945 by making wars obsolete. The importance of free trade was demonstrated most clearly when the world tried the alternative—protectionism—in the 1930s and experienced a devastating global depression and a horrendous world war as a result. Although measures to help the losers of free trade are needed, the huge benefits countries have obtained from free trade should not be given up easily.

The same cannot be said for the free movement of capital. This part of globalization often enlarges global imbalances and increases cries for protectionism in deficit countries while undermining domestic monetary policy everywhere. Countries such as Malaysia actually recovered faster when they scrapped the free movement of capital that had been destabilizing their economies. Since it is not at all certain whether free capital movement, especially of the short-term variety, adds value to the global economy, thorough research on when to allow and when not to allow such flows should be part of the effort to contain protectionism in all post-LTP pursued countries. Until conclusive research is available, policymakers facing the choice between free trade and free portfolio capital movements should definitely opt for the former.

With less-than-perfect investors and less-than-perfect economic and political integration, it is hoped that policymakers will be pragmatic and not beholden to the unproven ideology such as neoliberalism when addressing the problems of capital flows, exchange rates, and trade imbalances. This means there is still something policymakers can do for working families before surrendering to unfettered globalization or the other extreme, protectionism. But if no action is taken on capital flows and/or exchange rates and if trade imbalances are allowed to expand unhindered, the resulting social backlash against free trade in the pursued countries might force some governments to choose protectionism, in what would be the worst of all possible outcomes.

# CHAPTER 10

# Rethinking Economics

B efore the discovery of the other half of macroeconomics, economists had to come up with all sorts of explanations for phenomena they could not explain with their conventional framework, which is based on a profit-maximizing private sector. Those phenomena included prolonged economic stagnation and unemployment, and the explanations put forward included allusions to structural problems, expectations (of deflation), secular stagnation, and "external shocks." These explanations are in some ways similar to the explanations astronomers gave for the movements of the planets before Copernicus realized it was the earth that was circling the sun and not the other way around.

## Structural or Balance Sheet Problems?

Allusions to structural problems are a common retreat for economists when their conventional macroeconomic policies fail to produce the expected results. Too often, however, they do so without realizing that other factors— such as balance sheet problems or a lack of investment opportunities—can also produce similar results.

Economists tend to focus on structural issues because Ronald Reagan and Margaret Thatcher made the public aware of the importance of structural or supply-side issues. In contrast, balance sheet problems or shortages of investment opportunities were never discussed in economics departments or business schools until quite recently.

A large number of economists and policymakers therefore jumped onto the structural reform bandwagon in both post-1990 Japan and post-2008 Europe. But the Reagan and Thatcher era in the U.S. and UK could not be more different from the post-bubble period in Japan and Europe. At the time of Reagan and Thatcher, both the U.S. and the UK were facing high inflation and interest rates, incessant labor disputes, and large trade deficits. In present-day Japan and Europe, inflation and interest rates are both extremely low, labor disputes are rare, and trade accounts are deeply in surplus. Moreover, the economies were doing fine and responding well to conventional macroeconomic policies before 2008 in the West and before 1990 in Japan. This makes it difficult to argue that the economy is stagnating because of age-old structural issues.

But because of mainstream pundits' near-exclusive focus on structural reforms, Japan has wasted a tremendous amount of political capital and precious time on such policies over the last 20 years, as has Europe for the last eight. In the U.S., meanwhile, policymakers understood within the first two years of the GFC that the country was actually suffering from balance sheet problems and not structural issues. The U.S. is doing much better than Japan or Europe today because it did not waste any time debating structural reform policies. Indeed, it is the only country that did not fall into the structural reform "trap", even though many of its economists were confidently (if not arrogantly) lecturing the Japanese on the need for such reforms only a few years earlier.

## Structural Reforms Require Correct Narrative

The lack of investment opportunities typical of countries in a pursued phase is indeed an argument for structural reform. This is because deregulation and other structural reform policies can raise the return on capital at home. What must be made clear, however, is that structural policies are needed to address problems that existed *before* the economy fell into a balance sheet recession. In other words, structural reforms are necessary, but they are not the answer to the sudden deceleration in economic growth after the bubble bursts and the private sector begins deleveraging. For these much more urgent problems, fiscal stimulus, not structural reform, is needed.

The policymakers who peddled structural solutions for the post-2008 stagnation lost credibility with the public when their policies failed to produce a recovery within the expected timeframe. That loss of credibility then allowed outsiders and far-right political parties make substantial political gains, especially in Europe.

In Japan, former Prime Minister Junichiro Koizumi's favorite slogan, "no economic recovery without structural reform", and his opposition to fiscal stimulus were therefore totally inappropriate for a country that was actually suffering from massive balance sheet problems. During his five-year tenure, Japan's private sector was saving an average of 9.5 percent of GDP in spite of zero interest rates. Not surprisingly, the economy continued to stagnate during and after his structural reform efforts.

Ten years have passed since then, and Japan's private sector has finally repaired its balance sheet. The remaining challenge for Japanese policymakers is to fend off pursuers from behind, which is indeed a structural reform issue. The third "arrow" of Abenomics—structural reforms—is designed specifically to increase the return on capital at home by increasing domestic investment opportunities via deregulation and market-opening measures.

The problem is that the public was told 15 years ago that structural reforms would lead to economic recovery, but the promised recovery never materialized. Feeling betrayed, people are now rightfully skeptical of structural reforms of any kind. Many are tired of hearing the term itself.

What is missing, then, is a proper narrative for why the third "arrow" of Abenomics is required. The new narrative must clarify that these reforms are needed to make the economy innovator-friendly and more flexible and thereby raise the return on capital at home while allowing the country to take evasive actions to fend off pursuers from behind. While the second "arrow" of fiscal stimulus is countering the still-large after-effects of a balance sheet recession such as debt trauma and consequent excess private-sector savings, bold implementation of the third arrow is essential if Japan wishes to regain escape velocity from stagnation and remain an advanced country.

A similar distinction is also needed in Europe. It must be made clear that while structural reforms are necessary to increase the return on capital at home and fend off pursuers from behind, they are no substitute for the fiscal stimulus that is needed to counter the balance sheet recessions engulfing the region since 2008.

## Summers' Secular Stagnation Thesis

When Larry Summers first discussed secular stagnation in 2013[1], the U.S. was in the midst of a balance sheet recession in which the private sector was saving over 7 percent of GDP at zero interest rates. He subsequently noted[2] that the return on capital in the West began falling in the 1970s, long before the global financial crisis erupted in 2008.

It should be obvious that Western economies have experienced such a sudden loss of economic momentum since 2008 because they are suffering from serious balance sheet recessions following the collapse of the housing bubble. Alvin Hansen, who first coined the term "secular stagnation" in

---

[1] See Lawrence H. Summers' webpage on secular stagnation: http://larrysummers.com/category/secular-stagnation/.
[2] E.g., at a private conference held in Paris on June 4, 2015.

1938, also did so at a time when the U.S. was in the midst of the greatest balance sheet recession of all, the Great Depression, and the unemployment rate was 19 percent.

At the time of Hansen's speech, however, nobody in Germany was talking about secular stagnation. There, speedy, sustained, and substantial fiscal stimulus implemented to fight the balance sheet recession had completely eradicated the recession and brought the German unemployment rate down to just two percent in 1938 from a high of 28 percent in 1933. The fact that both Hansen and Summers brought up the issue of secular stagnation during balance sheet recessions, and that Germany—which had overcome its own balance sheet recession by 1938—was not suffering from such stagnation, suggests that balance sheet recessions are actually the main driver of "secular stagnation."

The post-1970 decline in the return on capital, however, is likely due to the fact that Western economies were all entering the post-Lewis Turning Point (LTP) pursued phase by the mid-1970s, when Japan started chasing them. From that point on, a growing number of manufacturers in those countries found that the return on capital was higher abroad than at home. Many of them decided to buy from or invest in the pursuing economies themselves, which at the time included Japan. Shrinking capital investment in the advanced countries then led to slower growth in productivity and wages.

This pattern of emerging economies taking away investment opportunities from the developed countries will continue until all economies have long passed their Lewis Turning Points and the return on capital has been more or less equalized. Although China has passed the LTP already, India and many other economies have a long way to go. The current transition process is therefore likely to continue for many years to come.

The above pattern can be explained by applying the framework of Figure 3.3 in a global context. Most countries can reach the EQ level of wages for ordinary workers in a relatively straightforward fashion if they follow the correct policies for economic development. These include providing a good education for the workforce, creating the necessary infrastructure, eradicating corruption, encouraging entrepreneurship, and opening up the economy.

For wages to grow beyond their EQ levels, however, wages for workers in all other countries must reach their EQ levels so that employers no longer have the option of finding cheaper workers elsewhere. This means individual countries can look forward to income growth until wages reach their EQ levels, but at that point the EQ level of wages effectively becomes the ED level of wages in Figure 3.3, applied in a global context. In other words, these countries must wait until all slack in other labor markets is eliminated for wages to resume rising. And the world is still decades away from what might be called the "Global Labor Market Maturity Point (GLMMP)," where all countries have reached their EQ level of wages. This means that workers in pursued countries should start improving their skills now instead of waiting for the global economy to reach its GLMMP, when the general level of wages might start rising again.

## Beware of Fake "External Shocks"

Economists are also fond of using the term "external shock" to describe what happened after 2008. This implies that the event originated outside the economy and therefore could not have been predicted (hence the "shock"). The author would agree that 9-11 was an external shock that he himself had failed to predict (which is why he, along with many economists of the National Association of Business Economists, was in the World Trade Center building in New York City when the attack took place). But to call the Lehman bankruptcy and the subsequent GFC an external shock is preposterous.

For years before Lehman, the existence of a housing bubble financed with Collateralized Debt Obligations (CDOs) containing subprime mortgages loans but carrying outrageously high ratings from corrupt rating agencies was well known. Once the bubble burst, the overwhelming amount of leverage in the system meant that economies *had* to fall into balance sheet recessions. In that sense, what happened after 2008 was largely *endogenous* to the system: it was not caused by unpredictable external factors.

When the crisis unfolded, economists, including former Fed Chairman Alan Greenspan, argued that it was a "once-in-a-hundred-year event" that could not have been predicted. Others called it a "perfect storm" or an "external shock." These terms all imply that economists should not be blamed for failing to predict it.

A young but brilliant Brazilian investor who incurred heavy losses in 2008 decided to leave the field altogether when he heard such statements from prominent economists. He thought that if the financial world contains dangers that even Alan Greenspan and other famous economists cannot anticipate, he would rather take up a different profession that did not expose him to such unpredictable perils.

After wondering for several months what profession to pursue, it occurred to him that if there was one person on this earth who saw the crisis coming, then 2008 was not a perfect storm. It simply meant that the big names in economics had the wrong models in their heads. After conducting the kind of extensive research that was typical of his style, he did find a few who had seen it coming, and the author was honored to be included in this very short list. The fact that the list was so short, however, is testimony to the fact that the economics profession has gone badly wrong for far too long.

The point is that the condition the economy was in prior to the "shock" is absolutely critical in understanding how it will subsequently respond to various policy actions. The nature of the shock itself is also important in predicting what follows.

For a purely external shock such as 9-11 in the U.S. or 3-11 in Japan[3], the economy may take a year or two to recover, although it depends, of course, on the magnitude of the event. But a highly leveraged economy will invariably take many years to recover when a bubble eventually bursts because millions of underwater private balance sheets must be repaired. Although the collapse itself may be triggered by some external event, the long and painful balance sheet recession that follows is no shock at all. Apart from events such as 9-11, economists should not use the term "external shock" to describe a simple lack of understanding of what was happening in the economy (including unsustainably high leverage) prior to the shock.

## Beware of Fake Allusions to "Expectations"

There is a great deal of literature in economics on expectations, especially on inflationary expectations. Indeed, those who are pushing for continued monetary stimulus on the face of repeated failures of central banks to reach inflation targets argue that such efforts are needed to "anchor expectations." But people's expectations are fundamentally based on what they see happening and what they have experienced in the past.

In post-bubble Japan, where commercial real estate prices fell 87 percent nationwide, the typical CEO was busy repairing his firm's balance sheet by using corporate cash flow to pay down debt. He was also aware that most other CEOs in the country were doing the same thing. With no borrowers to take funds out of the financial institutions and inject them into the real economy, it was obvious to these executives that no amount of central bank liquidity injections would increase the money circulating in the economy. And with no way to increase the money circulating in the economy, it was clear to them that monetary easing could not boost economic growth or inflation rates.

In this environment, the announcement of a two percent inflation target by the central bank will have no impact at all because CEOs realize that such a target is unattainable. Since the escape from negative equity is a matter of survival for businesses, they also have no choice but to continue deleveraging until their balance sheets are repaired. But if they continue their deleveraging, there will be no credit growth and no inflation.

---

[3] Tsunami that devastated Northeastern Japan on March 11, 2011.

Banks are also not allowed to lend money to businesses with balance sheet problems. The resultant undershooting of inflation targets by the central bank then reinforces these CEOs' understanding of the economy while undermining the credibility of monetary authorities and economists who pushed for these targets.

In such a world, the announcement that a central bank has raised its inflation target from two percent to four percent does not lower these CEOs' expectations of future real interest rates, because the original two percent target was not credible to begin with. This is the reality, and it has nothing to do with expectations. Anyone who cared to ask CEOs why they are deleveraging when the central bank is posting a 2 percent inflation target would have gotten this answer[4].

This also means that there is a disconnect between central bankers (and their economist friends, along with some market participants noted in Chapter 2), who are still operating on the assumption that the economy is in Case 1 or 2, and the rest of the population, who correctly understand that the economy is in Case 3 or 4. After all, they are the ones busily repairing their balance sheets. This is the case of CEOs and the general public having the correct model of the economy in their heads, while the economists do not.

When the economy was in a golden era (in Cases 1 and 2), in contrast, most CEOs were busy procuring funds to increase their productivity- and capacity-enhancing investments. Financial institutions were also lending out all available funds, raising the money multiplier to its maximum value. In such a world, a central bank could contain inflation by limiting the supply of reserves because the availability of reserves *was* a constraint on money and credit growth. This is why the three lines in Figures 2.9 to 2.11 moved together before 2008 in the West and before 1990 in Japan. The credibility of the central bank was also very high, especially when it was successful in taming inflation. But that is not the environment advanced countries find themselves in today.

There are many economists, including some at the Fed, who still fear that the fall in inflationary expectations will lead to economic stagnation "as happened in Japan." But this is an extension of the 1960s and 1970s mentality, where ingrained inflationary expectations that were formed in part due to inappropriate monetary policy had to be eradicated by drastic tightening measures (starting in October 1979) in order to restore price stability. Their view is that if inappropriate inflationary expectations can be crushed with severely restrictive monetary policy, then inappropriate deflationary expectations can also be corrected with highly *accommodative* policy.

---

[4] Admittedly, the question will have to be asked very carefully and somewhat indirectly because no CEO would admit that his or her company has balance sheet problems.

But post-1990 Japan and the post-2008 Western economies stagnated not because of deflationary expectations caused by inappropriate monetary policies, but rather because of private-sector balance sheet problems and higher overseas returns on capital, both of which have nothing to do with expectations or monetary policies. Without addressing these real issues with fiscal and structural policy actions, no amount of monetary easing will improve the economy or enhance the public's expectations of the future.

The point is that instead of treating "expectations" as some sort of a variable for policymakers to play with, economists should find out why people are behaving the way they are. The example of Japanese CEOs offered above indicates that they ignored monetary accommodation not because they had somehow acquired deflationary expectations but because they knew from their own debt-minimizing actions that *there was no reason why monetary easing should work*. Once these fundamental drivers of behavior are understood, economists should make far fewer allusions to expectations than they do today.

## Rethinking Macroeconomics

Macroeconomics is still a very young science. It began when Keynes, who recognized the existence of fallacy-of-composition problems in a macro-economy, came up with the concept of aggregate demand in the 1930s. With only 85 years of history, it is like a toddler when compared with centuries-old disciplines such as physics and chemistry. For example, Nicolaus Copernicus discovered the workings of solar system in 1530, and Isaac Newton discovered the universal law of gravity in 1687. These monumental discoveries took place 250 to 400 years before Keynes developed the concept of aggregate demand in 1936. As a young science, economics has been able to explain only a limited range of economic phenomena. Its youth also makes it prone to fads and influences.

The profession's immaturity was amply demonstrated by the fact that only a handful of economists saw the Great Recession coming, and even fewer predicted how long it would take to recover from it. Most also failed to anticipate that zero interest rates, massive quantitative easing, and inflation targeting would fail to bring about inflation within the forecast time.

These fundamental failures stem from the fact that most macroeconomic theories and models developed during the last 85 years assumed that private-sector agents always have both attractive investment opportunities and clean balance sheets (i.e., that they are maximizing profits) and therefore are willing to borrow if only the central bank lowers real interest rates far enough. In other words, these economists' mindsets remain stuck in the golden era, when economies are typically in Cases 1 and 2. They have not realized that most advanced economies today are not only in the pursued phase but are also experiencing balance sheet recessions, i.e., they are squarely in Cases 3 and 4.

By presuming that there are always willing borrowers, economists have assumed away the two most critical challenges to economic growth: the availability of domestic investment opportunities worth borrowing for and the existence of businesses with clean balance sheets that are able and willing to take on the risks of those investments. While the public is desperately waiting for economists to come up with policy recommendations to get the economy in Cases 3 and 4 to grow again, the economists themselves have largely assumed away the problem of growth because their models are assuming that the economy is already in Cases 1 and 2.

## Abrupt Reversals Difficult to Handle in Conventional Models

It was also assumed, sometimes implicitly, that the responses of economic agents to changes in prices and other external factors are always continuous. As Brendan Markey-Towler of the University of Queensland pointed out, traditional economics is based on the implied principle of universal substitutability, which means that a change in relative prices will always create a reaction in the economy[5]. For example, if the price of good A rises relative to the price of substitute good B, a certain number of consumers will stop buying A and start buying B. From this perspective, which assumes that changes in prices—including interest rates and exchange rates—always lead to corresponding changes in the economy, it is natural to assume that a sufficient decline in real interest rates will always encourage willing borrowers to step forward.

It was this kind of thinking that led the economist Paul Krugman to argue that the monetary authorities should opt for a four percent inflation target if a two percent target was not working. It also led some central bankers to conclude that if zero interest rates were not adequate, they should take rates into negative territory. The assumption here, of course, is that in the world of universal substitutability there should be at least *some* response to their policy actions.

When businesses and households experience actual or technical insolvency, however, their responses are highly discontinuous as they shift

---

[5] Markey-Towler, Brendan (2017a) *Foundations for Economic Analysis: The Architecture of Socioeconomic Complexity*, Ph.D thesis, School of Economics, University of Queensland.

abruptly from profit maximization to debt minimization. Debt minimization is also an urgent process because a technically insolvent business faces extinction unless it can quickly emerge from that state of negative equity. If the true state of the company's finances becomes known, no supplier will do business with it unless it pays in cash given the imminent possibility that it will seek bankruptcy protection. Financial institutions are also prevented by law from lending money or rolling over loans to insolvent borrowers in order to protect depositors. Many of the firm's best employees may also leave for other companies.

What this means is that the principle of universal substitutability does not apply when individuals and businesses face insolvency, because they not only stop borrowing money abruptly but also start paying down debt, which is the exact opposite of borrowing. And this shift, as observed after 2008, happens regardless of how low the central bank takes interest rates.

The problem is that economists who were trained under the assumption that universal substitutability is always valid find it exceedingly difficult to understand that there can be such disconnects and abrupt reversals in human behavior. As a result, their theories and models are often incapable of incorporating sudden shifts and reversals in private-sector behavior.

## Obsession with Mathematics Is Killing Macroeconomics' Credibility

The reliance on universal substitutability became essential when mathematical modeling became an obsession (or fad) for mainstream economists. Today, many in the profession would not consider anything that is not expressed in mathematical terms (such as this book) to be serious economics. But for mathematical equations to be useful (i.e., differentiable), models have to assume universal substitutability so that the behavioral changes of economic agents remain smooth and continuous. That, in turn, makes these models useless when households and businesses are forced to make abrupt changes or even reverse their behavior because of balance sheet concerns or other problems.

Economists such as Eggertsson and Krugman (2012)[6] have argued that their models indicate that monetary easing is still effective even in a Fisher–Minsky–Koo environment, and that inflation targeting and quantitative easing (QE) should work. The fact that Krugman himself admitted three

---

[6] Eggertsson, Gauti B. and Krugman, Paul (2012) "Debt, Deleveraging, and the Liquidity Trap: A Fisher-Minsky-Koo Approach," *The Quarterly Journal of Economics*, 127(3), pp. 1469–1513.

years later that these policies have failed to be "game changers"[7] in the real world suggests that their models and equations did not fully incorporate the possibility that universal substitutability would not only disappear but also change signs following a bubble collapse.

In view of the fact that the discipline of macroeconomics was born in the midst of the most abrupt shift to debt minimization in history, the Great Depression, the use of mathematics that cannot accommodate such disconnects in human behavior makes little sense. The fact that only a few economists were able to predict the Great Recession and its long and unpleasant aftermath says a lot about the usefulness of mathematical tools in understanding the economy.

The advanced mathematics used in astrophysics succeeded in landing a man on the moon. The advanced mathematics used in economics (and the professors who ply the trade) failed to predict not only the biggest macroeconomic event since the Great Depression and the birth of macroeconomics, but also the substantial changes to the effectiveness of monetary and fiscal policy after 2008.

Astrophysicists could land a man on the moon because the moon does not change direction abruptly. Economists failed to predict the Great Recession because people react to events and change direction *all the time*. And some of those changes can happen quite abruptly. By relying on mathematics as their primary tool, economists are often treating people as they would treat planetary objects like the moon or Mars, and not as thinking and reacting individuals.

## The Power of Plain Language in Economics

Economists may have latched on to mathematics because of what George Soros called "physics envy."[8] Indeed Soros has been arguing for decades with his theory of reflexivity the importance in economics of treating businesses and households as thinking and reacting entities.

At the same time, economists have a huge advantage over physicists in that they are analyzing the behavior of people just like themselves. Economists are themselves workers, consumers, savers, and investors. Economists even have the luxury of directly asking households and businesses why they

---

[7] International Monetary Fund (2015) "IMF Survey: Top Researchers Debate Unconventional Monetary Policies," Maurice Obstfeld and Gustavo Adler, *IMF News* on November 20, 2015. www.imf.org/en/news/articles/2015/09/28/04/53/sores111915a.

[8] Soros, George (2009) "Soros: General Theory of Reflexivity", *Financial Times*, October 27, pp. 11 www.ft.com/content/0ca06172-bfe9-11de-aed2-00144feab49a.

are doing what they are doing. Indeed they could have asked the Japanese CEOs why they were deleveraging when interest rates were zero. Unfortunately, very few did.

This means that nothing in economics is outside human cognitive experience. Everything in economics, including the behavior of households and businesses, must be explainable in plain language. As Alfred Marshall said, economics is a science of everyday life[9].

This is the opposite of physics, which cannot describe the movements of comets or electrons without using mathematical tools. Physicists also get nowhere by asking a comet or an electron why it does what it does.

This means it should be possible to spell out in plain language the assumed or expected behavior of individual consumers or businesses in an economic theory or model, mathematical or otherwise, to see whether it makes sense. In other words, it should be possible to determine whether the model is treating humans as planetary objects or as thinking and reacting beings by writing out in plain language what the model expects of households and businesses. The problem is that once the elegant-looking mathematical models have been deciphered and translated into plain language, it will be discovered that many of them do indeed treat people as comets and electrons.

When the author took part in a debate on trade frictions in Japan with a professor known for his elegant mathematical models, the professor inadvertently spelled out in plain language what was happening in his model. From that description, it was "discovered" that a worker who had lost his job to imports in his model would immediately find another equally well-paying job. But if that were the case, there would be no trade frictions to start with.

Trade frictions exist because people in importing countries are losing jobs and income. In real life, a worker who loses his job to imports will have to go through years of retraining to regain the income he enjoyed earlier. In many cases, his income may never recover fully. It is this difficulty that causes trade frictions. The economist's model, however, was saying that there should be no trade frictions because there are no income losses. This "discovery" effectively ended the debate.

Practitioners of economics, therefore, should constantly check to see what their models expect households and businesses to do. Students of economics need to be constantly asking professors to explain in plain language what is happening to households and businesses in their mathematical

---

[9] Markey-Towler, Brendan (2017b) "Poetry and Economics: Maintaining our Link to Humanity," from Brendan Markey-Towler's blog, July 24. https://medium.com/@brendanmarkeytowler/poetry-and-economics-maintaining-our-link-to-humanity-532785047f0e.

models. Only then can they judge for themselves whether the model makes any sense.

Put differently, because of the discipline's half-century-long infatuation with mathematics and the belief that mathematically formulated economics is the only "legitimate form" of economics, important phenomena falling outside its assumptions—such as balance sheet recessions and a lack of investment opportunities—have been completely overlooked. As a result, the economics taught at universities often applies only to non-bubble, largely closed economies in a golden era where balance sheet problems and a shortage of investment opportunities do not exist.

But under those conditions, who needs economists? Economists are needed when the economy is in Case 3 or 4, i.e., when there are the numerous counter-intuitive fallacy-of-composition problems mentioned in Chapter 1 that only trained economists can see through and analyze. Unfortunately, most economists today are only trained to look at economies in Cases 1 and 2 (or their models only work in those cases). Hence the public's ongoing disappointment with economists and their friends in the establishment.

Moreover, most economists simply *assumed* a rate of long-term "potential" growth based on the trend growth of capital, labor, and productivity and argued that policymakers should strive to bring the economy back to that growth trajectory. But such "potential growth rates" mean absolutely nothing when businesspeople on the ground are either unable (because of balance sheet concerns) or unwilling (because of a lack of investment opportunities) to borrow money and invest it at home. This also suggests that conventional economics has no meaningful theory of economic growth: economists have assumed away all the relevant questions the public expects them to answer.

The biggest concern for the economics profession at this juncture in history should be that the parents, students, and taxpayers who pay for or subsidize college tuition will eventually realize that what passes as "economics" in universities has very little to do with reality. When the public realizes that the vast majority of economics professors had no clue about the Great Recession, which cost eight million jobs on both sides of the Atlantic, it may want to cut funding to economics departments altogether.

New economist groups such as the World Economics Association with 13,500 members and the Institute for New Economic Thinking are keenly aware of this deficiency in the profession and are working hard to make the discipline relevant for society again. Professor Takamitsu Sawa[10] of Kyoto University is also issuing warnings that the funding for economics

---

[10] Sawa, Takamitsu (2016) *Keizaigaku no Susume: Jimbun-chi to Hihan-seishin no Fukken (Introduction to True Economics: Re-integration of Humanities and Critical Thinking)*, Tokyo: Iwanami Shinsho, p. 52.

departments in universities might be cut by the Japanese Ministry of Education[11] if the profession's unrealistic obsession with mathematics is not corrected. Unfortunately, many if not most economics professors continue to teach the same old material, as if 2008 had never happened and that the golden age is just around the corner. This means the profession as a whole must reinvent itself before the public realizes what it is actually happening.

## Economics a History of Changing Fads

Young disciplines, like young people, are easily influenced by fads. When macroeconomics was in its formative years in the 1940s and 1950s, most Western economies had passed the LTP and were in their golden eras with no one chasing them. New products were continually being invented, and people were optimistic about the future. Their balance sheets were also strong, thanks to the astronomical government spending during the war that had repaired the balance sheet damage wrought by the Great Depression. With strong demand for funds from the corporate sector, the economy was squarely in Case 1 or 2.

While the extraordinary effectiveness of fiscal policy in lifting the developed economies out of the Great Depression during World War II was obvious for everyone to see, Keynes, who argued for such policies, never realized that fiscal stimulus should be used *only* when the private sector is minimizing debt, i.e., when the economy is in Case 3 or 4. Because of this fatal omission by him and his followers, the postwar fad among economists was to believe that fiscal policy could solve most problems.

With private-sector balance sheets already repaired, however, the government's attempt to fine-tune the economy with fiscal policy in the 1950s and 1960s only resulted in more inflation, higher interest rates, and a general misallocation of resources. Although it still took Americans a full 30 years after 1929 to repair their balance sheets and overcome their debt trauma (long- and short-term U.S. interest rates did not return to the average levels of the 1920s until 1959), the fact that economies in the West were in a golden era meant that inflation was becoming an ever-larger problem. By the late 1960s and early 70s, the emergence of inflation caused significant loss of relevance and credibility for Keynesian economics.

When the inflation reached double-digit levels and became a national concern in the late 70s, the pendulum shifted to the opposite extreme, with people like Milton Friedman arguing that monetary policy and smaller government were the answer to most problems. They argued that central banks

---

[11] Full name: Ministry of Education, Culture, Sports, Science and Technology.

should be able to control inflation by controlling the money supply, and the Fed actually adopted a policy of money supply targeting in October 1979. Although that policy did not work as smoothly as expected, the enthusiasm for monetary policy among academic economists was such that some even tried to rewrite history by arguing that the Great Depression could have been avoided with better use of monetary policy by the Fed[12].

When the private sector lost its head in a bubble and sustained massive balance sheet damage, first in Japan in 1990 and then in the West in 2008, the advanced economies were already in the pursued phase, with falling demand for funds from private-sector businesses. The economics profession, however, was still beholden to a golden era mindset and golden era monetary policy.

Although all advanced economies were squarely in Case 3 or 4 by then, many economists argued for more monetary accommodation—even though fiscal policy is the only tool that can address a recession caused by a disappearance of borrowers. Fiscal policy was mobilized soon after Lehman's failure at an emergency G20 meeting held in Washington, D.C. in November 2008. By 2010, however, the orthodoxy had regained its grip on power and forced participating countries in the G20 summit in Toronto that year to halve their fiscal deficits, effectively throwing the global economy into reverse.

Policymakers who realized soon afterwards that the Toronto agreement had been a mistake, including former Fed Chair Ben Bernanke and current Chair Janet Yellen, issued stern warnings about the "fiscal cliff" to ensure that government continued to serve as borrower of last resort. That helped keep the U.S. economy from shrinking. Japanese Finance Minister Taro Aso also recognized this danger and included fiscal stimulus as the second "arrow" of Abenomics in late 2012. Their actions provided essential support for the Japanese and U.S. economies, and unemployment rates in the two countries fell to the full-employment levels of 2.8 percent and 4.3 percent, respectively.

In the Eurozone, however, no such understanding emerged in policy circles, and millions are still suffering from unemployment and deprivation because member governments are required by the Maastricht Treaty, which never considered Cases 3 and 4, to do the opposite of what is needed to fight balance sheet recessions. It is truly ironic that it is the Germans who are imposing this fiscal straitjacket on every country in the Eurozone even though they were the first to discover the effectiveness of fiscal policy in fighting balance sheet recessions in the 1930s. This was famously noted by Joan Robinson, a British economist and contemporary of Keynes, when

---

[12] See Koo (2008), op. cit, Chapter 3.

she said, "I do not regard the Keynesian revolution as a great intellectual triumph. On the contrary, it was a tragedy because it came so late. Hitler had already found how to cure unemployment before Keynes had finished explaining why it occurred."[13]

Economies do adjust given sufficient time. After eight years of doldrums and painful internal deflation, European countries such as Spain and Ireland are finally starting to improve. But there is no room for complacency given that flow-of-funds data for the region (Figure 7.2 to 7.5) continue to show massive deleveraging by the private sector. Indeed, there is a contradiction between the improvements in peripheral economies made possible by internal deflation and falling wages on one hand and the ECB's attempts to rekindle inflation by introducing massive quantitative easing and negative interest rates on the other. Most countries also remain below their pre-2008 peaks in terms of industrial production and real GDP per capita.

Nazi-like political parties have gained ground in Europe because people have been suffering from balance sheet recessions but the ill-designed Maastricht Treaty prevents their center-left and center-right governments from doing anything about it. Indeed, the whole continent is beginning to look a little like Germany under the Allied Powers in the early 1930s.

A few percent of the people in any country may hold xenophobic, far-right, anti-immigration views, but the ability of politicians and political parties espousing such views to garner significant support in the U.S., the UK, and France—countries that have traditionally been champions of democracy and human rights—needs to be closely monitored inasmuch as it suggests a huge loss of credibility for the established center-right and center-left parties and their economist advisors. In other words, the emergence of outsiders and extreme-right parties underscores voters' unhappiness with orthodox thinking. It is urgent, therefore, that people be made aware of the other half of macroeconomics (i.e., Cases 3 and 4) and how to address it with fiscal stimulus before the next Hitler arrives.

In the U.S., Donald Trump is pushing for infrastructure spending, which is the *right* thing to do in an economy where the private sector is still saving close to 5 percent of GDP at very low interest rates (Figure 1.1). Fed officials, including Vice-Chair Fischer, welcomed Trump's infrastructure spending proposals because they understand that the U.S. economy still needs its government to function as borrower of last resort. Given the truly sorry state of infrastructure in the country, it should also be easy to find public works projects that have social rates of return in excess of low U.S. Treasury bond yields.

---

[13] Robinson, Joan (1972) "The Second Crisis of Economic Theory," *American Economic Review* 62(1/2), pp. 1–10.

Unfortunately, this understanding of the economy is not shared by Trump's own party, which controls both the House and the Senate. And the Tea Party faction is dead-set against increasing government spending for any reason. This means the U.S. economy could still fall off the fiscal cliff if Republicans manage to overrule the president before the U.S. private sector is ready to resume borrowing.

## Appropriate Policy Response Depends on State of Economic Development

More generally, economists must wake up to the fact that the world they have been assuming, where monetary policy is effective because there are ample investment opportunities and the private sector has a clean balance sheet, describes only one half of the macroeconomic picture (Cases 1 and 2). In the other half, the private sector is minimizing debt because of balance sheet problems or a dearth of domestic investment opportunities (Cases 3 and 4).

The behavior of economic agents and the effectiveness of macroeconomic policy also change depending on the stage of economic development. These stages, in turn, have huge implications for inflation, growth, and the appropriate form of monetary or fiscal policy.

Economies in the golden era are fundamentally inflationary because wages, consumption, and corporate demand for productivity- and capacity-enhancing investments are all increasing. This means that the central bank must be vigilant against inflation during this period in order to ensure economic stability.

In the pursued era, however, economies are fundamentally non-inflationary because wages are stagnant, consumers are fastidious, imports are flooding the market, and businesses are cutting back productivity and capacity enhancing investments at home. If private-sector demand for funds falls below the level of savings even at very low interest rates, the government must mobilize fiscal policy and act as borrower of last resort to stabilize the economy.

The economy can also move from Case 1 to Case 3 or 4 very quickly after a bubble bursts. Even though the government and central bank have the tools needed to nudge the economy from Case 4 to Case 3 in one to two years, it may take years, if not decades, for an economy in Case 3 to return to Case 1.

Only fiscal policy can support an economy in Case 3 or 4, and it must be left in place until the private sector is ready to borrow again. Although that may seem to be a tall order given the size of the public debt in most advanced countries, bond yields fall to extremely low levels when the private sector is minimizing debt and government is the only borrower remaining.

These low yields are the market's way of telling the government that if any public works projects are needed for the nation's future, this is the time to implement them. Many public works projects also become self-financing at these very low bond yields.

Indeed, the most important task for policymakers in Case 3 and 4 economies is to assign their best and brightest to an independent commission to identify and implement public works projects capable of earning a social rate of return in excess of these ultra-low government bond yields. Instead of the independent central bank, which played a key role in stabilizing the economy during the golden era, it is the as-yet-to-be-created independent fiscal commission that must play a central role in stabilizing the economy during the pursued era.

This commission will have to continue finding self-financing projects until private-sector borrowers return. Such projects will increase the national debt, but they will not increase the burden on future taxpayers because they are self-financing. This is a policy option that was not available in Cases 1 and 2, when interest rates are much higher and self-financing public works projects are much more difficult to find.

In terms of monetary policy, the authorities should recognize that the advanced economies are in Cases 3 and 4, which means that monetary policy is not as effective as it was during the golden era, but the economies themselves are also fundamentally non-inflationary. In this environment, central banks' all-out efforts to meet inflation targets using such tools as quantitative easing and negative interest rates have not only failed to achieve their targets but have also saddled these economies with excessive risk taking and a consequent misallocation of resources, including frequent mini-bubbles. Additionally, they have left authorities with the daunting task of draining the excess liquidity that is now sloshing around the banking system.

Because trying to rekindle inflation in a fundamentally non-inflationary environment does far more damage than good, central banks should distance themselves from inflation targets and other legacies of the golden era. Instead, central banks should lead the policy debate in the direction of fiscal policy, as Ben Bernanke and Janet Yellen have done with the expression "fiscal cliff." They must inform the public that the government needs to play a central role in stabilizing the economy when private-sector businesses are no longer absorbing all the savings generated by the household sector, even at very low interest rates.

They should then find the least disruptive path to remove the excess liquidity in the banking system in order to normalize monetary policy. They must also do so before falling behind the curve on inflation and asset price bubbles.

# Difficulty of Maintaining Fiscal Stimulus in Peacetime Democracies

This policy re-orientation should be spearheaded by the central bank not only because it is the entity that collects the flow-of-funds data, but also because its credibility is at stake: a central bank should not be pushed into adopting policies such as inflation targets that it cannot expect to achieve when the economy is in Case 3 or 4. It has to convince the public, whose knowledge of economics comes entirely from golden-era textbooks stating that fiscal deficits are something to be avoided, that times have changed. Banks and institutional investors, who confront this shortage of borrowers on a daily basis, should also contribute to the debate by telling academics and politicians what is actually happening in the financial sector.

In other words, until universities begin explicitly teaching students about the other half of macroeconomics, the central bank (and its friends in the banking and institutional investor community) must take the lead in this debate because it will be monumentally difficult for elected leaders to convince the public that the economy is actually in the other half and that government must act as borrower of last resort to keep the economy going. Most will not even try because the risk of being labeled a pork-barrel politician is too great.

As a result, even those leaders who understand the need for speedy, substantial, and sustained fiscal stimulus will only propose it when the economy is in desperate shape. The rest will simply choose the path of least resistance, which means that they will go along with the usual anti-deficit chorus.

Because government spending, unlike monetary easing, always adds to GDP, the economy will react positively to such expenditures even if the private sector is still deleveraging. Those initial positive signs, however, will prompt the anti-fiscal-policy chorus to push for fiscal consolidation, only to see the economy fall back into a balance sheet recession. That will prompt another round of fiscal stimulus, only to be aborted again when the economy shows another round of positive initial signs. At best, therefore, fiscal stimulus is applied in an on-again, off-again fashion that is nowhere near sufficient to pull the economy out of Cases 3 and 4. That lengthens the recession and leads to a loss of public confidence in established political parties and economists.

In the meantime, those who have lost jobs or businesses will become increasingly desperate. Some may even backtrack on human rights progress if they feel a Nazi-like government is the only way to break through a policy orthodoxy that works only when the economy is in Case 1 or 2. In order to prevent such an outcome, financial market participants—including the central bank—who confront the shortage of borrowers on a daily basis must speak out, and schools must teach students about the other half of macroeconomics so that democratically elected leaders need not explain why fiscal stimulus is required when the economy is in Cases 3 and 4.

Paul Krugman, who fully understood the need for fiscal stimulus from the beginning in the post-2008 West, nonetheless expressed his disbelief at the author's adamant opposition to additional monetary easing. But the author was flabbergasted by the fact that 80 to 90 percent of the policy debate after 2008 was focused on monetary easing, when 80 to 90 percent of the problem originated in a lack of borrowers, which monetary policy is ill-equipped to handle.

Krugman, on his part, correctly realized early on that there was no political appetite in Washington for additional fiscal stimulus beyond the initial $787 billion package unveiled in early 2009. However, that was also true in Japan in 1997, when the whole country was obsessed with the need for fiscal consolidation. Both the IMF and the OECD were also putting strong pressure on Japan to cut its budget deficit.

When the author and his assistant Shigeru Fujita became the only two economists in Japan[14] to warn publicly that fiscal consolidation would destroy the economic recovery, it was an extremely unpopular and risky stance to take. But when their prediction came true and the economy collapsed, policymakers were able to change direction quickly because there was already an alternative road map that had been provided by the author. The point is that economists must continue telling the public what is needed even if there is no political appetite for it. If their prediction comes true, the public will change its mind, and that is the best an economist can hope for.

Chinese philosopher and educator Ku Hung-Ming once said it is not the educated or uneducated who cause problems, but rather the presence of a large number of half-educated people[15]. By half-educated, he meant people who *think* they know something but in fact do not. Naturally, not everyone can be educated on all issues at all times. The problem arises when policymakers turn out to be only half-educated on their area of policy responsibility.

The author was a panelist at a 2017 conference held in Europe when a central bank governor said "if Mr. Koo's argument is correct, then Italy and

---

[14] Koo, Richard and Fujita, Shigeru (1997) Zaisei-saiken no Jiki wa Shijo ni Kike: Zaisei-saiken ka Keiki-kaifuku ka ("Listen to the bond market for the timing of fiscal reform"), *Shukan Toyo Keizai*, February 8, pp. 52–59.
[15] Ku, Hung-Ming (1915) *The Spirit of the Chinese People*, Beijing, 1915, reprinted in Taipei, 1956, p. 106.

France should be the champions of economic growth because they both have large public sectors." He knew about the author's recommendation for fiscal stimulus, but he was only half educated on the central point of the author's argument—that such a policy should be used *only* when the economy is in Cases 3 and 4, i.e., when the private sector is minimizing debt.

The size of the public sector or public debt *before* the economy fell into a balance sheet recession is therefore irrelevant to the discussion of post-2008 economies. The high levels of government spending and debt in France and Italy were probably harmful to their economies before 2008 if they were in Cases 1 and 2. What the author was trying to point out in the panel was that it was a mistake for France and Italy to reduce their deficits to meet Maastricht criteria *after 2008*, when their private sectors had shifted from profit maximization to debt minimization despite near-zero interest rates.

If the absence of borrowers is due to a lack of worthwhile investment opportunities at home, the government must not only implement (self-financing) fiscal stimulus to stabilize the economy, but should also carry out supply-side reforms of the tax and regulatory regimes to maximize domestic investment opportunities. If the lack of investment opportunities is due to the fact that the country is being pursued, policymakers must also understand that the problem will not go away anytime soon and that a long-term fiscal and supply-side responses to increase the return on capital at home are needed.

This means that policymakers should review each and every regulation and tax and ask whether it is maximizing the creative and innovative potential of the population. They should also review the way the educational system is structured to determine whether it is preparing students to think critically and independently so they can create new products and services that will enable the country to survive and prosper in the post-LTP pursued phase.

Policymakers should also recognize that tax and regulatory regimes that were appropriate in earlier years, when there were numerous low-hanging investment opportunities and nobody was chasing them, may no longer be appropriate when those opportunities are exhausted and the country must come up with new products and services to stay ahead of its pursuers.

Maximizing incentives for those capable of creating new ideas and products may require a new social consensus on why such policies are needed in a pursued era. The public must be shown that what was fair and desirable in the golden era may not necessarily be fair and desirable in the pursued phase. In some cases, the government may also have to direct fiscal spending toward the development of cutting-edge technologies—in effect serving as *innovator* of last resort.

## Better Borrower Surveys and Flow-Of-Funds Data Needed

More generally, the economics profession should demand that governments and central banks in all countries collect data from borrowers similar to those collected by the Bank of Japan in its *Tankan* survey (top of Figure 8.7). Such data will make it possible to tell whether the constraint to economic growth is on the borrowers' side (Cases 3 and 4) or on the lenders' side (Cases 1 and 2). If such surveys indicate that lenders are willing to lend but borrowers are not borrowing, then it can be inferred that the problem rests with the borrowers.

By supplementing such surveys with interest rate and flow-of-funds data like those shown in Figures 2.3, 2.5 to 2.8, 2.16, and 2.17 as well as Figures 7.1 to 7.6, and 7.8, it is possible to see what borrowers are doing with their financial assets and liabilities. If borrowers are not borrowing or actually paying down debt despite very low lending rates, they are likely the source of the problem, which means that fiscal policy should be mobilized to overcome the constraint to growth.

If the borrower survey indicates that lenders are unwilling to lend, it can be concluded that the problem lies with the lenders. By supplementing this information with interest rate and flow-of-funds data for the financial sector, as shown in Figures 8.8 to 8.12, one can determine whether banks are trying to expand lending or economize on capital. If lending rates are high (even if policy rates are low) but lending is still contracting, the problem is probably with the lenders. In that case, monetary easing and bank rescue policies such as capital injections should be mobilized to overcome the constraint to growth.

The economics profession should also demand that governments and central banks improve the accuracy and timeliness of their flow-of-funds data. In some countries such as Netherlands and Austria, this data is only available annually. In other countries such as Taiwan, the data comes out too late to be of any use. In the U.S. and in Germany, this data has been subject to huge revisions.

As explained in the author's previous book[16], compiling these data is a massive and costly undertaking with great room for improvement. In spite of all the resources authorities have spent to compile this data, most economists still appear unable or unwilling to use it, even though it is essential in determining whether growth is being held back by the lenders or the borrowers. Now that there is a better understanding of the importance of these data in identifying which half of macroeconomics the economy is in, perhaps more economists will make use of them in the future.

---

[16] Koo (2015), op. cit., pp. 143–148.

# Summary and Conclusions

During the golden era, when private-sector investment opportunities were plentiful and interest rates were high, economists rightfully focused on strengthening the ability of monetary policy to rein in inflation while disparaging profligate fiscal policy. But that era ended in the 1970s for the West and in the 1990s for Japan.

Once the economy is in the pursued phase and the private sector often becomes a net saver even at very low interest rates, the effectiveness of monetary and fiscal policy is reversed. In particular, once the government becomes the last borrower standing, the effectiveness of monetary policy comes to depend on the size of the government's borrowings, because it is the only entity able and willing to borrow money from financial institutions and inject it into the real economy. Policymakers must therefore shift their focus from easing monetary policy to building an independent commission to seek out viable infrastructure projects so that the government can, in good conscience, continue to serve as borrower of last resort.

Economists should also recognize that multipliers and elasticities that were obtained in an earlier stage of economic development may be totally useless during the current pursued phase. These parameters can also change, sometimes drastically, within the same phase, depending on whether the economy is in Cases 1 and 2 or in Cases 3 and 4. For example, even if an economy is fundamentally in a golden era, the collapse of an asset bubble could leave it in Case 3 or 4 with no private-sector borrowers. That is basically what happened to the U.S. during the Great Depression and to Asian countries during the currency crisis of 1997.

At the global level, it must be recognized that there were enough losers from "free trade" in the U.S. in 2016 to put protectionist Donald Trump into the White House. In reality, however, they are the victims of free flows of *capital,* which is distorting exchange rates and trade flows. Since it was free trade (together with the nuclear deterrent) that made war obsolete and brought about the greatest prosperity in human history, it must be defended against unfettered capital flows, which are exacerbating trade imbalances and spawning protectionist pressures. This means policymakers cannot be indifferent to trade imbalances and exchange rates.

Economists must also examine the efficiency and welfare implications of *unbalanced* free trade and ask how long such conditions can be sustained, both economically and politically. Balancing every bilateral trade account is neither possible nor desirable in a world of 200-plus countries, but allowing trade imbalances to grow without limit is also an unsustainable policy. This means that economists must come up with measures to keep trade imbalances within manageable limits.

The already substantial size of social backlash against free trade in pursued countries also means that the easy days are over for emerging countries exporting all they want without opening their domestic markets for imports. Export-led growth based on comparative advantage is fine, but these countries must open their markets faster or accept higher exchange rates if they want to continue enjoying access to the markets of pursued countries.

Economists must also investigate the efficiency and welfare implications of cross-border portfolio capital flows when other factors of production are not free to move. Instead of simply assuming that anything that increases the freedom of the private sector will increase its welfare, they must determine under what circumstances such flows should be free and under what circumstances they should be constrained.

At the most fundamental level, the economics profession must realize that, apart from the early stages of industrialization, which are characterized by a surplus of low-hanging investment opportunities, shortages of borrowers have always been a bigger problem for growth than shortages of lenders. The poor economic performance and low productivity growth of advanced countries today stem from the fact that households continue to save for an uncertain future, but businesses are unable to find sufficient investment opportunities with a high enough return on capital at home to absorb those savings.

Instead of making facile assumptions about "trend growth rates" and assuming that there are always willing borrowers, economists need to confront head-on this shortage of domestic investment opportunities with a sufficiently high return on capital. The availability of investment opportunities and willing borrowers should never be taken for granted. This is particularly true in countries that are in balance sheet recessions or are being pursued, a group that includes virtually every advanced economy in the world today.

# References & Bibliography

*Asahi Shimbun* (1988) "Endaka 'Seiho-Hannin-Setsu' ni Kyokai ga Irei no Hanron ('Accusation that life insurers are responsible for strong yen is absurd')," in Japanese, March 30, 1988, pp. 9.

Australian Bureau of Statistics. *Australian National Accounts.*

Banca d'Italia. *Financial Accounts.*

Banco de España. *Financial Accounts of the Spanish Economy.*

Banco de Portugal. *Financial Accounts.*

Bank for International Settlements. *Effective Exchange Rate Indices.*

_____. Residential Property Price Statistics.

Bank of England. *M4 and M4 lending excluding intermediate OFCs.*

_____. *Notes and Coin and Reserves Balances.*

Bank of Greece. *Financial Accounts.*

Bank of Japan. *Average Interest Rates Posted at Financial Institutions by Type of Deposit.*

_____. *Deposits, Vault Cash, and Loans and Bills Discounted.*

_____. *Flow of Funds.*

_____. *Loans and Bills Discounted by Sector.*

_____. *Monetary Base.*

_____. *Monetary Survey.*

_____. *Money Stock.*

_____. *Reserves.*

_____. *Tankan.*

Bernanke, Ben S. (2010) "What The Fed Did and Why: Supporting the Recovery and Sustaining Price Stability," *Washington Post*, November 10, 2010. www.washingtonpost.com/wp-dyn/content/article/2010/11/03/AR2010110307372.html.

_____. (2017) "Shrinking the Fed's Balance Sheet," from his blog at Brookings Institution, January 26, 2017. www.brookings.edu/blog/ben-bernanke/2017/01/26/shrinking-the-feds-balance-sheet/.

Board of Governors of the Federal Reserve System (1976) *Banking & Monetary Statistics, 1914–1970.* 2 vols. Washington D.C.

_____ (2009) "Prudent Commercial Real Estate Loan Workouts," *Supervision and Regulation Letters*, SR 09-7, on October 30, 2009. www .federalreserve.gov/boarddocs/srletters/2009/SR0907.htm.

_____ (2012) "Transcript of Chairman Bernanke's Press Conference," Washington D.C., April 25, 2012. www.federalreserve.gov/mediacenter/ files/FOMCpresconf20120425.pdf.

_____ (2015) "Transcript of Chair Yellen's Press Conference, December 16, 2015." www.federalreserve.gov/mediacenter/files/FOMCpresconf 20151216.pdf.

_____ (2016) *Monetary Policy Report*, submitted on June 21, 2016. www .federalreserve.gov/monetarypolicy/files/20160621_mprfullreport.pdf.

_____ (2017) "Transcript of Chair Yellen's Press Conference, June 14, 2017." www.federalreserve.gov/mediacenter/files/FOMCpresconf20170614.pdf.

_____. *Aggregate Reserves of Depository Institutions and the Monetary Base.*

_____. *Assets and Liabilities of Commercial Banks in the United States.*

_____. *Financial Accounts of the Unites States.*

_____. *Foreign Exchange Rates.*

_____. *Money Stock Measures.*

_____. *Selected Interest Rates.*

Cabinet Office, Japan. *Annual Report on National Accounts.*

_____. *Quarterly Estimates of GDP.*

Central Bank of Ireland. *Quarterly Financial Accounts.*

Central Statistics Office, Ireland. *Quarterly National Accounts.*

CNBC (2016) "Fed's Fischer: Markets Missing Mark on Future Rates," January 6, 2016. www.cnbc.com/2016/01/06/feds-fischer-uncertainty-has-risen- in-markets-unsure-of-n-korea-news-impact.html.

Cooper, Richard N. (1997) "Should Capital-Account Convertibility Be a World Objective?" in Peter B. Karen et al. (ed.), "Should the IMF pursue capital- account convertibility?" *Essays in International Finance 207*, Princeton N.J.: Princeton University International Finance Section, May 1998, pp. 11–19.

Deutsche Bundesbank. *Financial Accounts.*

_____. *Monetary Aggregates.*

Directorate General of Budget, Accounting and Statistics (DGBAS), the Executive Yuan, Taiwan. *Consumer Price Indices.*

_____. *Monthly Average Earnings.*

Draghi, Mario (2015) "Introductory statement to the press conference (with Q&A)," ECB's press conference in Frankfurt am Main, January 22, 2015. www.ecb.europa.eu/press/pressconf/2015/html/is150122.en.html.

Eggertsson, Gauti B. and Paul Krugman (2012) "Debt, Deleveraging, and the Liquidity Trap: A Fisher-Minsky-Koo Approach," *The Quarterly Journal of Economics*, 127(3), pp. 1469–1513.

European Central Bank. *Euro Area Accounts.*

_____. *Minimum Reserves and Liquidity.*

_____. *Monetary Developments in the Euro Area.*

Eurostat. Harmonised Indices of Consumer Prices.

_____. *Quarterly National Accounts.*

Financial Services Agency, Japan (2016) "FSA publishes the status of loans held by all banks as of the end of March 2016, based on the Financial Reconstruction Act," on August 12, 2016. www.fsa.go.jp/en/regulated/npl/20160812.html.

Fisher, Stanley (2016) "Reflections on Macroeconomics Then and Now," remarks at "Policy Challenges in an Interconnected World" 32nd Annual National Association for Business Economics Economic Policy Conference, Washington D.C., March 7, 2016. www.federalreserve.gov/newsevents/speech/fischer20160307a.htm.

Flora, Peter, Franz Kraus, and Winfried Pfenning (eds) (1987) *State, Economy and Society in Western Europe 1815–1975. Volume II. The Growth of Industrial Societies and Capitalist Economies.* Frankfurt am Main: Campus Verlag.

Frydl, Edward J. (1992) "Overhangs and Hangovers: Coping with the Imbalances of the 1980s," *Federal Reserve Bank of New York Seventy-Seventh Annual Report for the Year Ended December 31, 1991*, pp. 5–30.

Greenwood, John (2016) "Successful Central Banks Focus on Greater Purchasing," *Financial Times*, May 31, 2016. next.ft.com/content/f7a98fb2-241f-11e6-9d4d-c11776a5124.

Hellenic Statistical Authority, Greece. *Gross Domestic Product.*

International Monetary Fund (2010) "Press Release: IMF Executive Board Approves €30 Billion Stand-By Arrangement for Greece," on May 2010. www.imf.org/en/News/Articles/2015/09/14/01/49/pr10187.

_____ (2015) "IMF Survey: Top Researchers Debate Unconventional Monetary Policies," by Maurice Obstfeld and Gustavo Adler, *IMF News* on November 20, 2015. www.imf.org/en/news/articles/2015/09/28/04/53/sores111915a.

_____. *International Financial Statistics.*

Italian National Institute of Statistics. *Quarterly National Accounts.*

Iwata, Kikuo (2001) *Defure no Keizaigaku ("The Economics of Deflation")*, Toyokeizai, Tokyo.

Jakab, Zoltan and Michael Kumhof (2015) "Banks Are Not Intermediaries of Loanable Funds—and Why This Matters," *Bank of England Working Paper*, No. 529. www.bankofengland.co.uk/research/Documents/workingpapers/2015/wp529.pdf.

Japan Bond Trading Company. *Long-term (10y) JGB Yield.*

Japan Real Estate Institute. *Urban Land Price Index.*

Japanese Bankers Association. *Financial Statements of All Banks.*

Koo, Richard (2001) "The Japanese Economy in Balance Sheet Recession," *Business Economics*, National Association of Business Economists, Washington, D.C., April 2001.

_____ (2003) *Balance Sheet Recession: Japan's Struggle with Uncharted Economics and its Global Implications.* Singapore: John Wiley & Sons.

_____ (2008) *The Holy Grail of Macroeconomics: Lessons from Japan's Great Recession.* Singapore: John Wiley & Sons.

_____ (2015a) *The Escape from Balance Sheet Recession and the QE Trap: A Hazardous Road for the World Economy.* Singapore: John Wiley & Sons.

_____ (2015b) "China and the U.S.-led International Order" in *How Do Asians See their Future?* edited by François Godement, European Council on Foreign Relations. www.ecfr.eu/page/-/ECFR130_CHINA_ASIA_REPORT_pdf.pdf.

_____ and Shigeru Fujita (1997) "Zaisei-saiken no Jiki wa Shijo ni Kike: Zaisei-saiken ka Keiki-kaifuku ka ('Listen to the bond market for the timing of fiscal reform')," *Shukan Toyo Keizai,* February 8, 1997, pp. 52–59.

_____ and Paul Krugman (1999) "Gekitotsu Taidan: Nihon Keizai Endaka wa Akuka ('Big Debate on Japan's Economy: Is Strong Yen a Bad Thing?')", *Bungeishunju,* November 1999, edited by Yasuhara Ishizawa, pp. 130–143.

_____. (2016) "The Other Half of Macroeconomics and Three Stages of Economic Development," at the conference of World Economic Association, *Capital Accumulation, Production and Employment: Can We Bend the Arc of Global Capital toward Justice?* http://capital2016.weaconferences.net/files/2016/05/WEA-CapitalConference2016-Koo.pdf.

Ku, Hung-Ming (1915) *The Spirit of the Chinese People,* Beijing, reprinted in Taipei in 1956.

Kuroda, Haruhiko (2013). "Quantitative and Qualitative Monetary Easing," speech at a meeting held by Yomiuri International Economic Society in Tokyo, April 12, 2013. www.boj.or.jp/en/announcements/press/koen_2013/ko130412a.htm/.

Maddison, Angus, (2006). *The World Economy. A Millennial Perspective (Vol. 1). Historical Statistics (Vol. 2).* Paris: OECD.

_____. "Historical Statistics of the World Economy: 1–2008 AD". www.ggdc.net/maddison/Historical_Statistics/vertical-file_02-2010.xls.

Markey-Towler, Brendan (2017a) *Foundations for Economic Analysis: The Architecture of Socioeconomic Complexity,* PhD thesis, School of Economics, University of Queensland.

_____ (2017b) "Poetry and Economics: Maintaining our Link to Humanity," from Brendan Markey-Towler's blog, July 24, 2017. www.medium.com/@brendanmarkeytowler/poetry-and-economics-maintaining-our-link-to-humanity-532785047f0e.

McLeay, Michael, Amar Radia and Ryland Thomas (2014) "Money Creation in the Modern Economy," Bank of England Quarterly Bulletin 2014 Q1, pp. 14–27 www.bankofengland.co.uk/publications/Pages/quarterlybulletin/2014/qb14q1.aspx.

Ministry of Employment and Labor, Korea. *Strikes Statistics.*

Ministry of Finance, Japan. *Budget.*

Ministry of Finance, Republic of China. *Finance Statistics,* in traditional Chinese.

Ministry of Health, Labour and Welfare, Japan. *Monthly Labour Survey.*

_____. *Survey on Labour Disputes.*

Ministry of Human Resources and Social Security, People's Republic of China. *Analysis on Supply and Demand of Employment Market in Some Cities,* in simplified Chinese.

Ministry of Internal Affairs and Communications, Japan. *Consumer Price Index.*

_____. *Report on Internal Migration in Japan.*

National Bureau of Statistics of China. *Consumer Price Index.*

_____. *Gross Domestic Product.*

National Statistics Institute, Spain. *Quarterly Spanish National Accounts.*

Nikkei Business (2015) "Tokushu: Nisen Mannin-no Hinkon (20 Million Japanese in Poverty)," in Japanese, *Nikkei BP,* Tokyo, March 23, 2015. pp. 24–43.

Oakley, David (2009) "A Bold Bid to Revive Lending," *Financial Times,* March 7, 2009. next.ft.com/content/9b3fd930-0a90-11de-95ed-0000779fd2ac.

OECD (2017) *PISA 2015 Results (Volume III): Students' Well-Being,* OECD Publishing, Paris, p. 71.

_____. *Unit Labor Costs and Labor Productivity.*

Office for National Statistics, UK. *Analysis of Real Earnings.*

_____. *Consumer Price Inflation.*

_____. *UK Economic Accounts.*

Piketty, Thomas (2014) *Capital in the Twenty-First Century.* Cambridge, M.A.: Harvard University Press

Population Division of the Department of Economic and Social Affairs of the United Nations Secretariat, *World Population Prospects: The 2010 Revision and World Urbanization Prospects.*

Real Capital Analytics. *Moody's/RCA CPPI.*

Real Estate Economic Institute, Japan. *Kinki-Ken no Manshon Hanbai Doko (Report on the Sales of the Condominiums in Kansai Area, Japanese only).*

_____. *Shuto-Ken no Manshon Hanbai Doko (Report on the sales of the condominiums in Tokyo Metropolitan Area, Japanese only).*

Robinson, Joan (1972) "The Second Crisis of Economic Theory," *American Economic Review* 62(1/2), pp. 1–10.

Rogoff, Kenneth S. (2016) *The Curse of Cash,* Princeton N.J.: Princeton University Press.

Sawa, Takamitsu (2016) *Keizaigaku no Susume: Jimbun-chi to Hihan-seishin no Fukken (Introduction to True Economics: Re-integration of Humanities and Critical Thinking),* Tokyo: Iwanami Shinsho.

Soros, George (2009) "Soros: General Theory of Reflexivity", *Financial Times,* October 27, 2009, p. 11. www.ft.com/content/0ca06172-bfe9-11de-aed2-00144feab49a.

Statistics Canada. *Financial Flow Accounts.*

_____. *Gross Domestic Product.*

Statistics Korea. *Flow of Funds.*

_____. *Internal Migration Statistics.*

_____. *Korea Statistical Year Book.*

_____. *National Accounts.*

Statistics Portugal. *Portuguese National Accounts.*

Stevens, Glenn (2003) "Inflation Targeting: A Decade of Australian Experience", address to South Australian Centre for Economic Studies April 2003, *Economic Briefings,* on April 10, 2003. www.rba.gov.au/speeches/2003/sp-dg-100403.html.

Summers, Lawrence H. (2009) "Rescuing and Rebuilding the U.S. Economy: A Progress Report", remarks at the Peterson Institute for International Economics, Washington, DC, on July 17, 2009. https://piie.com/commentary/speeches-papers/rescuing-and-rebuilding-us-economy-progress-report?ResearchID=1264.

Summers, Lawrence H. Secular stagnation. http://larrysummers.com/category/secular-stagnation/.

Swiss Federal Statistical Office. *Consumer Prices Index.*

_____. *Swiss Wage Index.*

Swiss National Bank. *Minimal Reserves.*

S&P Dow Jones Indices. *S&P CoreLogic Case-Shiller Home Price Indices.*

The People's Bank of China. *Balance Sheet of Monetary Authority.*

_____. *Depository Corporations Survey.*

_____. *Money Supply.*

Uchihashi, Katsuto (2009) *Shinpan Akumu-no Saikuru: Neo-riberarizumu Junkan (The cycle of nightmares: the recurrence of neoliberalism),* updated version, in Japanese, Japan: Bunshun Bunko.

United Nations, Department of Economic and Social Affairs, Population Division (2014) *World Urbanization Prospects: The 2014 Revision.*

_____ (2015) *World Population Prospects.*

U.S. Department of Commerce, Bureau of Economic Analysis. *Gross Domestic Product (GDP).*

_____. Personal Income and Outlays.

U.S. Department of Commerce, Census Bureau (2012), *2010 Census.*

_____. *Current Population Survey.*

Volcker, Paul A. (2001) "Jinsoku na Furyo-saiken Shori ga Hitsuyo daga Shori no Seigensokudo wa Daiji ('Prompt disposal of NPLs is needed, but so is setting a speed limit')," *Shukan Toyo Keizai,* June 23, 2001, pp. 58.

Wakatabe, Masazumi (2016) "Herikoputa Mane to wa Nanika (3) ('What Consititutes Helicopter Money?')", *Nikkei,* June 20, 2016.

Werner, Richard A. (2016) "A Lost Century in Economics: Three Theories of Banking and the Conclusive Evidence," *International Review of Financial Analysis,* 46: pp. 361–379.

Williams, John C. (2016) "The Right Profile: Economic Drivers and the Outlook," a presentation to Town Hall Los Angeles, February 18, 2016. www.frbsf.org/our-district/files/Williams-Speech-The-Right-Profile_Economic-Drivers-and-the-Outlook.pdf.

# Afterword

As can be gleaned from the text, I take economics, the science of everyday life, quite seriously. I take it seriously because I believe many human tragedies could have been avoided if the economists of the time had understood what was actually happening and had recommended the correct policy responses. In that sense, how well or poorly economists understand the world around them often has a direct bearing on the quality of people's lives. That was what prompted me to write books to share my thoughts with the general public on where our economies are going and what those developments mean for our daily lives. And that was in addition to my regular job as the chief economist of a research institute associated with Japan's largest investment bank[1].

Writing a book takes an enormous amount of time away from my family, and I am eternally grateful to my wife, Chyen-Mei, who allows me to spend so much time writing books like this one. I am also indebted to my daughter Jacqueline and my son Richard, both in the U.S., who kept up the family conversation via LINE so my wife would not feel too lonely.

This book would have been impossible without the help of my two able assistants. Mr. Masaya Sasaki, who prepared all the charts and checked the numbers, has long been the resident expert on flow-of-funds data, among many other things. Ms. Yuko Terado, who often works harder than I do, managed my schedule to ensure my health was not compromised despite demanding professional circumstances, both at home and abroad. I can never thank them enough for their hard work and dedication.

I am also extremely grateful to Mr. Chris Green, who was able to edit the manuscript of this book under a very tight schedule. This is our third book together, and I am fortunate to have someone who understands my thinking to do the editing work. Finally, I would like to thank Mr. Robert McCauley at the Bank for International Settlements for his comments on an earlier paper published by the World Economic Association.

---

[1] As a legal entity, Nomura Research Institute has been independent of Nomura Securities since 2001.

Someone asked me the other day where my inspirations come from. My answer: they come late on Sunday nights when I am under tremendous pressure to produce something useful to say to Nomura Securities' clients in my "Monday Meeting Memo". I hate to admit it, but I do better work under pressure. The ideas are tested first with Nomura's traders and dealers, and then with its global client base. Since these are all serious people managing billions of dollars every day, they never let me go off on a tangent, and any loose ends in my thoughts are usually laid bare by the end of Monday morning. The assistance, encouragement, and constructive criticism received from Nomura staff and clients over the last 34 years have therefore been invaluable in keeping me focused on the issues that matter, and I am forever grateful for their continuing support.

Richard C. Koo
October 2017

# Index